Small Is Necessary

Small Is Necessary

Shared Living on a Shared Planet

Anitra Nelson

First published 2018 by Pluto Press
345 Archway Road, London N6 5AA

www.plutobooks.com

British Library Cataloguing in Publication Data
A catalogue record for this book is available from the British Library

ISBN 978 0 7453 3423 3   Hardback
ISBN 978 0 7453 3422 6   Paperback
ISBN 978 1 7868 0188 3   PDF eBook
ISBN 978 1 7868 0213 2   Kindle eBook
ISBN 978 1 7868 0212 5   EPUB eBook

This book is printed on paper suitable for recycling and made from fully
managed and sustained forest sources. Logging, pulping and manufacturing
processes are expected to conform to the environmental standards of the
country of origin.

Typeset by Stanford DTP Services, Northampton, England

Simultaneously printed in the United Kingdom and United States of America

Contents

List of Figures, Tables and Boxes

FIGURES

TABLES

BOXES

Abbreviations

£	British pounds
$	dollars
A$	Australian dollars
€	Euros
3D	three-dimensional
ABS	Australian Bureau of Statistics
ACF	Australian Conservation Foundation
ACT	Australian Capital Territory
ADU	accessory dwelling unit
aka	also known as
BBC	British Broadcasting Commission
BedZED	Beddington Zero Energy Development
BICA	Bend of Islands Conservation Association
BREEAM	Building Research Establishment Environmental Assessment Methodology (UK rating system)
BVCLT	Beverly-Vermont Community Land Trust
bn	Billion
CA	California
CABE	Commission for Architecture and the Built Environment (London, 1999–2011)
CBD	central business district
CEHL	Common Equity Housing Ltd
CHP	combined heat and power
CIC	Catalan Integral Cooperative (Cooperativa Integral Catalana)
CLT	community land trust
CMHC	Canada Mortgage and Housing Corporation
CO_2	carbon dioxide
CO_2-e	carbon dioxide equivalent (carbon emissions)
COP21	21st Conference of the Parties (to UNFCCC)
COP22	22nd Conference of the Parties (to UNFCCC)
CRSP	Cooperative Resources and Services Project
CSA	community supported agriculture

DC	District of Columbia
DCLG	Department for Communities and Local Government
DELWP	Department of Environment, Land, Water and Planning (Victoria, Australia)
D_{ef}	ecological footprint distance
DELWP	Department of Environment, Land, Water and Planning (Victoria, Australia)
DIO	do it ourselves
DRE	Dancing Rabbit Ecovillage
E2C2	ecology and economics, community and consciousness (approach of Litfin)
ELZ	environmental living zone
ft	feet
ft^2	sq ft
GEN	Global Ecovillage Network
gha	global hectare (to quantify human ecological footprints and biocapacity)
GHG	greenhouse gas
GPS	global positioning system
HHP	Hockerton Housing Project
IDO	interim development order
INURA	International Network for Urban Research and Action
IPCC	Intergovernmental Panel on Climate Change
kW	kilowatt
$kWh/(m^2a)$	kilowatt hour (of energy) per square meter per annum
l	litres
LAEV	Los Angeles Eco-Village
LEED	Leadership in Energy and Environmental Design
LID	low impact development
Lilac	low impact living affordable community
m	metre(s)
m^2	sq m
MA	Massachusetts
MEF	Moreland Energy Foundation
MHOS	Mutual Home Ownership Society
NHF	National Housing Federation (UK)
NHF	National Housing Federation
NSW	New South Wales
NYC	New York City

NZ	New Zealand
NZ$	New Zealand dollars
OECD	Organisation for Economic Co-operation and Development
OPD	One Planet Development (as in Welsh policy)
p.a.	per annum
P2P	peer-to-peer
PIA	Planning Institute of Australia
PV	photovoltaic
RBCC	Round the Bend Conservation Co-operative
RIBA	Royal Institute of British Architects
RMIT	Royal Melbourne Institute of Technology (university)
S$	Singapore dollars
UK	United Kingdom
ULI	Urban Land Institute
UN	United Nations
UNFCCC	United Nations Framework Convention on Climate Change
UNRISD	United Nations Research Institute for Social Research
URL	Uniform Resource Locator
US	United States
US$	United States dollars
USTA	Urban Soil/Tierra Urbana
V	volt(s)
W	watts
WWOOFers	Willing Workers on Organic Farms
ZAD	Zone à Défendre

Glossary

Accessory dwelling units: unit partitioned out of a larger, say family, dwelling or detached dwelling alongside a larger one, aka Granny flats (Australia) or self-contained studio/unit/dwelling created for supplementary income, independent children and caregivers.

Affordable housing: for eligibility and statistical purposes variously defined. In Australia typically referring to housing that costs the household less than 30 per cent of their gross income to live in (includes mortgage or rental payments, insurance, maintenance, council rates and property taxes but not necessarily costs of essential services, such as operational energy and water services). All such definitions, standards and measures neglect aspects and spawn anomalies such as under-used dwellings and 'overcrowding', accommodation as in-kind remuneration for employment, 'energy poverty' and precarious employment.

Apartment block: separate multi-household dwellings each separately owned or rented, with potential for voluntary community bonds and sharing of resources, goods and services.

Baugemeinschaften, 'community building partnerships' or 'building communities': privately owned dwellings with collective ownership of shared spaces.

Baugruppen: self-administering building groups of owner-occupiers who collectively buy land, collaboratively design, and sometimes labour on, a multi-household build (*baugruppe*).

Cohousing: purposively co-located and connected neighbourhoods of multiple households, each household with a private dwelling but sharing, with their cohousing neighbours, specific common spaces (such as a common house), resources (such as community gardens and cars) and activities (such as preparing and eating meals). Such settlements have formal, legal, community governance arrangements covering rules for entry and exit, shared access, maintenance, fees and other sets of mutual obligations and expectations. Legal models and names for such arrangements are many and various, including cooperative, condo(minium) association and 'collective house' (Japan).

CoHousing: a generic European term for collaboratively designed and built housing spaces for multiple households that develop 'self-managed social architectures' to share activities and experiences, not just spaces and resources (see id22).

Co-housing: used, especially with respect to European models, to refer to multiunit housing that involves some level of self-organisation, as in collectively built, co-located and self-managed (collectively managed) housing. The comparable term in this work is the all-encompassing 'collaborative housing'.

Collaborative housing: a generic term for housing typically produced by professional and industry partners with prospective residents and, once established, maintained by household types that function as a community of residents who share amenities, facilities and spaces.

Communes: communal living with a 'common-purse', income-sharing, and making joint decisions over financial spending and numerous personal activities, i.e. operating as 'one household', sometimes a working and living arrangement, and/or all-under-one-roof.

Condo(minium) (NA): privately owned units on commonly owned land governed by an association of owners (similar to 'strata title' in Australia).

Consensual decision-making: the process of making a joint decision, which involves the time and space for open discussion by all participants of various issues and options, and an outcome that each agrees to hold to even despite certain misgivings. (Many groups have a modified consensual decision-making process where, say a 90 per cent, majority vote suffices in cases of deadlock or inappropriate delays.)

Cooperative housing: typically, where residents are members of a corporation that is the common owning body (US); where housing is owned by resident-members as a non-profit enterprise (Australia); where resident-members own shares (Germany).

Eco (prefix): projects with intentional Earth-friendly housing and ecologically sensitive householder practices, at the very least energy- and water-efficient housing, growing productive and ecologically sensible plants (typically using permaculture principles) and sourcing sustainably produced foods.

Ecological footprint: the amount of land necessary to supply the resources on which a resident's consumption relies.

Ecovillage: a relatively self-contained settlement of dwellings pursuing collective sufficiency and ecological balance within Earth's regenerative potential and limits, both locally and globally.

Garden city: urban settlement planned to maximise green spaces, typically green parklands surrounding a mix of residential, commercial and light industrial developments.

Intentional community: a community whose members intend to maintain a self-governing community with self-defined goals.

Kibbutz: collective communities, both secular and religious, developed in the nineteenth century and initially based on agriculture, with around one-third still income sharing; up to two per cent of Israel's population still live in kibbutzim.

Low impact development (LID): developments intended to create a whole-of-life equilibrium with their productively used natural surrounds (thus, 'low impact communities').

Marginal rental housing: highly managed housing, with fewer occupancy rights than for mainstream private and social housing tenants, and some degree of shared facilities and spaces. Examples include boarders in boarding houses and tenants in residential parks (with caravans and/or other types of mobile homes, including manufactured houses).

One planet development/living: applies the standard measure of potential and actual ecological footprints at both global and local levels to achieve and keep the level of resources residents consume within the earth's regenerative capacity.

Over-crowded housing: an international standard is the OECD indicator, which divides the total number of rooms in a dwelling by the number of its residents; however, many countries focus instead on the number of residents compared with bedrooms. As with much data on averages, national statistics often blur considerable underuse or overcrowding typical of specific regional or demographic cohorts.

Participatory decision-making: serious engagement, often involving multiple stakeholders, using discursive, appreciative inquiry and many consensual decision-making techniques but allowing voting.

Pocket neighbourhoods: clustered dwellings surrounding shared open space, such as a courtyard or street, where households share responsibility and enjoyment of that space.

Share(d) house(hold) – aka a collective or joint household, cooperative house: typically, a rented house (sometimes a mansion), where personal rooms are private spaces and the rest of the space is shared, maintained and governed in non-hierarchical ways. Rules and protocol apply to householder members' monetary contribution to the collective rent (all equal or different, say according to room size, amenity, and single, couple or family occupancy), splitting bills, buying, preparing and eating food, visitors, and tolerance of certain activities, including noise. Sharing a house is sometimes called **cohouseholding** or **coliving**.

Social housing: modest housing managed by government or not-for-profit bodies and specifically rented to those on low or low-medium incomes.

Squatting: inhabiting or doing other activities in a private property – thus making it a squat – without the permission of the owner (or leaseholder) whether for individualistic purposes or with a collective political rationale.

Tactical urbanism: applies a classic action research method and result for a suite of initiatives such as road calming, intersection repair, quirky block improvements and popup spaces (including cafes, benches, parklets and park-mobiles).

Tenement: separate dwellings (including single rooms) in a block of such, rented by tenants.

Tenant: deriving from the Latin 'to hold' (*tener*), to have use-rights over a property, a resident who rents their dwelling/property from a landlord (owner).

Utopian settlements: housing generally dominated by highly idealistic, well-defined and detailed plans and principles (a name emerging from such developments in the later nineteenth century).

NOTE

Throughout this work, dates in brackets next to names of buildings refer to the year in which their construction was completed or when they started to be inhabited for the residential purposes in question.

Acknowledgements

I benefitted enormously from a three-month writing fellowship at the Rachel Carson Centre for Environment and Society of the Ludwig Maximilian University of Munich (2016–2017). This centre, a joint initiative between the university and the Deutsches Museum in Munich, has been supported substantially by the German Federal Ministry of Education and Research. In terms of writers and writing, it is the foremost international interdisciplinary centre for research and education in the environmental humanities and social sciences in the world. I thank all the dedicated staff at the centre and all the other fellows who read and constructively critiqued my work, and with whom I discussed generic writing issues and current environmental impasses.

I thank David Castle, Senior Commissioning Editor at Pluto Press, for his patience and support through delays of all kinds. This project began as a joint initiative with my late partner Frans Timmerman with whom I co-edited the Pluto Press book, *Life Without Money: Building Fair and Sustainable Economies* (2011). Soon after we signed the contract for *Small Is Necessary*, Frans was diagnosed with motor neurone disease (aka Lou Gehrig's disease and amyotrophic lateral sclerosis). For around two years the project was put on hold as I cared for him and later grieved his death. However, Frans' input into the initial concept and design of the project, and his steadfast support for such a work remained an inspiration.

I do not simply study, but have experience of, collaborative housing. In Victoria (Australia), I participated as an owner-builder in a mudbrick self-building scheme (mid-1980s), an all under-one-roof living-working rural commune (mid-1990s) and a residential peri-urban conservation cooperative (late 1990s). For several months I was a visiting resident of two impressive and enduring intentional communities located in east coast states of the United States. I thank all the people with whom I lived, and engaged, in these life journeys.

Alternative communities attract a good deal of grassroots attention and visitors, as well as being composed of a range of long-term and short-term residents – all these kinds of people taught me more about the frustrations and potential of collaborative living than learning, reading or talking in academia or professional contexts. At the same time, I cannot lightly dismiss all the informative discussions I have had with colleagues, architects, designers, planners, builders and other sustainability experts of all kinds. All of them, far too many too mention personally even as a short list, I thank profusely for confirming my prejudices and changing my mind, as the case might be.

Last, but not least, I am very grateful to acknowledge those from whom I obtained copyright permission to reproduce numerous images for this book:

Photographer Mike Crowhurst and Commonground intentional community (Central Victoria, Australia) for the photo of Commonground's main building in Figure. 1.1.

Architectural photographer Nic Granleese (Melbourne, Australia) for the photo and Emilio Fuscaldo (Nest Architects, Melbourne) for the content of Figure 1.2.

Photograph of Birmingham (UK) back-to-backs (Figure 2.1) courtesy of UK National Trust Images/Robert Morris, Image ref 153032.

Adam J. Green Architect (Evansville, Indiana) for his rendering (Figure 2.2) of the Peters-Margedant House in Evansville, Indiana (US).

Taxiarchos228 at the German language Wikipedia, CC BY-SA 3.0 (https://commons.wikimedia.org/w/index.php?curid=11829063) for the photograph (Figure 3.3) of Habitat '67 in Montreal (architect, Moshe Safdie).

Patrick Blanc for the photograph, Figure 3.4, of Caixa Forum Madrid, May 2010, designed by Herzog and de Meuron Architects, and the vertical garden wall by Patrick Blanc.

Boeri Studio, and photographer Paolo Rosselli for the photograph of the Bosco Verticale 'Vertical Forest' Milan apartments, Figure 3.5.

Ivan Brodey (photographer Oslo, Norway) for the photograph of Boxhome (Rintala Eggertson Architects) Oslo, Norway, Figure 3.6.

Rintala Eggertsson Architects and artist John Roger Holte (Oslo, Norway) for sketches of Boxhome, Figure 3.7.

Photographer Frank Oudeman/OTTO for the photograph of East Village Studio, NYC (Jordan Parnass Digital Architecture), Figure 3.8.

The three floor plans in Figures 4.1–4.3 – from pages 67, 142 and 93, respectively, in Terence Conran, *Small Spaces: Inspiring Ideas and Creative Solutions*, originally published by Conran Octopus, London 2001 – are used courtesy of Octopus Publishing Group.

The photograph (Figure 5.1) of Summerland Mansions, St Kilda (Melbourne, Australia) is courtesy of Heritage Victoria.

Laura E. Fitch, architect (Amherst, Massachusetts) for her early schematic design rendering for Jamaica Plain Cohousing, Figure 5.2.

Simon Dale (photographer) and 'www.beingsomewhere.net' for the exterior (Figure 6.1) and the interior (Figure 6.2) of a Lammas dwelling.

Sustainable Projects Ireland (specifically Peadar Kirby) for the masterplan sketch of Cloughjordan Ecovillage (Figure 6.3) and Davie Philip for his photograph of ploughing at Cloughjordan Community Farm (Figure 6.4).

Jim Barmore, photographer of Dancing Rabbit Ecovillage, an aerial view (Figure 6.5) courtesy of Dancing Rabbit Ecovillage.

carpaneto.schöningh architekten (Berlin) and photographer Ute Zscharnt (Berlin) for the photograph of Spreefeld, Figure 7.1.

Post- (architectural practice, Perth) for the photo and sketch of a tiny house (West Australia) they designed, Figure 8.1.

Katja Testroet for a photo of a Ceilidh at Tinkers Bubble in south Somerset, England, Figure 9.1.

Kim Wyon (photographer) and VisitDenmark for Figure 9.2, a photograph of Christiania.

Introduction

1

Less Is More:
Living Closely on a Finite Planet

This introductory chapter outlines why, and how, small and shared housing is a stepping stone towards environmentally sustainable livelihoods and socially convivial lifestyles this century. After sketching the global challenges that small and shared housing can address, I sketch out what small and shared living means on a personal level. Then I describe the structure of this book which, selectively reads the past (Part I), reviews the present (Part II) and speculates on the future of collaborative housing (Part III) at a time when economic and environmental challenges threaten life as we know it, even our species-life per se. *Small Is Necessary: Shared Living on a Shared Planet* addresses those massive challenges in constructive ways to show how community-based activities could make us live more sustainably.

THE CHALLENGES THAT FACE US

The enduring Great Recession following the Global Financial Crisis of 2008 unsettled households across the world. There have been negative impacts on work opportunities, incomes and government support for affordable social housing, contributing to unstable house prices and unfavourable terms of credit for purchasing homes. In some regions precarious employment, declining incomes and fewer government services have driven people to cities ill-equipped to cater for rapidly expanding numbers of job-seekers demanding a range of basic services. It has become commonplace for house prices to have risen alarmingly in capital cities, with impacts on rental demand and costs. By the mid-2010s, particularly in Europe, substantial migrations had contributed to temporary and permanent resettlements. Finding appropriate and affordable housing has become a widespread challenge, particularly for young and elderly singles, especially women whose savings and incomes are typically lower than similarly aged men.

This is a chronic crisis and, writing in 2017, the prognosis remains bleak. According to a Resolution Foundation Study, 90 per cent of 18–34-year-old Britons will be unable to afford their own homes and will be confined to renting by 2025.[1] This deterioration in housing afford-ability is replicated across the United States (US), Canada, Australia and New Zealand (NZ). On the one hand, housing industry sources often complain that regulatory constraints on land use containing the boundaries of cities are responsible for rising land and home prices.[2] On the other hand, remarkably high house prices in Australia, amongst other nations, have been attributed to the availability of more onerous home loans at low interest rates, which translate into lower mortgage repayments, and the preparedness of owner-occupiers to devote a relatively high proportion of income to housing costs.[3] Another upward pressure on prices has been international investment, responsible for a two-tier real estate market developing in global cities, typically in capitals such as London where the mean house price was roughly double that of other parts of England in 2014–2015.[4]

Still, the trend to house price increases has been neither uniform nor universal in cities, regions or countries. For instance, with respect to other Organisation for Economic Co-operation and Development (OECD) countries, house prices and household debt multiplied remarkably in Sweden, Norway, France, Chile, Belgium, Israel and Denmark between 2000 and 2015, yet dropped in Portugal, Japan and Greece over the same period. Where house price hikes occurred they often flowed on to rental increases, especially in the US, and in Australia where there is low competition from that minor proportion (circa 4.5 per cent) of stock that is social housing (modest housing managed by government or not-for-profit bodies specifically for those on low incomes).[5]

Meanwhile, in terms of demand for housing and land for residential development, global population keeps rising. In 1800, there were just 1 billion (bn) human residents of Earth. We grew, increasingly rapidly, to 6bn in 1999, then to 7bn by the end of 2011. The projected 1.1bn rise between 2015 and 2030 is expected to swell most urban areas outside Europe by around 15 per cent. These averages deceive, in as much as they do not adequately represent places where populations will either shrink to leave unoccupied housing or, alternatively, increase remarkably. Indeed, the Australian capital of the state of Victoria, Melbourne, is expected to double its population to 8 million by 2050 from 4 million in 2012.[6]

The challenge is not simply one of fitting in more residents on limited land. Mainstream housing in the Global North absorbs materials and energy in its construction and everyday operation, contributing significantly to resource depletion and global carbon emissions. Settlements on coastal fringes and wholesale clearance of woodlands and forests have impacted heavily on animal habitats. In contrast to human increases, since 1970 populations of other vertebrate species have diminished by more than 50 per cent.[7] The WWF 2014 *Living Planet Report* shows that our ecological footprint (the area required to supply the ecological goods and services we use) has increasingly over-reached the earth's regenerative biocapacity since the mid-1970s.[8] So much so that, by the mid-2010s, we were regularly consuming 50 per cent more than the earth could replenish. More disturbingly, the 2016 *Living Planet Report* indicates that, if we follow current trends we will exceed Earth's regenerative capacity by around 75 per cent as soon as 2020.[9]

There are strong direct and indirect connections between housing and the over-use of Earth's resources. In 2010, all types of buildings worldwide accounted for 32 per cent of total global final energy use, contributing significantly to global warming – a development which not only threatens multiple ecological systems across the globe but also makes the future of the human species uncertain.[10] The Intergovernmental Panel on Climate Change (IPCC) has warned that increasing population, urbanisation and development threatens even more deleterious impacts in the future. Yet the IPCC also signals significant potential for reducing energy used in both the construction and use of residential building. Feasible low-cost achievements rely on compliance with strengthening government standards to improve building codes for construction and retrofits, policymakers attending to effective urban infrastructure and planning, and multiple voluntary lifestyle changes. How we house ourselves, live in our houses, and go to work and other daily activities, all have potential to significantly reduce carbon dioxide emissions and global climate change.

MANAGING OUR FUTURE TO BE 'SMALL' AND 'SUSTAINABLE'

Given that we are struggling with affordability and breaching environmental limits, this book explores future directions of housing and household consumption towards more compact and shared lifestyles to enhance both social and natural environments alike. Through decades of experimentation, activist-residents, community-oriented policymakers and non-government organisations have developed successful and enduring models. *Small Is Necessary* examines the benefits and challenges of creating smaller and more efficient living spaces using various collaborative housing models, such as cohousing, ecovillages and communal housing in cities, suburbs, peri-urban fringes and regional areas. All such models refer to households that share building and outside spaces and facilities in self-managed ways.

The book's title develops on a rich lineage. The classic *Small Is Beautiful: Economics as if People Mattered* by 'E. F.' (Ernst Friedrich) or 'Fritz' Schumacher was originally published in 1973 (London: Blond & Briggs) and argued the environmental efficiencies of modest lifestyles for sustainability. Several years later, in 1981, George McRobie's *Small Is Possible* (New York City: HarperCollins) offered a variety of small operations and appropriate technologies to illustrate Schumacher's ideas in action. Much later, in 2008, Lyle Estill sketched another practical, economic and spatial dimension in *Small Is Possible: Life in a Local Economy* (Gabriola Island: New Society Publishers). Similar to Rachel Carson's *Silent Spring* (1962, Boston: Houghton Mifflin Company) the emphasis in *Small Is Necessary: Shared Living on a Shared Planet* is on avoiding the consequences of business-as-usual peril.

Clearly, any focus on sustainable housing and lifestyles must engage with the broader social, economic and environmental contexts for sustainable household practices. Therefore, in this book, I ascribe to Edwards' and Hyett's simple and constructive definition of the contested term 'sustainable housing' as 'housing that creates sustainable communities in a resource-efficient manner'.[11] Notwithstanding the criticism of Guy and Moore – regarding Edwards' and Hyett's rather technical approach to sustainable housing – taken on its face value, this definition encompasses environmental and social aspects at a neighbourhood scale, and focuses holistically on broad-scale social and material contexts where local cultures and government policies can encourage and maintain sustainable practices.[12] The term 'sustainable communities' emphasises inter-generational and reproductive aspects, as well as local economies and cultures. Beyond a state that an individual or household might attain alone, say by purchasing or retrofitting their home and garden appropriately and adopting more environmentally efficient practices, the concept of sustainable communities appreciates sustainable housing in a dynamic context of conjoined socio-cultural, political and economic environments that establish and maintain sustainable practices in holistic ways.

HOW COMPACT AND HOW COMMUNAL?

In contrast to the economic interest of residential developers and the building sector to sell bigger houses to smaller households in suburbs and shoebox apartments in skyscrapers to investors who charge exorbitant rents, *Small Is Necessary* discusses the contradictions and challenges posed by current and future needs for shared and compact living. I am a critical advocate asking, for instance, whether high-density inner-urban living, as touted by many government policymakers, really does achieve a smaller ecological footprint than more collaborative suburban models. Similarly, I engage with debates on small and shared housing that historically separated many social and environmental movements.

The traditional left response to urban overcrowding and substandard housing was to call on the state to provide affordable individualised housing. This line failed, first, as many governments post-Second World War tended to respond by developing bureaucratically run public monuments that were neither friendly, aesthetic nor well-integrated. Second, under the influence of neoliberalism later in the twentieth century, states withdrew from direct provisioning of housing as part of cost-cutting and privatisation measures. Moreover, the traditional party and union-based left clashed in organisational ways with the diverse and growing 'alternative' movements' emphases on agency, collectivism, self-sufficiency and squatting – experimenting with models of alternative lifestyles, including communal living, creating alternative technologies and techniques for building, supplying energy and water, and dealing with waste, and self-provisioning for food and clothing. If these 'alternative' forms of living have become more central to a sustainable future, the traditional left maintains strong positions in asking central questions around the line between modest and sufficient housing, and cramped, noisy and insecure shelter.

Various models of collaborative housing are examined in this book, from non-relatives owning a house together and sharing their lives as a household unit, through to ecovillages that can include thousands of residents. A key question across all models focuses on preserving privacy and individuality. Despite the challenges of making such models work, I argue that collaborative housing can offer social support for young and old, singles and families alike, while providing environments where sharing networks and local cooperation can flourish. Shared housing encourages sharing knowledge and skills, addressing a neighbour's problem cooperatively, rather than individualistically ignoring or competing against them, say through conspicuous consumption. Teasing out all the environmental and human factors that contribute to more sociable, liveable and sustainable neighbourhoods, *Small Is Necessary* develops a practical framework for assessing what works best in different contexts, to satisfy different needs and achieve the most appropriate solutions for residents.

Small and shared living is a sensibility and art practised in appropriately built, or altered built, environments within rural and city landscapes that remind us that we belong to planet Earth. Small and shared living depends on skills and knowledge that develop and balance our needs for gregarious sociality and privacy. Small and shared living is about a modest haven, fondly called 'home', socialising in streetscapes and 'greenscapes' nearby, working at home or in a conveniently located shared office space, where – thanks to the Internet and cloud storage – the world is our oyster.

Imagine a room of one's own in a household where facilities and living spaces inside and out are shared, along with tending and harvesting from a collective food garden. Small and shared is about well-planned neighbourhoods and good public transport, which ease the frustrations and irritations of everyday working and socialising. It's about choices, greater equality and connectivity between us, and a more sustainable balance with nature.

'That's the sales pitch,' I hear you sigh. 'What about the shambolic, crowded and dirty joint household I lived in when I was a student? To avoid all the conflicts and mess, I spent as much time as possible at friends' houses and dreamt of a flat of my own or a house big enough for a family to share with my soul-mate. I don't want anyone telling me what to do in my own home. Coliving sucks!'

This is where personal skills and community knowledge about coliving and collaborative housing are essential. It's why community-minded residents, architects, developers, builders, policymakers, regulators, public service providers, businesspeople, funders and financiers need to develop joint visions and processes for establishing built and social environments that incubate and facilitate modest collaborate living. In cultures of small and shared living, environmental efficiency is the norm or ideal, and space is convivial. Residents accept household principles about who uses what, when and how – and benefit from joint cleaning and cooking schedules. Mutual support and care is at hand. The neighbourhood is planned for private and group activities. Noise and pets are controlled. When people have differences that interfere with what they each want, they problem-solve for win-win results.

It is complex, but the skills of self-organised community-based living can be learned and applied. After all, the city has long been regarded as the epitome of civilisation and, equally, the community-oriented character of a traditional village is a widely held ideal. This book features successful living models and experiments in cities and rural regions where people have set about collectively addressing current challenges of affordability, environmental sustainability and yearning for community by establishing households and neighbourhoods that are modest yet 'enough', and shared but secure and organised.

LEARNING FROM EXPERIENCE

This research interest evolved from my life's journey. I was brought up in a small nuclear family but benefited from my grandfather living with us for four years when I was young. When my father researched in Wales, we spent months at a time living with different relatives. I boarded at school for a short period, which was my worst experience of shared living because of the imposed rules and regimentation. Afterwards, as a young adult, I lived in joint households 'for better or for worse' – great learning experiences! Sharing homes with different partners also honed my skills in negotiation and conflict-resolution.

However, none of those experiences improved on living in two residential cooperatives for almost one decade. One was an all-under-one-roof living and working intentional community, Commonground (Central Victoria; see Figure 1.1). The other was Round the Bend Conservation Cooperative (RBCC) on the peri-urban fringe of Melbourne, whose residents collectively manage a 130-hectare woodland, where each of the 32 shares entitles the shareholder-household to a site for a house built and managed under collectively developed and collectively monitored regulations. Effectively, this cooperative is 'eco-cohousing', which is examined in Chapter 5. RBCC resident members have few shared resources beyond their land but significant joint responsibilities for the natural environment. There have been barriers to easy entry and exit due to member approval processes and the failure of lending institutions to offer appropriate models for buying in and out of such collectively owned property. I found that two long-term experiences of community 'self-management' – a curious term given what we are really talking about is 'collective management' – were deeply empowering on a personal level.

Figure 1. Commonground intentional community, Central Victoria, Australia

Source: Mike Crowhurst, photographer

Still, when I've lived by myself I have rarely felt 'alone', possibly because I have always been active in my immediate neighbourhood or wider diverse place-based community. Today, I live in Castlemaine, Central Victoria, Victoria being the most southern mainland state on the eastern coast of Australia. Castlemaine is known for its strong social and sustainability values and an artistic and diverse quasi-urban culture. The nonmonetary, sharing, solidarity and social economy practices that have become subjects of much social and scholarly interest in recent years were always part and parcel of the way I lived and loved, gave and received.

These experiences of shared living in economic spaces – mine was the smallest house built on the conservation cooperative – have informed this text in equal measure to information gleaned from key practitioners, experienced professionals and academic experts, the books I've read, and the audio-visual material I've listened to and watched in order to write it. Experience is the great teacher. But, equally, following wise advice can minimise or prevent bad experiences. Collective living showed me that good planning and processes can be learned, and that adapting tried and true processes in flexible ways saves frustration, time and energy. I learned that wholesome cultures of shared living can be established, or be absent, and that such cultures exist as a critical form of what is often referred to as 'social software'. However, I often wonder whether relationships and values are not, in fact, the very real hardware of societies?

Experience showed me that governments and regulations, as well as mainstream social norms, often frustrate the smooth implementation or running of collective arrangements. Despite the diversity of the modern 'family' household, local, state and Federal politicians, bureaucrats, financiers, business people, builders, developers and appliance manufacturers have tended to cling to a dominant notion of the primary household as a nuclear-style family. For a long time in Australia, the United Kingdom (UK) and the US, banks have refused lending money for collectively purchased property unless, say, everyone guaranteed the repayment of the loan, which might well be smaller and offered on higher interest rates than for individual homeowners. The idea of sharing energy sources or waste-disposal schemes has often sent bureaucrats – with their simple sets of rules and regulations for residential neighbourhoods laid out in a patchwork of private properties – into a 'Can't do', 'Never done' mode. This book shows how and why the economic and political tide is turning in favour of 'alternative' collaborative housing.

My experiential observations are supported by wider reading and studies that I have conducted as a researcher for the Centre for Urban Research, RMIT University (Melbourne, Australia) in a range of projects – many funded by the Australian Housing and Urban Research Institute – on housing affordability and sustainability, mortgage default, boarding houses, caravan and manufactured housing parks, and developing 'greenfield' suburbs. You will see, then, that all the arguments I mount are framed in reference to relevant literature and supported by evidence mounted in endnotes.

READERSHIP AND SCOPE

This book was written because the growth of interest in small, sustainable and affordable housing and shared living is increasing. While subjects of the popular television program 'Grand Designs', which is hosted by architect Kevin McCloud, generally spend hundreds of thousands (even millions) of British pounds on creating homes that fail sustainability criteria simply on the basis of size, viewers voted the episode on Ben Law's small £28,000 sustainable hand-built woodlands house as the 'best ever'.[13] Similarly, another popular episode focused on a modest and inexpensive two-roomed house and studio built in sympathy with its idyllic surrounds on Skye.[14] Furthermore, there was great interest when host Kevin McCloud developed a community-oriented social-housing model, Haboakus, though he dropped eco-aims early on due to classic market-straightjackets conflicting with professional and market-led community-building.[15]

On the other side of the world, in Australia, when ideas journalist Michael Short wrote an article in the Victorian state daily *The Age*, in 2015, on ten solutions to Melbourne's housing crisis – namely floating apartments, converted shipping containers, modular and prefabricated spaces, neat subdivisions of land, retrofitting an old house to make two, or an old factory to make many more homes, rooftop gardens and tiny houses – his article quickly trended as the newspaper's most read.[16] This interest is fuelled by the surge of experimentation in novel areas of alternative housing. In a more mainstream context, Figure 1.2 shows an 80sq m home, a 'backyard' infill development on circa 180sq m created by subdividing a block in a Melbourne inner suburb. With sustainability features such as the green roof, it was the first example of a 'Less Is More' home in a series of *Assemble Papers* (an e-journal that explores both 'small footprint living' and a 'culture of living closer together').[17] Similarly, in North America, the 'tiny house' movement has burgeoned with increasing models of tiny house settlements (Chapter 8) offering the added benefits of collective living.

Concentrating on the Global North, this book refers selectively to developments and scenarios in Europe, the UK, North America, Japan and Australia and NZ since the mid-twentieth century. Drawing

Figure 1.2 A modest infill development in an inner suburb of Melbourne (Nest Architects)

Source: Nic Granleese, photographer

on existing literature and policies related to housing and planning developments in various settings, it poses fresh questions and offers some original insights. As such, this book will interest all those seeking more diverse, liveable and sustainable housing. It is a field-guide for academics, students, professionals, activists and citizen interest groups in a range of areas – affordable and sustainable housing and urban planning, architecture and design, the financing of housing and the sociology of everyday life – as well as associated policymakers that influence, or are influenced by, diverse housing choices.

BOOK STRUCTURE

This book is divided into three parts – on past developments, current trends and likely futures. However, even in Part I, the focus is on recent developments in as much as housing and households of the past are reviewed on the basis of twenty-first century themes of sustainability and affordability. The analysis is inclusive of a diversity of household types and economic circumstances but precludes specific analyses of cultures, gender, ethnicity and race due to lack of both space and sufficient relevant research. Throughout the book discussion centres, instead, on social movements supporting affordable and appropriate housing whose concerns inform and coincide with the prerogatives of small and shared housing.

The book starts by reviewing the history of housing and households, with a special emphasis on relevant changes during the twentieth century. Remarkably, the typical household shrank from an extended intergenerational family with several children to a conventional nuclear family with a couple of children and, finally, a range of parent–child households with de facto couples, same-sex couples, step-families, single-parent households and blended families. Towards the end of the twentieth century, higher separation and divorce rates and extended average life spans had resulted in a diverse mixture of predominantly smaller households, many with single half-time parents and elderly couples or singles. Most significantly for housing, on average, households diminished from circa 4.5 to 2.5 members.

At the same time as household sizes contracted, in certain countries such as the US, Canada and Australia, newly built houses especially in outer-city suburbs grew in size right up to the 2008 Global Financial Crisis, significantly triggered by residential mortgage defaults. The trends and counter-trends to 'McMansions' were not as marked in Europe. Indeed, in Britain, the persistence of smaller houses has been detrimentally associated with poor housing stock. In most cities across the world, as populations rose depressing slum living became more apparent. Today, up to one-third of Earth's urban residents (1bn people) still live in slums.[18] So, even if for different reasons, in most countries the growing ecological case for smaller residential footprints was at odds with mainstream ideals for larger housing in spacious land developments. The apparent novelty of the mainly North American tiny house movement illustrates the distance between mainstream and alternative ideals.[19]

Meanwhile, during the last few decades, an increasing range of residents, urban planners, architects, government agencies and activists have recognised – even if implicitly rather than, as here, explicitly – that *coupling shared with small* makes greatest social and ecological sense.

They have observed, drawn on and benefited from numerous insights gained from various experiments since the 1960s, when a generation evolved that was prepared to challenge 'the Establishment' by living in alternative ways – and from a more recent generation, many of whom who regard 'green' as an axiom. Today sustainable urban innovations appear in places as far apart as Barcelona (Spain) and Melbourne (Australia), and feature significantly in inner-city, suburban and peri-urban cohousing and ecovillages in Europe and North America. Today, the drivers range from self-organising residents and proactive governments to niche markets created by entrepreneurs recognising the demand for sustainable, community-oriented developments.

Small Is Necessary tells this story, showing the potential for smaller and shared models of housing to meet current and future social and environmental challenges.

Parts: past, present, future

Part I reviews how inner-urban housing always tended to be compact and remained so as more households moved to cities. While detached houses in North American and Australian suburbs tended to increase in floor space right up to the Global Financial Crisis, apartments and town houses in cities such as London, Tokyo and New York City had always been characterised by compact, high-density living, blending modern with traditional designs. Clever interior design appeared critical in small inner urban spaces, where householders incorporated technological advances in household appliances and furniture – from kitchen wizardry to sofa beds and foldaway wall beds – in symbiosis with working more outside the home and flourishing streetscape cultures.

However, tiny private urban spaces became socially insular nuclear-family pressure cookers. Moreover, while achieving valuable energy savings in sectors such as transport, the overall consumption of many households in compact cities such as New York are not environmentally sustainable. In such locations apartments have not meant cheaper housing either; micro-apartments have been attractive to investors in the mid-2010s because they attract higher rents space-wise. These factors, along with deindustrialisation, the rise of information economies, city pollution, pockets of disadvantage, gentrification and suburbanisation have shown weaknesses of a simple small and compact urban model.

Chapter 2 focuses on very select historical developments: reflecting the rise of capitalism, the home retreated from a workspace to a place of respite and diversions from work except, of course, for beavering housewives. Today, home has re-emerged as a work base for growing numbers of self-employed, contractors and e-workers. Many urbanites opted for life in a detached or semi-detached house in suburbs with demographic changes in household composition and size influencing, interacting and clashing with developments in house styles, floor plans and house sizes over the twentieth century. Meanwhile, owner-occupier dwellings have become a strange amalgam of capitalist commodity and asset – impacting on house and apartment prices.

Chapter 3 focuses on apartments to find that many of their environmental, social and economic limitations and potential were clear very early on – replicated across geographies and multiplied as industrialisation and urbanisation both expanded and contracted. Green apartments, micro-apartments and utopian apartment living all come in for scrutiny. While current policies and plans for future cities favour medium- to high-density, compact and 'smart' urban developments, such apartments are often unaffordable, and not even environmentally sound and appropriate living spaces. Social inequities and ecological unsustainability appear closely integrated in analyses involving apartment size.

Chapter 4 walks right into apartments, reviewing their interior sustainability and dwellers' sustainability practices beyond their dwelling. The implications of domestic technology and household consumption are discussed. Modest and comfortable, cleverly designed and used apartments, are identified and characterised. However, despite market forces claiming that what they offer is a response to demand, we find that real resident engagement might well be key to decisive improvements in the affordability, sustainability and sociality of residential planning and buildings.

In short, Part I covers the persistence of, and countertendencies generated by, small private household living in highly urbanising infrastructures. These narratives highlight push and pull factors leading to the *small and shared* social and environmental developments examined in Part II, where a clear distinction is drawn between eco-cohousing and ecovillages.

The eco-cohousing Chapter 5 starts with smaller collaborative initiatives, such as a house, land, and farming enterprise co-owned by three or more non-related residents. Many and various cohousing models are testimony to bottom-up pressures to escape alienated lifestyles typified by a career 'rat-race' and stereotyped male–female roles in households. Over the four decades since cohousing projects began, designs have tended towards smaller private areas, larger common facilities and greater eco-efficient and environmentally friendly features.[20]

A spirit of social empowerment, visions of shared collective housing and concerns about the environmental costs of mainstream urban living have encouraged urban and peri-urban ecovillages in the UK and Europe (Chapter 6). The specific ecovillages discussed show clear achievements in terms of ecological footprint measures. I highlight well-established projects that have pioneered ways of addressing the economic, social and environmental needs for compact housing by sharing common spaces and facilities through to those that integrate collective sufficiency in work-and-live arrangements.

By the twenty-first century, professionals, bureaucrats and politicians in certain countries, such as Germany, developed strategic and subtle responses to needs for environmental sustainability and social cohesion in cities. Part III examines outstanding examples of such top-down and bottom-up transfusions, involving sophisticated engagements between residents and the authorities servicing them, creating more environmentally robust and socially appropriate landscapes. As such Part III examines developments introduced in Part II but in the broader context of urban landscapes, urban planning and local governance. As a way to consider the future scaling-up of small and shared living, and shared landscapes, each chapter focuses on a specific driver: the state (Chapter 7), the market (Chapter 8) and grassroots communities (Chapter 9).

These three chapters offer models of, and principles for, extending smaller footprints and shared living spaces across urban and rural landscapes. Practical examples include European models where architectural and cultural heritage are preserved by community-oriented developments; an Australian environmental living zone, which evolved after principles established in a neighbourhood residential cooperative were readily adopted by local private landowners and households; and a post-capitalist eco-industrial village established by ex-squatters in the remains of a Catalan factory village replete with hacker space and environmental remediation projects. I discuss participatory governance and sharing economy initiatives to show how communities in collective spaces have forged skills readily transferable to urban planning and governance, becoming a catalyst for participatory design in cities.

Another theme shows how nature has been, and can be, brought into cityscapes with cohousing and urban ecovillages as the beating heart of these efforts. Alternative technology and energy sources offer new opportunities for efficiently servicing residential housing; infrastructure and vital service providers are developing models known as co-management and co-production. Here, sharing household equipment, resources and services meets collaborative consumption, nonmonetary swap and barter networks, and community-supported agriculture. There are emerging initiatives for household and neighbourhood collective sufficiency integrated into holistic patterns for city and rural living.

CONCLUSION

In summary, small and shared housing and living is a 'necessary but not sufficient' principle for more environmentally sustainable livelihoods and socially convivial lifestyles. In arguing that the future direction is to smaller and more shared living spaces, I am not so much signalling a totally new future as a return to historical social norms. However, equally, our future will not be a simple return to the past, if only because other factors, such as population growth, environmental pressures, technological developments, and the still antagonistic trend of certain market forces, mean that the movement for small and shared living has come from various quarters as a countertrend to mainstream ideals and has an environmental rationale specific to our time.

In short, whether for environmental, affordability or social reasons, sharing is becoming a natural and necessary complement to small. *Small Is Necessary* offers constructive critiques and a state-of-the-art summary of a range of existing developments and future possibilities appropriate for various contexts, pointing out attractive, feasible housing solutions for enjoying more with less.

PART I

Compact Urban Housing

2

Once We Were Small:
Traditional and Contemporary Homes

In conversation and popular culture, 'home' is associated with a haven, privacy, comfort, kin and mutual support.[1] A home might be inherited and represent ties of kinship. A house might be lovingly, or for solely practical reasons, owner-built. A tenant might feel either insecure and resentful or secure and grateful. Owner-occupiers' houses co-exist as a use value, a dwelling, and as an asset, for renting out or for potential sale. Most significantly, in terms of mobility (say migration or moves driven by aspiration), notions of home assume complex associations beyond the 'house' and 'family' to encompass neighbourhoods, towns, regions, even nations, adopted homes or lost 'homelands'. In these senses, home is both a landscape and a belonging to community. In short, the house as a 'home' is a socio-material concept inseparable from 'household' and set in wider spatial, socio-economic and cultural contexts.

This chapter focuses on select developments over the last few centuries as the production and experience of home reflected the rise of capitalism in the United Kingdom (UK), Europe, North America, Australia and New Zealand (NZ). In this process home morphed from a workspace to a place of respite and diversions from work except, of course, for the 'housewife' who busily maintained the home and household. The house succumbed to capitalist production processes, becoming a commodity and asset whether built by small or large building companies as a one-off spec home, as one amongst many in a housing estate, or as a unit in a multi-storey housing block. Many urbanites opted for life in a detached or semi-detached house in suburbs. Over the past century, demographic changes in household composition and size have influenced, interacted and clashed with developments in house styles, floor plans and house sizes. Most houses supplied on the market are environmentally unsustainable, many are unaffordable for people on average (let alone low) incomes, and perpetuate alienation rather than encourage genuine community in authentic neighbourhoods.

In short, under significant economic, environmental and social challenges, the home has been subject to competing pressures and ideals and now presents a challenge. This chapter explores this evolution, avoiding generic topics associated with apartments (treated in Chapter 3) or sustainability-specific changes in the interiors of apartments and dwellers' practices within and beyond their apartments (Chapter 4). In the context of the argument for smaller and shared housing, this chapter shows how the size of dwellings has grown very quickly in a relatively short period of time. More modest living had been much more the norm during the last few centuries of human history. Similarly, history shows larger and more varied households than are seen to be typical in the Global North today. In short, such historical characteristics are closer than contemporary mainstream housing and lifestyles to the ideals and practices of smaller and shared living 'alternatives' explored in later parts of this book.

WORK, HOUSEHOLDS AND HOUSE SIZE

In pre-industrial times, able household members worked sociably at, around or from home. Industrialisation relocated work away from homes that would, instead, turn into units of consumption, education and clean domesticity. Just as private housework was generally performed by women and servants, the productive cash economy was dominated by men. Data from New York City (NYC) shows a climb in numbers of men working away from home from fewer than 5 per cent in 1800, to 20 per cent by 1820, and 70 per cent by 1840.[2] While this level of change was neither as swift nor uniform across most regions and countries, housing everywhere would become an appendage to commercial activities, which reorganised expectations and obligations between couples, and parents and their children. For housewives, homes were productive-cum-consumptive units as they cared for household members, cleaned the house, provided meals, laundered and mended clothes – making home and work synonymous. In contrast, for household members working outside home, it became a place of relaxation, leisure and pleasure. Meanwhile, social changes associated with rising capitalist classes and power impacted differentially on house sizes, space, use and location.

The 'family' household

In *The Making of Home*, Judith Flanders argues that the romantic leitmotif myth of a traditional tight-knit nuclear or extended family was prompted by disconcerting conditions attending the rise of capitalism, industrialisation and urbanisation. In reality, for centuries families were mobile and mixed affairs, losing and adopting (especially young) members because of deaths and cohabiting with other families. 'Family' gatherings at Christmas, marriage and funerals meant community as well as kin. In short, the 'image of a family of the past gathered together around a dinner table was a novelty of modernity, and of plenty' rather than historical reality.[3]

Similarly, a Canadian study across the twentieth century data shows that the percentage of children living with both parents was highest relatively recently, in 1961 (94 per cent). A similar number of children lived in single-parent families in 1931 (12 per cent) as in 1981 (13 per cent), although most often with a widowed parent in 1931 and a separated one in 1981. In 2011, 11 per cent of Canadians aged up to 24 years lived in blended (or step-) families.[4] In 2011, a mere 9 per cent of family households contained non-immediate family members while 31 per cent had done so in 1901. Clearly the 'family' household has never been either as complete or as cohesively kin as popular culture and contemporary politicians suggest.

However, Flanders does argue that, for a few centuries, a relatively exclusive nuclear family unit did become relatively normal across north-western Europe, with its women, children and household workers subservient to a male head. Meanwhile, in most other areas of Europe and its colonies, single adults lived in various multi-nuclear and extended-family households based on kinship, cultural norms and practicality. In the nineteenth century, single rooms in boarding houses or lodgings also became respectable homes for singles and young couples in Britain and the United States (US).[5] Furthermore, it was not unusual to find houses, rooms and beds shared by family members and visitors. Of greatest significance to our study here, people shared living, eating and sleeping spaces, which were often relatively small.

The English house of the nineteenth century

An income above £150 per annum identified middle-class English family households during the first half of the nineteenth century and, by mid-century, Burnett estimates that one in six English people comprised this 'tier of middle classes'.[6] Middle-class homes were located away from workplaces and their pollution, generally had at least six rooms, and were bigger households than working-class ones partly because they included servants, and separated public (male) from private (female) areas as well as family-only areas from activities involving deliveries and door-to-door salespeople.[7] Gendered spheres determined household experiences and practices.[8] The genteel housewife made the home an antidote to the challenges, threats and alienation of commercial production; home was for intimacy, relaxation, religiosity, care, cleanliness and nurture.

While middle-class households reflected managerial male authority in the workplace, urban geography highlighted the capitalist class divide. Working-class tenements and boarding houses in Britain's industrial cities were close to their polluting workplaces, overcrowded, noisy, under-ventilated and dank, with communal water and toilets clustered in courtyards. In the mid-nineteenth century, one working-class area of Leeds had more than 200 dwellings occupied by an average of 11 people per dwelling and more than two residents for every bed (beds and bedding were expensive). Even 'back-to-backs', replacing slums in the nineteenth century, had just a few rooms and three shared-party walls, with 'privies' and standpipes – along with their users – exposed to a courtyard or the street.[9] Similarly in the US, by 1900, two-thirds of the residents of NYC (2.3 million out of a total of 3.4 million) lived in pokey, dank tenements with poor facilities that had a negative impact on health and mortality rates.[10] Some escaped in the following decades, as urban areas of the US were populated with small row houses of a few 'public' and 'private' rooms.[11]

Although workers in nineteenth century Britain experienced tiny, crowded and poorly built housing, 'back-to-backs' – as in Figure 2.1 – were of a higher standard than the rural labourer's cottage. Many benefitted from courtyard spaces where residents shared toilets, water services, play areas and child-care. Based on 1851 England-wide data, revealed in an 1864 inquiry, Burnett suggests that the vast majority of residents lived in one or two-bedroom cottages where the average 7ft (2.13m) height and 10ft by 10ft (3.05m by 3.05m) bedroom would bed four or five people.[12] Meanwhile, European house-building practices inspired tiny single-storey structures of one room built in colonial settlements of the eighteenth and nineteenth centuries. Later, such modest structures were extended, renovated and replaced with larger houses and more rooms. Subdivision created the 'bedroom', which was 'largely an invention of the late eighteenth and early nineteenth centuries'.[13]

Figure 2.1 Birmingham (UK) back-to-backs

Source: ©National Trust Images/Robert Morris, Image ref 153032

'Overcrowding', meaning two members per room over 10 years of age – younger children counted as 0.5 – became the main criterion for assessing English housing when, in 1891, the measure of household members per room was substituted for one based on members per dwelling. Burnett characterises this as simply 'a tolerant minimum' given that it still 'allowed a three-roomed house to contain two adults, four children and any number of babies without falling foul of the definition.'[14] The inexact measure of a 'room' has persisted in Organisation for Economic Co-operation and Development (OECD) statistics where vagaries in sizes of rooms, even the 'average room', endure. This is significant because the number of rooms per resident is the OECD proxy for levels of overcrowding; recent data suggest that the average dwelling in OECD member countries (and of Switzerland) offers 1.8 rooms per person.[15]

The English house of the twentieth century

If income determined space in English homes of the nineteenth century, its influence diminished in the twentieth century. The standard was raised to 1.5 occupants per room, one that almost 17 per cent of households failed in 1911, but fewer than 3 per cent did in 1961. Once more than one member per room signified overcrowding, in 1971, the proportion falling short of that standard soon dropped from 6 per cent to 3 per cent, in 1981. Of course, averages conceal considerable variations in house (and household) size; a house with the same number of rooms often accommodated both the swelling family and, later, its aged 'empty nesters'.[16]

During the past century house size was less related to an English family's income than to tenure type and location. Owner-occupiers ballooned from 29 per cent in 1950 to 60 per cent in 1983. In 1962, three-quarters of private homes built for owner-occupiers with mortgages were around 750–1000sq ft (70–93sq m). Owner-occupier households tended to have more space than those of renters mainly because the typical clients of council houses had comparatively larger families. By 1983, 29 per cent of housing was rented from local authorities compared with just 11 per cent in private market rentals (a sharp reduction from 58 per cent in 1947). The council house was a lower-middle-class creation which, by the 1970s and 1980s, offered more spacious and sanitary conditions, private bedrooms for boys and girls, 'a garden which developed healthy children and sober husbands', and a modest level of comfort, even if in a depressing environment and involving long waiting lists for applicants.[17]

For decades, the Parker Morris Report of 1961 remained a reference point for UK housing reform, emphasising space and heating as basic needs. Minimum standards for floor space started from 350sq ft (33sq m) for a one-person dwelling, including 30sq ft (2.8sq m) for storage, through to 950–1100sq ft (88–102sq m) for a household of six, including 50sq ft (4.65sq m) for storage with an option for 20sq ft (1.85sq m) storage outside. Its recommendations meant costly improvements, which were only incorporated by all local authorities once they became mandatory in the late 1960s. Never forced on private housing providers, in 1980 the space standards were relinquished in the public sector in favour of cost limits, in line with neoliberal sentiments, and the demographic fact that household sizes were smaller.[18]

Mixed developments and high-rise flats built since the early 1950s were coming under increasing criticism. Similar developments characterised US high-rise public housing that 'isolated and warehoused poor citizens' and suffered from a 'deplorable lack of security and maintenance'.[19] The 1985 Inquiry into British Housing recommended greater investment, the removal of tax deductions related to mortgage interest, and local authorities transformed from direct providers of housing to facilitators and regulators of private and not-for-profit social housing.[20] Such neoliberal trends characterised social housing in many other nations.

The Greater London Authority reintroduced a standard, in 2011, referred to as 'Parker Morris + 10%', although in most details and configurations the standard proved more spacious than 110 per cent of the Parker Morris Standards. In contrast to this ideal, Morgan and Cruickshank have shown that new builds in the 2010s tended to be sub-standard by this measure and that 'the vast majority (79 per cent) of English homes are near or below the minimum acceptable size, as defined by the *London Housing Design Guide*' of 2010, proof of the perceived smallness of contemporary British dwellings and the need for space labelling per householder.[21] Indeed, the UK ranks low in actual housing space and standards in any international comparison.[22]

Of course, workers with higher skills and incomes enjoyed housing of a higher standard than casual and unskilled workers or those in sectors such as mining but enhanced housing conditions and size tended to improve all social scales, if unevenly, during the past century.[23] Still, London remained a special case. By the 1920s, electricity, water and gas services along with internal toilets and baths had connected houses and improved English living standards. However, only half of London's working-class housing had running water inside as late as 1934.[24] Even in 1966, Greater London had more tenements than the rest of England, almost one-quarter of households shared their house – considered pejoratively – and homelessness was more likely.[25]

Meanwhile, by the 1960s, fewer servants and children per family, and a speculative building industry determining supply led to the 'average middle-class house' appropriately shrinking from six or more to four or fewer bedrooms. At the same time, Burnett contends that 'the dwelling-house continued to be a prime indicator of social status for a society in which class-consciousness had not greatly receded' and the building sector would play on this factor.[26] A detached house in a suburb became the ideal. Householders wanted central heating and a place for the car on their plot. Most significantly, the North American and Australasian suburban house would swell in size during the twentieth century, even as household sizes fell.

THE PRODUCTION OF HOUSING AND SUBURBS

The typical conurbation that we call a 'city' generally incorporates a broad area of settlements of variable density and service convenience, satellite cities and suburbs. In Britain, the suburb was established by trains: two in every five US households had a car by around 1935 whereas just 2 million out of 46 million English residents owned a car by 1939.[27] Nevertheless, the car spread, enabling significant suburban growth – expanding cities right across the globe. As such, city growth became a major focus of developers and builders seeking commercial opportunity and, in reaction, attracted much socio-cultural critique.

Moreover, urban expansion offered utopian movements an opportunity to experiment with alternative models, discussed in later chapters. It suffices here to point to the independent model workers' villages that industrialists established, in the late nineteenth century, to quell revolutionary currents and guide reform within a protestant working-class ethic. Furthermore, a movement for 'garden cities' – green parklands surrounding a mix of residential, commercial and light-industrial developments – was started by Ebenezer Howard, associated with Chicago's re-planning around city parks, although the first intentional garden city was in Letchworth, Hertfordshire (UK).[28]

In the 1920s, the modernist architect Le Corbusier ventured into plans for entire cities that deconstructed the roomed plan of homes into progressive, communal spaces surrounded by functional, minimal and clean built-in cupboards, storage and appliances, with generous windows and doors opening onto gardens. But this modernist aesthetic and communal spirit did not extend to the real growth areas of homes in suburbia. When open plan did become fashionable in houses on developers' estates, later in the twentieth century, its communal potential was contradicted by segregated spaces for children, teens and adults, and diluted by the alienating impacts of personal digital devices. Even though by mid-century, Patrick Geddes' 'regional city' model gained attention, again there was marginal impact on mainstream inner-urban and suburban developments.[29]

With the growth of the market society houses had become commodities but their particularly long life as a use value (a functional home) and opportunities for lease and re-sale made them a quasi-asset for owner-occupiers and a direct working asset for investors.[30] With the rise of the residential construction industry creating housing on a manufacturing scale, cities rippled out in suburban circles, construction became a major engine of gross domestic product in many countries, and financial sectors increased loans dedicated to mortgages.

Initially, houses designed by developers not only expressed the pressures of costs and availability of materials but also re-created cultural nostalgia. The 'colonial' (1870s) style spread throughout the US, just as Tudor replicas were rolled out in Britain, and Germans evolved a neo-traditional Altdeutsch gables and ornamental craftwork both inside and out that persisted well into the twentieth century.[31] Housing estates featured various styles, replicas and new developments, including the rise – and fall – of rooms for specific activities, especially leisure, from playrooms and rumpus rooms to theatre rooms and games rooms.

In North America, Australia and New Zealand, average house sizes were larger than in the UK and Europe. Government limits on Australian house sizes – aiming to ration construction materials during the Second World War – lasted till 1952. The 1200sq ft (111sq m) limit for timber constructions and 1250sq ft (116sq m) for brick, were considered so austere that many regarded initial builds simply a first stage. When restrictions lifted, the maximum became a minimum local government standard for new builds! However, compact designs persisted due to labour and material costs. In the early post-war years, residential gardens typically included a garage for a car just off the street, a small paved terrace or timber deck adjacent to the house, a porch for the front door, lawns, a pathway to a clothes line, and substantial space for growing vegetables, herbs and fruit trees.[32] In short, while certain marginal movements strove for connected, cohesive, compact, modern and green cities, suburbanites were making their homes and gardens a multiplicity of interior-centred and very private 'castles'.

Manufacturing the suburbs

The attraction of living in detached or semi-detached homes on small lots, facilitated by government housing policies and owner-occupier financial schemes, and access and time to travel to work meant that, after the Second World War, suburban residential development boomed for a few decades in the US, Australia and Canada. Suburbs and their engine, speculative house-building activity, arose earlier in the UK with middle-class relocation facilitated by new transport options. Significant local authority social-housing developments between the world wars, 'cottage estates in garden suburbs', merely 'institutionalised for the working classes the process of suburbanisation which the middle classes had followed since at least the middle of the nineteenth century'.[33] By the 1980s, a semi-detached suburban house with three bedrooms was 'home' for half of Britain's population.[34] Similarly, three-quarters of Australia's population lived in suburbs by the early twenty-first century.

In the US, Levittown (Long Island, NYC) epitomised mass production of speculative residential construction with almost 17,500 homes established between 1947 and 1951.[35] The 'King of Suburbia', building developer William Levitt used a small number of simple single-storey designs created by his brother Alfred, setting the houses across landscapes like tent cities. Levitt referred to his enterprise as 'manufacturing' rather than 'building'. The interiors of Levittown houses had a TV and hi-fi built in, covenants excluded minorities (such as African-Americans) and Levitt declared their inhabitants too busy to be Communists! Yet, the 1948 Housing Bill, 'a rare act of American socialism' enabled home-buyers and speculative builders alike to pursue their dream of a home of their own and profit, respectively.[36] Although the level of government support would wane, by 1970, US suburbs housed more residents than lived either in rural or in urban areas and, by 2000, more than half the US population were suburbanites.[37]

However, certain suburbs did contain, typically architect-designed, examples that broke commercial moulds. In the late 1930s, Frank Lloyd Wright started designing residential buildings in the 'Usonian' style. They proved aesthetically pleasing, environmentally friendly, comfortable and functional homes, but failed to live up to the intention of even middle-class affordability. Yet his colleague, William Wesley Peters, did design and realise a 552sq ft (51sq m) affordable worker's cottage, made of simple materials and blending into, and set far back on, its small lot – see Figure 2.2. Although it had only two bedrooms, it housed a family of six during the 1940s. The Peters–Margedant House – removed from its original setting to a university campus nearby in mid-2016 – demonstrates to an unusual degree the hard-to-achieve trio of environmentally sustainable, affordable and socially cosy. An exquisite diamond-pendant shape, the house features wide eaves and doors opening onto a paved courtyard. An internal brick wall had a fireplace with hood and grill to conserve and re-distribute heat along with hinged panels for opening to ventilate the house. The house was sealed with aluminium foil insulation. One, only now obvious, environmental blemish was the external oak boards

– dipped in creosote, a toxin the risks of which were not well-publicised and regulated against until the 1980s.[38]

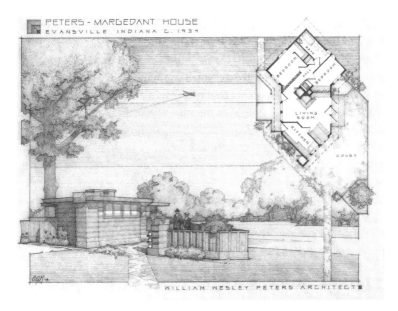

Figure 2.2   Peters-Margedant House, as rendered by Adam Green

Source: Adam J. Green Architect

Breaking the planning and settlement mould of suburbs, Merchant Builders, pioneers of architect-designed project homes in Melbourne, piloted clustered housing on the peri-urban fringe in the 1970s. Although homes in their Winter Park development occupied as much space as neighbouring low-density estates, ten houses on six acres were sited in two groups of five around a 1.5-acre central park. This model never got off the ground, but not due to lack of commercial success of the pilot case. Still, in the mid-2010s, houses there sold for 50 per cent above the local average despite extra operating costs in time (or gardener fees) to keep up their extensive native gardens.[39] Indeed, the main suburban fare had its detractors.

Socio-cultural critique of suburbia

The lyrics of 'Little Boxes' – written by Malvina Reynolds (1962) and made famous by Pete Seeger's 1963 hit – encapsulated the cultural critique of suburbia. Full of boringly similar houses, shoddily built – Reynolds coined 'ticky-tacky' – and clustered like tombstones, suburban housing seemed to embody ultra-ordinary mass-produced lives. US architectural and planning historian Lewis Mumford advised 'vigorous countermeasures' to the 1950s suburb. He saw a rational pull to the suburbs in the desire to live in a healthier, greener, more spacious and relaxed space than a city centre but pointed out that the popularity of suburbia buried its potential in developments that were 'not even a cheap counterfeit, but rather the grim antithesis' of their ideals. Furthermore, the car that enabled suburbs to exist also became a mandatory part of suburbanite life, ironically polluting the suburban dream of fresh air with exhaust, entangling their space with freeways and car parks, and causing fatalities on a war-scale.[40]

Architect Robin Boyd has traced the evolution of the Australian suburban cottage as far back as the 1820s, just decades after the 1788 invasion and subsequent settlement, declaring the suburb victorious by the end of the Second World War:[41]

Australian cities, spreading at an even single-story thickness over the land, were now the largest, per head of population, in the world. The little man could still build his own private castle, but it might be beyond the reach of the pipes and wires which conveyed twentieth century comfort, and it would certainly be so remote from his work that at least one-eighth of his waking hours would be taken in travel. The planner asked: How much longer can we go on like this? ... [W]ill not our big cities choke themselves out like over-stimulated weeds? ... How dull can life become?

Such critiques were labelled elitist. Weren't suburbs working-class achievements? Estate purchases were affordable and suburban living simply reflected a different, not necessarily inferior, lifestyle. In contrast, by the twenty-first century, critiques could legitimately claim that suburbs typically lacked both environmental sustainability and affordability. Largish estate houses on the edges of cities have become expensive options because of higher running costs and poor location. Houses in outer suburbs, peri-urban or 'growth area' suburbs, tend to be further from work and school than those living in city centres, with household members more dependent on cars as they travel longer distances for all their daily activities.

Meanwhile, commercial pressures to keep offering a bigger-is-better commodity for rising prices meant that the average size of newly built houses in countries such as Australia and the US reached absurd proportions by the time of the Global Financial Crisis in 2008, especially once demographic shifts were taken into account (as outlined in the Unsustainability section below). Furthermore, neither efficient size nor ideal location featured strongly in commercial strategies to romantically promote new estate developments as quasi-communities in the early twenty-first century. Rather, the features of compact size and ideal location were reserved for marketing apartments and condominiums in the inner city and along rapid transport nodes (discussed in Chapter 3). It must be emphasised that inner-city versus suburban living have existed in a dynamic struggle. 'The Great Inversion' is how urbanist Alan Ehrenhalt has referred to the relatively recent reversal of decay and poverty in the inner suburbs of US cities with central city residential convenience and opulence trumping suburban neglect, a trend already set in European and Australian cities by the twenty-first century.[42]

DEMOGRAPHIC SHIFTS AND AFFORDABILITY

Significant demographic shifts in household composition and size over the last 150 years have had slow, delayed and even contradictory impacts on house designs and construction. Irrespective of the rise and fall of the social housing sector as an alternative in many countries during the latter half of the twentieth century, market supply and affordability have conditioned choice. Given the longevity of built housing, the construction sector's drive to make profits, and umpteen individual choices determining renovation and extensions, the real estate market straddles old and new homes of great variety in terms of quality and context. The result has been a disconnect between households' needs and what 'the market' offers.

Demographic shifts

At the start of the nineteenth century, the European household averaged around five residents. This was double the average number occupying a dwelling by the early 2010s.[43] In 2011, the NZ average household size was 2.6 members, with both England and Japan at 2.4 and Scotland 2.2. In many countries the trend is expected to continue to even smaller household numbers. For example, the average Australian household size diminished from 4.5 members in 1911 to 2.5 in 2001.[44] Indeed, by 2026, the number of single-person Australian households is projected to rise somewhere between 57 and 105 percent of the 2001 level.[45] Perversely, the trend in house sizes has been in the opposite direction so, in less than two decades (between 1984–1985 and 2002–2003), the average floor area of new houses leapt from 162sq m to 228sq m while other (attached) newly built residences such as apartments also grew from 99sq m to 134sq m. In New South Wales (NSW) the average house size reached 245sq m.[46]

The 'First Demographic Transition' was related to health, characterised by dropping fertility rates, falling mortality rates and improved management of illness, disease and disabilities, allowing residents to age in place, at home, alone, for longer. The result was more one-person households and smaller family households. A cluster of social changes drove the 'Second Household Transition'. The fragmentation of nuclear households – divorce rates increased from the 1970s – meant more sole-parent families and the creation of blended families as divorcees remarried. One-person households rose in number as more young female and male students and workers lived independently and delayed marrying, and even after having children chose to 'live together apart'. There has been greater and more open acceptance of different household types, from joint households and collectives to same-sex couples. Such a variety of demographic shifts has made more, and more frequent, transitions between household arrangements more likely.[47]

Adding to these kinds of shifts has been a rise in mobility. Increased mobility has increased types as well as changes in residences, which are made into homes, sometimes splitting households and recreating others. As employers offer more 'fly-in, fly-out' work, such workers have two distinct (work and home) residences; workers and managers are required to spend periods interstate, or to move for years at a time for work in other regions or countries (sometimes leading to permanent moves or bringing a partner back to live in their home country); work has become less permanent and reliable, retrenchment and unemployment more common, leading to movements to gain more opportunities to work; and young people, especially, choose to see the world by working casually in a range of jobs overseas. These more complicated residential arrangements are harder to track for policymaking purposes.

Since the 1970s, women in industrialised regions, especially cities, have spent considerably more time in the workplace, despite contributing comparatively greater effort than their male partners on household chores and care of household members, especially children. This has meant greater access to home loans and, generally higher levels of credit, for single female, heterosexual couple and family households. More women working outside the home has had a downward impact on fertility levels and pushed up levels of one-person households. Arguably, the existence of two working parents has increased purchases of multiple 'time-saving' household devices and appliances for preparing and cooking food, cleaning and maintaining the home.

OECD data for distinct household formations during the early years of the twenty-first century shows a degree of variety according to country – see Table 2.1. In the US, even when the 'proverbial "typical household" accounted for only 15 per cent of the population', in 1980, 'single-family homes remained a sanctified ideal, protected by strict zoning regulations, popular media, and government agencies'.[48] The single family home

Table 2.1   Types of household by household type (%), 2011 (or nearest available)

	One-person households	Couple without children	Couple with children	Sole parent households	Other household types
Australia	23.9	25.9	31.0	10.5	8.7
Belgium	34.1	28.4	23.1	7.7	5.0
Canada	27.6	29.5	26.5	10.3	6.1
Denmark	37.5	27.9	22.2	6.2	6.2
France	33.8	28.5	25.6	7.3	4.8
Germany	37.3	31.2	20.6	5.5	5.5
Greece	25.7	30.6	27.8	4.2	11.6
Ireland	23.7	24.5	32.7	8.8	10.3
Italy	31.1	27.8	27.1	5.4	8.6
Korea	23.9	15.4	37.0	9.2	14.5
Netherlands	36.4	30.6	25.7	5.6	1.7
NZ	23.5	28.1	28.9	11.2	8.2
Norway	39.6	23.2	25.4	7.2	4.7
Poland	24.0	23.7	28.9	7.7	15.7
Spain	23.2	29.9	30.4	5.9	10.6
Sweden	36.2	27.9	24.3	6.6	5.0
UK	30.6	28.4	22.4	8.5	10.1
US†	26.7	28.21	20.2	9.6	15.3

Source: Select data, rounded to one point, drawn from OECD Family Database, Table SF1.1.A Types of Household, 2011 of 'SF1.1 Family size and household composition' in *Indicators*, as in the 7 September 2015, pp. 3–4 – http://www.oecd.org/els/family/SF_1_1_Family_size_and_composition.pdf

remains a popular aspirational dream, a myth serviceable for the kind of housing supplied by the market and epitomised in the grand 'McMansion' of US suburbs, but a myth all the same as any semblance of the family household as a stereotype has, in fact, disappeared.

Tenure and affordability

To some extent, demographic shifts associated with the 'Second Household Transition' were conditioned by, and conditional on, affordable options related to tenure. The devastation of urban areas in post-war Europe had prompted governments to directly supply housing, subsequently influencing both housing styles and tenure. In Europe and the UK there were more opportunities than in the US or Australia to rent affordable social (public) housing during the 1950s through to the 1970s. The extent of social housing in the UK and Europe de-incentivised private investment in rental properties, which were important housing sectors in the US and Australia. Across most countries neoliberal policies since the 1980s have favoured selling off public housing stock (for instance in rent-to-buy programs), substituting direct supply for support of social housing provided by non-profit sectors, and subsidies to private landlords to offer properties for affordable, below- or low-market rents.[49] In response, across all countries considered in this book, there has been a swing to owner-occupation and private sector provision of both owner-occupier and rental housing.

According to United Nations data, a century ago the proportion of owner-occupiers as a percentage of total national households varied considerably: 70 per cent in the UK, 68 per cent in the US and 66 per cent in Canada, the largest proportions were in Spain (82 per cent) and Ireland (80 per cent) whereas Germany (42 per cent) was only marginally higher than Sweden (40 per cent) and Switzerland (34 per cent).[50] Germany has a hybrid private–government social housing scheme whereby individual landlords receive a public subsidy for offering their property under state rent and tenancy regulations. Similarly, Sweden developed a stolid social housing sector post-Second World War and maintains strong regulations on private landlord rental properties.[51] Yet the withdrawal of state housing provision in most countries has resulted in growing unaffordability in the open market. A recent OECD study summarises data on affordability stressing the extent of households 'overburdened' with the cost of housing: one in seven rental households and one in ten mortgagors have to reserve at least 40 per cent of their disposable income to cover their housing costs; one in seven households suffers from overcrowding, and a similar proportion has no interior flushing toilet; social housing is severely limited in quantity and, therefore, access and eligibility.[52]

Honing in on one tenure in England, the 2013–14 *English Housing Survey* highlighted that, although European tenants paid an average 24 per cent of their take-home pay on rent, the English average was 47 per cent and in London (where 23 per cent of English renters reside) the proportion was 72 per cent.[53] Especially given that 36 per cent of English renters formally live in poverty, partly attributable to high housing costs, saving for a deposit is extremely difficult. Furthermore, renters have minimal protection for stable housing; the standard contract is for just 6–12 months (similar to Australia, where the norm is one year). While private rental conditions pressure residents towards home ownership, high rents make this kind of solution unachievable. The 2014–15 *English Housing Survey* calculated the average (mean) weekly rent for social housing as £99, for private rental £179 and, in London £298, and revealed that the proportion of private renters doubled between 2002 and 2015, by which time almost half of 25–34 year olds lived in private rental housing.[54]

While every other OECD country has distinct levels of housing inadequacy – varying numbers who are homeless or in mortgage stress – income-related data indicate broad characteristics shared across OECD countries regarding household type and tenure. Not surprisingly, those on lower incomes are less likely to be owner-occupiers, with 30 per cent renting through the private market and 9 per cent in social rental housing. While one in three sole parents occupy private rentals, fewer than one in seven two-parent households rent. Similarly, almost three times the number of sole-parent households compared with two-parent households live in subsidised housing. While a significant minority of senior-only households continue to pay off mortgages, 70 per cent of senior-only households in OECD countries completely own their home. Most young adults continue to live at home as they complete tertiary studies, train or start work.[55]

Marginal housing

The complicated tenancies and practicalities of those living in a distinct version of suburban-style living – in caravans, 'trailers', mobile or manufactured homes in residential or mobile home parks – highlights the vulnerability to exploitation of both owner-renters and renter-renters and the extent of unaffordability of housing in the US. 'Owner-renters' own their mobile home, even if – like many other owner-occupiers – they are in debt purchasing it, yet they must, at the same time, pay rental for a site and associated facilities and services to locate their home. Meanwhile, 'renter-renters' rent both the mobile home and their site. An Australian study categorises mobile homes in a suite of 'marginal rental housing' – 'highly managed or controlled housing, with fewer occupancy rights for tenants than in other forms of private rental and social housing, and some degree of shared facilities and spaces'[56] – to conclude that, where satisfactory living conditions were affordable and management reliable and respectful, this form of housing can be reasonable and an enjoyable experience. However, in Australia, as in the US, residential or mobile home parks are notorious for lack of value for money, poor physical and social conditions, criminality and precarious security of tenure.

In 2016 Breville reported that there were seven times the number of affordable mobile homes and households (8.6 million) than low-rent homes and households (1.2 million) in the US. The 20 million residents of mobile homes – 12 million in private parks where they at least rent a site and pay for shared facilities and services – include almost one-quarter of all US retirees. Fifteen per cent of housing in New Mexico is mobile homes. Although a site is rented and the home mobile, the size (say 75sq m) of manufactured dwellings and the ways in which they settle on site make moving expensive and a lot more effort than many elderly residents can face.[57] In Australia such parks often occupy zones – along coasts and rivers subject to flooding or adjacent to industry – where no other types of residential housing are allowed and managers can readily move residents on if their proposals to re-develop the site are approved by council.[58]

Given the failure of the public and private sectors on both environmental sustainability and social affordability fronts, individuals, groups and professionals have driven grassroots experiments and partnerships, significant examples of which are explored in the rest of this book. It suffices here to point to a well-promoted professional-cum-commercial initiative aimed at addressing housing affordability by Chilean architect Alejandro Aravena (Elemental).

Aravena has re-introduced a traditional 'incremental housing' approach (and the 'platform for change' intent of Lima's Proyecto

Experimental de Vivienda), designing simple, quality dwellings in well-serviced locations appropriate for expansion following household needs and finances. This is mainly achieved by designing porch-like roof structures of various sizes in the initial build, portending DIY fill-ins. Moreover, Aravena's well-known Monterrey project (2010) incorporated 'collective space' for up to two dozen households between public spaces and private households. Establishing 'half of a good house', a townhouse or apartment of 40sq m, with the medium density courtyard-style block leaving spaces for further stages, the completed plan for a low-storey complex with relatively modest 59sq m and 76.5sq m dwellings of four bedrooms would seem to satisfy a series of economic, environmental and social standards. Furthermore, in 2016, drawings of such incremental residential designs were released by Elemental as an open-source resource.[59]

Nevertheless, one detractor has pointed to the neoliberal 'more with less' homeownership bias of Aravena's projects and contends that, after several years, an Elemental Quinta Monroy project was worse for wear, even 'scarcely better than the shanty towns they replaced'.[60] Similarly, while lauding activist architecture, McGuirk has lamented that an incremental approach is 'questionable urbanism', 'dispiriting monoculture' and 'lacks idealism'.[61]

The examples in this section show that mainstream ways of addressing affordability tend to be marginal, neither widely accessible nor without risks of exploitation and insecurity. In short, statistics and trends across many countries show why the growing unaffordability and insecurity of mainstream housing, for both tenants and owner-occupiers, have become push factors towards collaborative housing solutions explored in the rest of this book.

UNSUSTAINABILITY

The expansion of capitalism has involved extensive resource use as well as activities reliant on non-renewable energy. Residential buildings and householders contribute in active and passive ways to over-consumption of resources and energy. 'Active' contribution refers to all the direct and obvious environmental costs of residential construction and extensions, yearly maintenance and everyday operations. By the twenty-first century, energy-saving building and household practices were encouraged and demanded through local, state, regional and national policies, plans and regulations. New building regulations have focused on minimum environmental ratings for homes, educational programs and householder subsidies, especially to install water- and energy-saving devices and appliances.

'Passive' over-consumption refers to less direct and more insidious practices, such as living in a poorly serviced suburb in a larger-than-necessary house that demands more energy and water use to inhabit, clean and maintain than living more modestly in a better location. Passive factors tend to be neglected by planners and policymakers who incentivise denser developments close to established infrastructure and services rather than regulate to constrain sprawl and set maximum house sizes to prevent and reverse carbon emissions.

Table 2.2 indicates the highly variable average size of newly built dwellings by country and certain cities. The table shows that, in the late 2000s, Australian homes being constructed were 4.7 and 2.8 times bigger than new builds in Hong Kong and the UK, respectively. Indeed, per capita calculations show each Australian had almost 6 and 2.7 times the amount of space than residents of new builds in Hong Kong and the UK, respectively. For several years, Australia has ranked as producing

Table 2.2   Floor space of new builds in 15 countries, 2009

Country, region, city	Average size, new-build dwelling	Average floor space per capita
Hong Kong	45	15
Russia	57	22
Urban China	60	20
UK	76	33
Italy	81	31
Sweden	83	40
Japan	95	35
Spain	97	35
Germany	109	55
France	112	43
Greece	126	45
Denmark	137	65
Canada	181	72
US	201	77
Australia	214	89

Source: Statistics drawn from Lindsay Wilson, 'How big is a house? Average house size by country', April 2013 – http://shrinkthatfootprint.com/how-big-is-a-house

the biggest new houses in the world, making it a focus of debates on the relationship between environmental sustainability and dwelling size.

Certain energy-efficient building studies and rating systems that focus on use practices in existing homes indicate that larger houses are more energy efficient in megajoule (MJ) per sq m than smaller ones. Such research fails to include the higher life cycle energy demand of bigger buildings, particularly embodied energy, and the efficiency of primary, not just thermal, energy required as well as per capita impacts. Stephan and Crawford have shown that the broader perspective reverses the rule of thumb to: 'larger house sizes result in significantly higher embodied and operational energy use and associated environmental impacts'.[62] Their case study was in Melbourne, a capital growing more quickly than any other in Australia and in a state where average house sizes grew from 229sq m^2 in 2003–2004 to 248sq m in 2011–2012.[63] They concluded that, if Australian houses were more modest, say 100sq m, this might more than halve their embodied material and energy costs over a 50-year period.

Similarly, another Australian case study, by Clune et al., has argued that house size is the most significant factor in addressing thermal efficiencies in residential buildings. Indeed, Clune et al. pointed out that the fact that Victorian house sizes increased between 2003 and 2009 limited, by 38 per cent, the effectiveness of a simultaneous mandatory improvement in thermal efficiency whereby builders had to comply with a 6-star, rather than a 5-star, rating. Moreover, carbon dioxide equivalent (CO_2-e) reduction targets of 80 per cent might be met if house sizes were contained, along with built-in improvements in thermal energy, with the added benefit of 'significant housing affordability impacts'. To illustrate, if Australian houses were reduced to the size of the average UK house (76sq m), the savings in terms of heating and cooling would be equivalent to mandating builders to enhance thermal energy in a 204sq m house to an 8-star standard (currently considered in state-of-the-art range). Clune et al. drew parallels between their findings and research on US housing and calculations by Güneralp and Seto showing that efficiency gains during the 1990s and 2000s had failed to offset actual increases in resource consumption and CO_2-e emissions worldwide. Consequently, Clune et al. have recommended applying a direct approach through restrictive building regulation setting maximum, not just minimum, sizes for Australian housing.[64]

In fact, community consultation by a housing company in the Australian capital city of Canberra found that participants would be prepared to live in a house around half the national average provided their most critical, and certain desirable, requirements were met. Indeed, Moore et al. have pointed out that smaller homes are especially suitable for older Australians living as couples or singles and for 20–35 year-old Australians who tend to favour smaller housing conveniently located to their everyday activities.[65] Restrictive regulations and market production and trade that responds more favourably to ethical and free choices to live more sustainably in smaller houses have special significance in Australia, where the number of households is increasing and projected to reach almost 12.7 million by 2036 – a 50 per cent increase from 8.4 million in 2011 – as household size stabilises or falls a few points. One-person households are expected to rise most, by two-thirds, while group households will fall marginally. Similarly, substantial falls in household size are expected in the UK, Japan, NZ and Japan.[66]

From the 1920s through to the mid-1950s, Japanese households averaged five members each whereas the 2010 census recorded less than 2.5 members per average household and more than 31 per cent were one-person households. Two-thirds of Japanese households (21 per cent of total households) contained one person of 65 or more years of age, three-quarters of them female.[67] Similarly, it is expected that 38 per cent of UK housing stock will be occupied by single-person households by 2026. Because of efficiencies of scale, sole-member households can use 50 per cent more energy per person than those living in couple-households, and an aging demographic means thermal performance of homes will be increasingly important since health and wellbeing of seniors partly relies on comfortable room temperatures.[68] Calculations based on US Department of Energy data from 2001 suggest that, if household size is held the same, larger compared with smaller dwellings and detached compared with attached buildings show greater consumption, on average, by 17 and 26 per cent respectively.[69] Furthermore, a study of Chinese cities concluded that household size was the main determinant of differences in per capita residential carbon emissions, with occupants in smaller households contributing disproportionately more to emissions.[70]

TWENTY-FIRST CENTURY FLUX

This chapter has examined very select characteristics of land settlement and lifestyles over the last couple of centuries. While homes generally lost their function as workplaces during the eighteenth and nineteenth centuries, their location for e-working and bases for tradespersons, self-employed professionals, contractors and niche wholesalers has only grown in the twenty-first century, along with more precarious work and a higher proportion of semi-retirees. While the average household has fewer members, compared with a century ago, the average house size is larger, which magnifies energy inefficiencies and resource overconsumption. Similarly, sprawling low-density urban development has increased environmental costs by clearing and other land use changes. Outer suburban residents require extra infrastructure and greater use of vehicles for transport of people, goods and services. Such environmental impacts have dispersed and delayed economic impacts and significant contributions to dangerous carbon emissions.

This chapter ignored apartments which, arguably, address all the shortcomings of detached one-storey homes in terms of their environmental extravagance, alienation and even lack of affordability. Surely compact, smaller developments in neighbourly blocks are the way of the future? The next two chapters explore evidence supporting and contradicting this conclusion found in the chequered history of the apartment as a built and social form, by examining the apartment as a context for household practices that might be more environmentally sustainable than those characteristic of households in detached dwellings, and by weighing up how socially appropriate – community-oriented, affordable, secure and homely – the apartment has been in reality, and in the here and now.

3

Apartment Living in Cities

The main type of housing that springs to mind as associated with small and shared living is the apartment, in an apartment block, in its natural social and urban environment, the city. This chapter selectively draws on a long-term and broad perspective of the apartment to show some of the weaknesses of concluding that this type of housing, apartments in compact cities, will solve either environmental challenges related to planetary sustainability or social challenges, namely affordability. In short, it looks at the apartment as a unit, 'a part' of a city – governed by politicians and bureaucrats and driven by entrepreneurs, specifically developers – whereas Chapter 4 journeys into the interior of the apartment and examines householders.

Many of the environmental, social and economic limitations and potential of apartments were clear early on in their development, to be replicated across geographies and multiplied as industrialisation and urbanisation both expanded and contracted. At the two ends of the spectrum stand the penthouse and the slum. Unfortunately, 'small' has been more associated with apartments of the poor than those of the wealthy. Similarly, sharing has remained more potential than reality in apartment living characterised by privacy, independence, mobility and absence. Developments in England and Australia are exemplary, as sketched out in this chapter alongside certain characteristics of European and North American apartment living.

Today, population growth and movements, demographic changes in household types, and environmental imperatives all offer new opportunities and cast new shadows on apartment developments in capital and global cities. This chapter explores such aspects of the real and actual development of apartments, in the contexts of utopian thinking on apartments, architectural innovation and the rise of 'green' and micro-apartments. Current policies and plans for future cities favour medium- to high-density, compact and 'smart' urban developments. This implies developing more apartments, as is happening in many cities.

However, historical experiences offer lessons for policy-makers. Cities such as London, Tokyo and New York City (NYC) have been defined by high-density apartment living for centuries. In the past decade such development has come in for many accolades. Urbanists, planners and architects are apt to refer to the blending of modern with traditional designs, and smaller, efficient and effective living spaces of apartments as the way of the future. But, how far have they been affordable, environmentally sound and appropriate living spaces?

THE 'APARTMENT': WHAT'S IN A NAME?

Apartment dwellings have existed in various forms – at least since ancient Roman times as *'insulae'* – to save land space and increase settlement density, often appearing side-by-side in a standard style. Apartment housing attended industrialisation and associated urbanisation as a product of the private market both as a necessary form of shelter for workers – initially often poorly built, tiny and with few facilities, adjacent to polluting and depressing factories (as 'tenements' or 'slums') – and as luxurious city habitations for work, rest and play for the rich. What we refer to generically as 'apartments' – derived from the Latin *partire*, to share or divide and, thus, *appartimenta* – have had numerous other names depending on the period, place and specific type of self-contained set of rooms separated, but a part of, the multi-unit and multi-storey residential building in question.

The Scots, whose upper class pioneered apartment living in the United Kingdom (UK) in the sixteenth century, referred to them as *'flaets'* (a floor or storey). 'Flat' would become common not only in the UK and Australia but also in the United States (US), later in the nineteenth century, for distinguishing private housing from working-class tenements. Elevators enabled 'apartment towers' and, ultimately, the 50-plus-storied 'skyscraper' replete with multi-dwelling units. Lush 'penthouses' evolved, juxtaposed to 'towers' characteristic of mass social housing in the 1950s–1970s, which became notorious as depressing eyesores. The twentieth century saw suburban expansion favouring two-(or three) storeyed 'walk-ups', such as 'garden apartments'. While the well-established 'duplex' was a unit extending over two floors, 'loft units' were created in the twentieth century out of ex-servant quarters and ex-factories. Specific definitions for 'lo-rise' and 'high-rise' blocks vary: in Canada, for instance, 'low-rise' refers to buildings with four or fewer storeys and 'high-rise' to five or more storeys.

Other names for apartments refer to forms of ownership: North American 'condos' –'condominiums' – where ownership of the unit is separate but common spaces are governed by the association of owners (similar to 'strata title' in Australia); 'cooperative apartments', where owners are members of a corporation that is the common owning body, are more common in Europe than North America or Australia; while 'tenements' and their 'tenants' (renters) derive from Latin for 'to hold' (*tener*), to have use-rights over, a property. It is most significant that matters of common concern falling under legal arrangements involving residents in multi-unit buildings are often managed by a third-party private or public company or a small number of active residents, and generally focus much more on issues such as whether pets are allowed in dwellings than on communal activities. The latter are voluntary, partial and limited, a shadow of the shared governance and sharing considered in Part II.

THE RISE OF MODERN APARTMENTS

Numerous types of apartments arose in different cities and countries throughout Europe, the UK, North America and Australia, developing distinctive physical and social characteristics related to the rise of new construction techniques, design trends and multi-unit social housing.

English working-class housing: from cellar-dwellers to terraces and council flats

John Burnett has created a scale of descriptors for standard English working-class housing in nineteenth-century industrialising cities, from the poorest cellar-dwellers, to lodgers and tenement dwellers – all in adapted cast-off housing originally belonging to the wealthy and referred to as 'rookeries' – to the more adequate multi-storied back-to-backs (illustrated in Chapter 2), which evolved from efforts of housing reformers. Some better-off workers were housed, by their employers or by private arrangement, in narrow two-storied 'through' terraced houses, a form of duplex more commonly held by a middle-class household, and benefitting from light, sanitary facilities and a patch of garden. However, workshop houses, philanthropic and other employer housing often took the form of high-density blocks of self-contained units. Speculative apartment building was poorly designed, cobbled together by subcontractors, often without sewerage, with tiny windows and walls that might be just half a brick thick.[1]

By 1901, some 60 per cent of English and Welsh tenement households lived in five or more rooms, and more than three-quarters of urban residents of US cities lived in apartments, from one-roomed bed-sit apartments, some serviced 'catering flats' through to larger family-sized apartments.[2] By 1914, a three-roomed flat in inner London was likely to cost more than renting a four-roomed suburban cottage – probably more due to the costs and difficulties of living distantly from work than with the quality or desirability of a London apartment.[3] Meanwhile the middle class considered flats expensive, poor quality and mostly, or even only, appropriate for bachelors, professionals or couples without children who could do without domestic help.[4]

After the First World War, brighter and roomier English council flats – each with a kitchen, toilet and bathroom – became the norm. The Greenwood Act of 1930 laid the basis for replacing slums through subsidies per capita, with higher subsidies for flats because they proved expensive to build. Conservationists and 'modern movement' architects advocated flats, which increased in number from the mid-1930s. Typically, such 'five-roomed' flats had four bedrooms, a living area, kitchenette, bathroom and toilet. Balconies were more popular than courtyards. Still, during that decade, there were fewer than 100,000 council flats (8.5 per cent of the housing stock). A Mass Observation study in the early 1940s revealed a small house and garden was most popular; only 5 per cent of participants wanted to live in an apartment.[5]

Given lifts and central heating systems, English mixed neighbourhood developments of the 1950s included high-rise and low-rise flats for families and singles, with public housing increasingly compact. The 1961 *Parker Morris Report* recommended 320–930sq ft (30–86sq m) minimum floor spaces on a scale from one- to six-member households, with 28–35sq ft (2.6–3.3sq m) storage of which 20sq ft (1.9sq m) might be outside. By 1969, most benefited from heating by a central boiler yet 85 per cent had just one or two bedrooms, compared with the interwar years when two-thirds had three bedrooms. In 1981, as discussed in Chapter 2, economic arguments led to discarding both Parker Morris and other existing standards.[6]

By 2014, the mean average floor area of an English dwelling was 94sq m, comprising a range of averages by sector: social-sector dwellings

(67sq m), private rentals (77sq m) and owner-occupiers (106sq m).[7] As discussed in Chapter 2, the average floor size of UK housing remains modest in international rankings, in theory making the transition to modest, low ecological footprint living easier than in settler colonial societies, such as Australia ('ecological footprint' referring to the amount of land necessary to supply the resources on which a resident's consumption relies).

The slow evolution of the apartment in Melbourne and Sydney

In the worldwide trend to create apartments by subdividing grand mansions, more than one-quarter of the 1200 houses with 20 or more rooms in the state of Victoria (Australia) in the 1890s were broken into flats, tenements and even hospitals. By 1921, only 569 mansions remained. With the Great Depression, ordinary houses were remodelled to accommodate an extra self-contained household with such secondary dwellings also called 'flats'.[8] Still, flats of all types only numbered 5 per cent of occupied dwellings in Australia in 1933, although they became more numerous during and after the Second World War.[9] McFadyen expressed a common sentiment: 'The flat dweller belongs to the floating population of the big cities and is of no value to the community, as a flat is not a home.'[10]

Indeed, religious anti-apartment lobbies convinced many Australian local councils to ban apartments from most residential zones. The vast majority of planners and academics advocating for compact living compromised by arguing that they were ideal for all but family households. So, during the twentieth century, apartments developed mainly as purpose-built accommodation for singles and child-free couples. 'Clendon', a suite of eight middle-class bachelor flats in a two-storeyed U-shaped block, designed by Roy Grounds, acted as a 1940s prototype in Victoria's capital, Melbourne. Each flat had a 'compact kitchen plan, the glass hatch which left the kitchen open to the living-room, the folding wall-bed and the squared obscure-glass screen inside the front door'. Apartments designed by Grounds featured an important encouragement to sharing – 'generous outdoor circulation', verandas and courtyards, so that 'even today they provide lessons on apartment living'.[11]

However, it was the New South Wales capital Sydney that boasted more than half of Australia's flats in 1947. Australian apartment purchasers would often buy off-the-plan or purchase upfront as shares in building construction after the Second World War, when governments started subsidising first-home buyers and caused a slump in investment in flats. Nevertheless, between 1954 and 1961 the increase in Sydney's apartments (28.5 per cent) – nine in every 10 were 'walk-ups' (detailed below) – far outstripped its population growth (17 per cent).[12]

Although referred to as minimalist or modest, as in international modernist or 'democratic modernist' style, three substantial blocks of apartments built in remarkable locations came to epitomise city housing for wealthier people around the world. Aaron Bolot's 10-storey Wylde Street Cooperative Apartments (1951), a building that elegantly curved to the north, established a precursor to strata title and associated common owners' management that became norms in Australian real estate. Robin Boyd's controversial Domain Park Towers (1962), Melbourne's first residential high rise (20 storeys of mainly two- and three-bedroom apartments of 90–135sq m), sits opposite the Royal Botanical Gardens. The first strata title apartment in Australia, Harry Seidler's Blues Point Tower (1962) was both unusually square and oriented on environmentally inspired north–east–south–west diagonals on a point close to Sydney's famous harbour bridge, with floor sizes starting from 30m².[13]

By 2001, just 16 per cent of Sydney's dwellings – and a tiny 5 per cent of Melburnian ones – were in apartment buildings three or more storeys high. Ten years later (2011), they had grown in proportion to 21 per cent and 7 per cent, respectively, with three-quarters of Melbourne's central business district (CBD) dwellings classified high-density,[14] compared with the broader City of Melbourne where higher-density housing accounted for only 29 per cent of stock.[15] In specific blocks where apartments dominate, densities are comparable with Dublin (Ireland), Athens (Greece) and Rio de Janeiro (Brazil), due to the rise of the micro-apartment (discussed below).[16] In contrast, a strong backlash even to low-rise apartment building has been spearheaded by the Save Our Suburbs! Movement resulting in planning limits across substantial urban areas where councils only permit one- or two-storey developments.[17]

Californian garden walk-up apartments

Sydney's and Melbourne's apartments were influenced by US apartment housing, which benefited from a surge in investment in the 1960s in the Californian garden walk-up apartment. According to Rubin, multi unit housing grew rapidly from 10.3 per cent to 37.3 per cent of US new builds 1956–1963, to accommodate baby boomer renters, studying or working before they settled down to family life at a later age than when their parents had married. Typically, two- or three-storeyed rectangular blocks in the shape of a U, garden–courtyard apartment buildings might feature a pool (Figure 3.1). Some walk-ups were built on pillars atop open or closed car parks, highlighting visual and functional impacts of the car on housing, an effect magnified because of their similarity to motels.[18]

Figure 3.1   Schematic impression of a Californian garden walk-up apartment

Although the courtyard and pool might have encouraged shared activities, the car-centrism of the Californian garden walk-up emphasised privacy and personal sufficiency, probably exaggerating their occupants' sense of alienation. In the 1960s, this type of apartment established multi-family housing in Taiwan's capital Taipei and, in 2015, still represented more than half of all Taipei's dwellings. Interestingly, there, this 'quintessentially modernist mid-rise block with a central stair hall and two units per floor' allowed for a distinctively collective form of urban living and evolved a unique 'merging of modernist ideologies with vernacular preferences', the latter specifically recognisable in their facades.[19]

Canada's condos

Analysing Canadian apartments (1900–1940), yet reflecting common perspectives worldwide, Richard Dennis has highlighted that 'luxury apartments were welcomed as evidence of metropolitan sophistication but more modest buildings were condemned as incipient slums, bad for business' and even referred to as 'living factories'. Apartments of the rich had fewer private servants than houses of the wealthy, or they replaced servants altogether with efficient modern appliances and onsite services. Many considered apartments inappropriate for families; close and cloistered living seeming to threaten privacy and morality and deprive children of space to play. Dennis reports how anti-apartment groups and planners prompting bylaws introduced in Toronto in 1912 viewed all apartments as unhealthy and anti-family, conflating tenements and subdivided houses with new spacious apartment blocks.[20]

Today, many Canadian apartments are rented or owner-occupied as condominiums ('condos') with different models of private ownership of dwellings, and 'shared' – in reality 'delegated' – governance and management of common areas and facilities for the whole property. Condominium tenure is not exclusive to apartments but, in 2011, apartments accounted for two-thirds of Canadian condominiums. Typically, condominiums are comprised of dwellings smaller than the national average, with fewer rooms and smaller households. Consequently, they have become a popular, more affordable, first-home-buyer option. Furthermore, the average size of a City of Vancouver one-bedroom apartment fell 2008–2013 from 668sq ft (62.1sq m) to 580sq ft (53sq m). In 2011, Canadian women were twice as likely as men to be sole owner-occupants, three times as likely if they were aged over 55 years, and women accounted for the highest proportion of single-parent condominium owners. Despite the opprobrium towards the apartment a century earlier, in 2011 Toronto boasted half of all the high-rise condominiums in Canada. Even though the detached dwelling is expected to remain dominant (as in many cities worldwide), owner-occupied apartments are expected to lead an increase in all types of Canadian housing through to 2036.[21]

Affordable apartment living in Berlin

The histories of many European cities have reflected similar urban development mixes of luxury versus tiny overcrowded apartments, and their councils led pressures for compact cities. In the latter half of the nineteenth century, Berlin expanded block by low-rise block in courtyard style. The wealthy occupied the street sides of buildings and the workers the inner courtyard-facing apartments – typically overcrowded, low-amenity accommodation.[22] Since the reunion of its eastern and western halves, Berlin has been characterised by vibrant apartment living, a traditional renter's city attracting young 'creatives' and professionals, initially through low rents.[23]

German housing policies have included a long-term standard compact with private landlords, subsidising affordable and secure rental for lower-income tenants – one of the most successful national affordable housing policies according to a range of socio-economic and environmental criteria.[24] Eligible apartments are required to be a maximum size, even though the subsidy is calculated per square metre. In the mid-2010s, 85 per cent of Berliners were tenants, 100,000 apartments were being constructed, apartments for tourists came under greater restriction, and more than 10 per cent of Germans lived in public housing apartments.[25]

If German policies are strong in supporting affordability – Austria and the Netherlands achieve well on this criteria too, due to their proportion of social housing, 22 and 31 per cent respectively[26] – there are still ways in which German urban apartment life could be improved. Hamburg's Right to the City movement demands affordable living space, shifting funding from automobile to public transport infrastructure and green parks because compact living conflicts with elements of social justice, conservation of nature and common space. By way of an example, Nicole Vrenegor refers to contemporary high-rise estates on the fringes of Hamburg; developed in the early 1970s, within an area of less than 1 sq km, Osdorfer Born houses 10,000 residents with just a bus to the centre for public transport.[27]

The Paris apartment

Apartments were built in Paris as early as the seventeenth century. By the nineteenth century the 'Paris apartment' was serviced inside by a concierge and outside by a boulevard, for sitting as well as walking. This model placed better and bigger apartments for the wealthy on the first floor, above retail and hospitality outlets on the street, with smaller apartments (initially reserved for servants) as the floors reached the top. In St Petersburg, a similar low rise 'dokhodny dom', built around a common courtyard, appeared and expanded with industrialisation. The 'Paris apartment' became a US favourite, especially in the mid-twentieth century, and the secure solidly built apartment block set on a main street above retail shops and professional offices remains a common model worldwide.[28] Courtyard styles endure in many European cities, such as Munich and Budapest, and are favoured by urbanists for incorporating green and community values into compact urban densification policies.[29]

In short, the development of apartments shows a mixed history: 'small' has been associated with substandard and low-income; and 'sharing' has been limited generally to simple access to use restricted common areas under pre-determined rules. However, the apartment is not only a unit in an apartment building but also a dwelling in a larger block of buildings in a neighbourhood city precinct, and apartment dwellers invariably rely on multiple urban services and infrastructure managed, contracted out and regulated by city councils.

THE STATE, CITY, APARTMENT AND CLASS

The semi-autonomous and interdependent relationship between state, class and market explains certain trends in the development of the apartment. This section considers the negative influence of the rise of public housing in the form of apartment blocks, the often overlooked public costs of cities, the apartment's natural home, and ways that income and wealth have continued to develop apartments with characteristic class distinctions.

Social housing apartments

Early on in industrialisation, various governments, charitable bodies and reformers set up model projects or programs involving direct intervention in the market because the speculative commercial building and real estate industries failed to supply sufficient affordable and appropriate houses for those on lower incomes. As direct providers of housing in the twentieth century, governments focused on large construction projects, specifically apartment towers. The apartment tower and skyscraper relied on the inventions of a safety brake for lifts and steel load-bearing skeleton frames because weighty and costlier lower storeys had supported light higher storeys in earlier 'tall' buildings.[30] Such building was not only expensive in terms of project management but also required massive injections of finance. The cost of public or social housing from a neoliberal, anti-welfare-state point of view – and social criticisms of the many 'brutalist', impersonal and depressive interventions – led to a withdrawal of direct state intervention later in the twentieth century. Meanwhile, apartment living per se was scarred with such negative associations.

The public cost of cities

Only massive public investments in water supply, sewerage systems and street cleaning limited infectious disease, contagions and other ill health in cities. In the US, NYC was a leader in state provisioning, starting with a quality water system in 1842. Sewerage followed, along with the cleaning of streets dirtied by horse and other animal excrement, and business waste.[31] Postal, radio, telephonic, Internet and other information and communications services were all easier, less costly and potentially more remunerative to establish in higher density urban areas with maximum potential users. In a similar way trains, underground rail and electrified streetcars (trams) and, more recently, sky/monorails have interconnected urban areas. The capitalist state supported such developments and relocation to urban apartments to service the needs of capital. At the same time capital city councils have benefited from charging visitors for access, say to parking for cars, and from state taxes that flow from poorer peripheral areas to the centre, with its headquarters of financial and commercial powerhouses. When operating costs and benefits of urban apartments are tallied up there needs to be a line (or two) accounting for the costs of such state-funded or subsidised amenities and facilities.

The apartment and class

Especially as Paris's population increased by 50 per cent in the second half of the nineteenth century, and working-class housing was disturbed by the reconstruction (the '*Haussmannisation*' of Paris), modest, typically two-roomed working-class attached dwellings were disparaged as family-unfriendly.[32] Yet, a recent study of court files and literature suggests that, in fact, the conviviality of apartments in well-populated areas facilitated surveillance of vulnerable children and meant that assistance was readily available when abuse was imminent.[33] Yet movements against multi-unit dwellings proliferated worldwide, including the US National Housing Association, which was established in 1909.[34]

These essentially middle-class movements denigrating apartments assisted socialists and liberals to make minimal reforms to apartment building codes and standards. Yet the anti-apartment lobbies idealised suburban houses and lots in the process. Still, apartments had their middle-class promoters who appreciated their economic and environmental benefits: referring in 1912 to Winnipeg and Edmonton, J. Pender West advocated apartment living for its cheaper communal heating, proximity to work, shops and other services, and assistance in snow clearance, so Canadians could better adapt to, or endure, their long winters.[35]

If, initially, the effect of the market on the form of housing for workers was decisive, urban historian Lewis Mumford points out another complementary effect, as early as the latter part of the nineteenth century, on the apartments of the middle classes. It was, he says, the 'unpremeditated revenge' of workers that – under 'the applications of capitalist standards' – middle-class apartments would shrink and lose decorative and amenity qualities even while remaining superior to working-class housing.[36] Yet the penthouse remains proof that the rich escaped such restraint. Furthermore, as urban apartment living has become more attractive, stock is bifurcating into larger and smaller 'micro' apartments.

Indeed, Redway has argued that planners advocating medium and high-density apartment living need to be more concerned with the growth in sheer size of city apartments. In the context of the average Australian householder's quota of space trebling, from an adequate 31sq m in 1933 to 91sq m in 2007 – just as houses grew 70 per cent (or more than 100sq m) between 1973 and 2007 – it is salutary to find that, in 2007, even new medium-density townhouses and low-rise apartments averaged 154sq m and high-density apartments 137sq m. In fact, during 2003–2004, two-thirds of high-density dwellings built in Australia had three or more bedrooms with at least two bathrooms. Redway stated that Australian building construction company AV Jennings would favour national policies for greater sustainability features in homes and costs could be offset by reductions in dwelling size.[37] Although the average size of new apartments had fallen to circa 130sq m in 2011, analysts suggest that the growth in micro-apartments (discussed below) is likely to have skewed the result.[38]

The city was a centripetal force throughout the nineteenth and twentieth centuries. If the wealthy once had a secondary city apartment to complement a main rural residence in earlier centuries, they tended more towards a city residence and country holiday houses in the twentieth century. In the twenty-first century, many rich people have – or have access to – several apartments scattered across the world in global cities. Serviced and other apartments catering for visiting business people and professional advisers, those involved on cultural or government projects or professional development (say conferences) and tourists, all represent a distinct real estate niche interlocked with similar accommodation in similar 'global cities'. The effect in such cities is a two-tier real estate market with the international market of overseas buyers forcing up prices that local nationals, typically, struggle to afford.

APARTMENTS AS HOUSING UTOPIAS

If the apartment seems less of a solution to collapsing our ecological footprints, what other ideals might it fulfil? Nineteenth-century US feminists dreamed about its social potential. Melusina Fay Pierce coined 'cooperative housekeeping' to refer to collectives of women economising on domestic labour through cooperation, thereby gaining a wage via charging men for their services.[39] Her ideas coincided with practical developments in apartments for the rich in the late nineteenth century, such as Haight House (NYC), where 20 family and 15 bachelor suites could take advantage of common cooking, eating and laundering facilities.[40]

Pierce envisaged apartments free of kitchens and laundries which, instead, would concentrate in separate buildings. In the twentieth century, such ideas of socialised domestic work were promulgated in various ways, for instance by Ebenezer Howard in London, as garden apartments and the garden city concept, and by the Heineman brothers, who designed a 'double bungalow with a connecting sliding door' to form either separate quarters for a couple or for joint activities of two, otherwise distinct, households in Los Angeles.[41]

Another example of the confluence of social utopias and urban design – explored by Dolores Hayden in *The Grand Domestic Revolution* – was proposed by King Camp Gillette in the 'millionaire socialist's book', *The Human Drift* (1894), before he moved onto his fully realised invention of the double-edged disposable safety razor blade. This 'skyscraper metropolis', multiple 25-storey buildings established in a matrix pattern for 6 million residents, was the ultimate in conservation; people resided, socialised and produced in a monumental steel-structured, brick and glass hive apparently leaving the rest of nature to proliferate unimpeded. Cooperative dining occupied three levels underground, superstructures were mainly high-rise apartment buildings while productive units were in food, training and entertainment clusters.[42]

While utopians like Gillette respected and appreciated nature, they were not environmentalists as we understand the term now, nor did they address environmental challenges that we face in the twenty-first century. Driven by feminist and socialist values, they did understand that the built environment structures and reproduces social relationships. They envisaged a built environment where personal space was separated from domestic activities, common areas were totally accessible to all, and domestic chores were shared – replicating industrialised cooperative non-domestic labour. Thus, the model of small was married with sharing to create, what I call, 'efficiency squared', efficiencies operating in two dimensions. However, three-dimensional efficiencies really require the integration of 'green'.

GREENING APARTMENTS

In Part II, various examples of groundbreaking environmentally sustainable multi-household low-rise housing models, such as BedZED (London) and The Commons (Melbourne), are discussed and analysed. Similarly, complementary planning initiatives arising from grassroots action and environmental movements involving professionals and politicians, show how urban developments can encourage local economies, 'pocket neighbourhoods', small parks, guerrilla gardening, 'tactical urbanism' and 'smart' sustainability. Therefore, this chapter centres on the commercial market and mainstream opportunities for apartment living today.

The challenge of reducing carbon emissions

According to the Intergovernmental Panel on Climate Change (IPCC), buildings accounted for one-third of energy-related CO_2 and three-fifths of halocarbon emissions worldwide in the 2000s. Most significantly, IPCC researchers concluded that a transition in this sector would offer the simplest and least expensive reduction in greenhouse gas (GHG) emissions. Even though current stock had built-in energy inefficiencies, the IPCC indicated that almost one-third of building CO_2 emissions could be cut by 2020 if a transitional strategy was successfully adopted. Easy improvements could be made through new builds but retrofits and reconstruction, especially wholescale as in apartment blocks, also offered strong potential for savings. For instance, the relatively simple changes to apartments – as shown 'before' and 'after' in Figure 3.2 – are estimated to reap reductions in energy use of 90 per cent.[43] They include pushing out walls to replace internal balconies with external ones shading a greater number of windows, placing solar panels on the roof, removing chimneys, and covering external doorways.

Small apartments in high-density communities have become central to the regeneration and intensification of global cities. Policymakers have seen the compact apartment as offering a context, in and of itself, for more or less sustainable household practices. However, holistic environmental assessments of the sustainability of apartment households show less potential. To pre-empt discussions in Chapter 4, the practices of householders cannot necessarily be contained, constrained or even driven by the design and other sustainability features of their dwelling. Furthermore, sustainability features of commercial purchases are often minimal, set by council building standards, and purchasers are limited by cost and what is on offer.

Certainly, with respect to 'stuff', the smallness of an inner-city apartment compared with a suburban detached dwelling seems to create an imperative to think twice before buying and to facilitate sharing appliances with neighbours. However, say in a block of mainly singles in micro-apartments – as discussed below – self-containment can mean replication of both minimal and comparatively under-used kitchen, laundry and bathroom facilities and appliances. Some apartments come with all white-goods already installed. If such appliances were all highly energy-efficient, this would enhance sustainability, but this is often not the case so the outcome might well be worse than if occupants self-selected white-goods.

Consuming in a city comes at a relatively high environmental cost once transport of goods and services is included. The measure of ecological footprint distance (D_{ef}) indicates the average distance natural resources are transported to service city needs, which is key to assessing, monitoring and improving environmental costs or benefits of living in cities.[44] For instance, even if certain city dwellers save money, time and

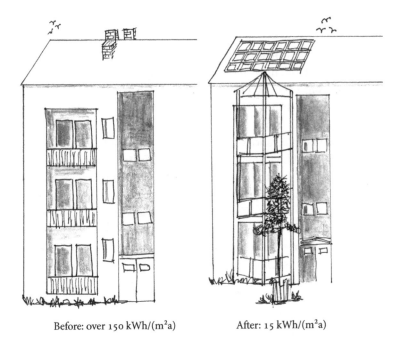

Before: over 150 kWh/(m²a) After: 15 kWh/(m²a)

Figure 3.2 Energy savings from German apartments retrofitted using passive house principles

Source: Sketch based on photographs in Diane Ürge-Vorsatz, slide show on her co-authored *Climate Change Mitigation in the Buildings Sector: The Findings of the 4th Assessment Report of the IPCC* – https://www.ipcc.ch

carbon emissions by taking public transport rather than a car to work, an holistic assessment might reveal air travel for their holidays in distant places erodes and even reverses the sustainability and other environmental gains of living a compact urban life.

Arguably, purchasing or renting an apartment offers fewer benefits, less diversity and options, than a detached house when it comes to sustainability features, such as solar or other renewable energy use, high levels of insulation, appropriate siting to maximise passive solar energy gains, and other design features maximising use of recycled construction materials and gardens, including roof and vertical gardens. If walls and furniture (such as wardrobes) are structurally inbuilt, this minimises flexibility. Occupants can end up in a state of hyper-alienation, surrounded by aloof residential neighbours with whom they have little or no conversation and simply share the odd pass-by in an echoing hallway and lift chamber. Alternatively, they might find apartment living facilitating a lot of sharing, from bulk food purchases to eating together, cooking for one another and sharing entertaining and activities.

Public transit-oriented development alongside apartment blocks is efficient but certainly not cost-free. Compact cities require a lot of attention from planning professionals and policymakers who propose, plan, establish, ensure finance for, and supervise the expanding or upgrading of all kinds of inner-urban infrastructure. Aside from commercial considerations and the creativity of the architect, councils set various building standards, many of which can work against sustainable practices. For instance, some councils insist on one car space per apartment but make a common bike rack or cage optional. Proactive sustainability councils offer incentives for apartment developments with sustainability features, such as collection and storage of rainwater for re-use, water-efficient tap fittings and landscaping, and collective grey-water systems. This might cost more upfront but saves on operating costs so, after some time, financial as well as carbon and other environmental savings accrue.

Many city building regulations are only starting to incorporate standards for adaptability and flexibility. Maximising how our built environment can be re-used, and the adaptability of space and functions was recognised by early-twentieth-century modernists, such as Le Corbusier. They acknowledged that flexibility is a critical characteristic for meeting social challenges such as aging in place and growing, and shrinking, family households. Such architects placed restraints on space, took a minimalist approach, prioritising efficiency and led, for instance, to folding furniture and multi-functional rooms that can be, say, a study in the day and dining room at night. Standardisation, a function of mass manufacture, called for adaptability in design and an aversion to the one-size-fits all or stereotypical Mr and Mrs Average. Adaptability can be achieved within a unit, an apartment building or compact neighbourhood by diversity of floor plans, enabling movement between habitations, housing designs, by making doors and hallways reasonably wide, and minimising stairs for whole-of-life, multigenerational use and for different needs and abilities. Common spaces for basic and social activities, such as laundries and roof-top gardens, also economise on space.[45] Yet dwellings characterised by such ideals are limited in mainstream urban markets and their cost is prohibitive for most people.

Urban affluence

Glowing sustainability evaluations of city living made by authors such as Glaeser in his *Triumph of the City* and Owen in his *Green Metropolis* can be roundly criticised for selective environmental foci.[46] Holistic analyses find that overuse of natural resources and energy are just as or more associated with consumption of food and other goods and services than with transport, household energy and water use which are the foci of many sustainability audits of city residents. For instance, a 2007 study indicated that the operating costs of houses and transport only account for around one-tenth of the ecological footprint of an average Australian, whose consumption exceeds many in North America and Europe.[47]

The same study showed that household use, construction and renovations accounted for around 25 per cent of the average Australian's total water use and 42 per cent of GHG emissions. Food, and other goods and services, accounted for the remaining 75 per cent and 58 per cent, respectively. Therefore, given its increasingly affluent character, urban apartment living can translate into highly unsustainable 'consumption hotspots':

> despite the lower environmental impacts associated with less car use, inner city households outstrip the rest of Australia in every other category of consumption. Even in the area of housing, the opportunities for relatively efficient, compact living appear to be overwhelmed by the energy and water demands of modern urban living, such as air conditioning, spa baths, down lighting and luxury electronics and appliances, as well as by a higher proportion of individuals living alone or in small households.
>
> In each state and territory, the centre of the capital city is the area with the highest environmental impacts, followed by the inner suburban areas. Rural and regional areas tend to have noticeably lower levels of consumption.[48]

Indeed, a 2015 study found that goods and services produced from resources and energy sourced elsewhere, and land necessary to absorb related CO_2 emissions, accounted for the bulk of the average Canberran ecological footprint, 8.9 global hectares per capita (2011–2012) or 3.5 times the then global average! The top five most damaging impacts were from use of electricity, hospitality venues, petrol, gas and transport.[49]

Given that carbon efficiency cannot compensate for growth in per capita consumption and population, analysts of causes of global GHG emissions (1990–2010) have concluded that, 'policy makers need to address the issue of affluence'.[50]

On a planetary scale, Girardet highlights the spatial and environmental perversity of parasitic cities dependent on global hinterlands – a range of ecosystems are stressed by flying, sailing and road-transporting basic needs into cities – production and distribution requiring much more energy than the calorie content of the transported food. He estimated that, by the late twentieth century, the ecological footprint of Londoners was 293 times its surface area, twice the surface area of Britain! A more detailed, and probably more accurate, City Limits study (2000) calculated a figure double that of Girardet.[51]

This critique redirects our thinking on individualistic lifestyles that naturally evolve within capitalism with production for trade, profit and growth eroding Earth's natural limits. Studies suggest that larger households living in smaller spaces, eating more communally, sharing and minimising consumption, and relying on locally grown and made basic needs, offer ways for us to achieve more sustainable practices. Nevertheless, innovative design and new technologies are popularly heralded as making urban apartment living sustainable. The next section shows a marred track record, especially in terms of unaffordability.

HABITAT '67 TO SKY HABITAT AND SKY FOREST

Early in his career, 'to re-invent the apartment building' for world fair Expo '67, architect Moshe Safdie scaled down a design for an ambitious complex of 1000 residences with streets and shops, to a remarkable 'block' of apartments that still sit Lego-style along the Marc-Drouin Quay of St Lawrence River in Montreal (Figure 3.3).[52] As if deconstructing brutalism, three rounded hills of 352 identical prefabricated boxes form steps and bridges invisibly intersecting, for access, via several lifts. Coming in one of 15 distinct sizes (60–160sq m), each of the around 150 apartments have access to a terrace set on an adjacent unit. The overall design of Habitat '67 by this American Institute of Architect's Gold Medallist (2015) created an impressive balance of simplicity and complexity, nature and manufacture, intimacy and community, and is still popular today.[53] Yet the building proved an expensive construction and the exposed concrete walls resulted in exorbitant heating bills.[54]

Figure 3.3   Habitat '67 today in Montreal (Moshe Safdie, architect)

Source: Taxiarchos228, photographer

Some of Safdie's original environmental intentions for Habitat '67 have been realised in his recent work Sky Habitat (Singapore). Its sloping residential towers contain 509 naturally ventilated apartments with balcony boxes, communal gardens and pools, interconnecting sky bridges, and a sunken car park.[55] Yet these luxury condominiums in a prime location are generously-sized for Singapore and, in December 2015, were being sold at an expensive median price of S$1.695 million.[56] Whatever environmental and economic gains in reduced operating costs, the high establishment costs and potential for affluent living diminish such work as genuine environmental and social advances.

Any discussion of green apartments cannot fail to mention 'vertical gardens', pioneered by French botanist Patrick Blanc in the 1980s, and prominent in recent policy discussions for contributing insulating effects for inhabitants and minimising the 'heat island' effect characteristic of contemporary cities. Often Blanc uses hundreds of different species to develop wallscapes with insulating and cooling properties, recycling water naturally through percolation from the top down to lower plants – as in Figure 3.4. For instance, he used 7600 plants to cover a 25m-high five-storey apartment wall on the corner of rue d'Aboukir and rue des Petits Carreaux in Paris.[57] Yet, 'green cities' and such green features are hardly new: in the fifteenth century, the Aztecs' Tenochtitlan – a remarkable city preceding what is now Mexico City – evolved steep food-producing terraces; Park Güell (Barcelona), one of Gaudi's major works, is replete with viaducts and irrigation systems to prevent erosion. Furthermore, Despommier expanded and applied vertical garden techniques to conceive a 'vertical farm'.[58]

Figure 3.4   Patrick Blanc vertical garden at Caixa Forum, Madrid (Herzog & de Meuron Architects, Basel, Switzerland)

Source: Patrick Blanc

A high-density residential development with adjacent apartment towers, both higher than 25 storeys, in Milan (Porta Nuova), is growing a 'vertical forest' (Figure 3.5). A collaboration between Boeri Studio and Arup, jutting ledges support 4.4 hectares of vegetation – more than 700 trees, 5000 shrubs and 11,000 groundcover plants – absorbing pollution and releasing oxygen, creating bird, animal and insect habitat, creating dappled light and shade, and dispersing noise. This development won architect Stefan Boeri the biennial International Highrise Award for 2014. Claimed to perform the same housing function as 5 hectares of urban sprawl, it is promoted as having 'high energy efficiency and environmental sustainability standards'.[59] However, in 2011, asking prices were reported of £560,000 to £1.7 million for a low-level 80sq m apartment through to a 200sq m penthouse with remarkable views.[60]

Furthermore, in February 2016, a generously-sized two-bedroom two-bathroom apartment with a 43 sq m terrace and car park in Porto Nueva had an asking price of €1,160,000 (£928,807) at a time when the average (and not insubstantial) house price in the UK was around a third of that (£288,000).[61]

Figure 3.5   Bosco Verticale (Vertical Forest) apartments, Milan (Boeri Studio, Milan)

Source: Photographer Paolo Rosselli (Milan) and Boeri Studio

Clearly, innovative architects have experimented in various ways to break up both the apartment block and the apartment itself – a self-contained, highly private and artificial unit – and to re-orient apartment buildings and their constituent units around community, neighbourhood and nature. But, given the tendency for such designs to prove unaffordable and generously sized – environmentally costly in seemingly invisible ways – we turn, instead, to more affordable and smaller conventional options, 'micro-apartments'.

MICRO-APARTMENTS

Edwin Heathcote refers to forementioned architect of Habitat '67 and Sky Habitat, Moshe Safdie, as one of several 'pod-fathers' whose designs were equally organic and futuristic. Another was artist-architect Constant

Nieuwenhuys, who made designs for an anti-capitalist city New Babylon (1959–1974, Amsterdam), where nomadic urbanites would play below stilted removable structures. Richard Rogers Lloyd's Building in London (1972) features prefabricated smart micro-apartments with a porthole style window. Kisho Kurokawa used pods to construct beehives of minimalist worker-homes, the most famous of which is Nakagin Capsule Tower (1972) – prompting commercial capsule hotels.[62]

Indeed, in contemporary Tokyo, we find the most extreme examples of stacked 'micro-apartment' capsule rooms without windows or doors in capsule hotels. 'The largest is 6½ feet deep by 5 feet wide,' Kahn reported of one capsule hotel, 'you can't stand up inside.' Initially aimed at late-night workers for an occasional short-night sleepover, some take up monthly rental in capsules where there is 'barely enough room for an adult to lie down completely flat'. Reported, in the early 2010s, as sometimes costing US$600–700 per month, young unemployed to hard-working, hard-playing professionals find here 'a shelf, perhaps a tiny television, and some poor lighting, and that's your home-sweet home'.[63]

A range of contemporary architects have applied themselves to designing tiny pre-fab units, which might be hoisted into place on the top of existing urban buildings for owner-occupation or rental tenancies (Figure 3.6). In this vein, Architects Rintala Eggertson's Boxhome in Oslo (Norway) created a prototype 19sq m two-storey timber and aluminium 'urban cave' – Figure 3.7 – most significantly for a quarter of the cost of a similarly sized urban apartment.[64]

Given that one working definition of a micro-apartment is 'a self-contained unit smaller than 350ft² [32.6m²] often found in either a mid- or high-rise, a new or a converted building', it is not surprising that views on micro-apartments slot into the slum and tenement mould, particularly when they appear en masse, say in student accommo-dation. So, it might surprise that a 2014 study by the US Urban Land Institute (ULI) found that, especially in compact cities – NYC, Boston, Washington, San Francisco and Seattle – micro-apartments tend to have lower vacancy rates and higher rents per square foot compared with larger local apartments. This is mainly due to the attractiveness of their typically central location and considerably cheaper rent, around 20–30 per cent of local larger apartments. Furthermore, a small survey referred to by the ULI suggested that almost one-quarter of renters in other kinds of apartments were attracted to micro-apartment living as an option despite concerns with lack of storage space.[65]

Figure 3.6   Boxhome in Oslo, Norway (Rintala Eggertson Architects)

Source: Photographer Ivan Brodey (Oslo, Norway)

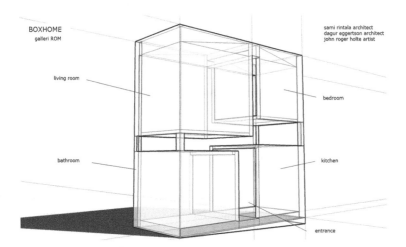

Figure 3.7   Sketches of Boxhome (Rintala Eggertson Architects, Oslo)

Source: Sami Rintala and Dagur Eggertson (architects) and John Roger Holte (artist)

The size of such apartments relies on commercial considerations, minimum size eligibility criterion for mortgage funds, and minimums set by local council regulations. Reducing minimum size rules often causes public controversy. In San Francisco and the District of Columbia that, of course, includes Washington DC, an apartment can be as small as 220sq ft (20.4sq m) while Dallas's minimum is 500sq ft (46.5sq m). ULI research indicated that a micro-apartment often needed to be 300sq ft (27.8sq m) to accommodate regular furniture and appliances and to be compliant with government standards.[66]

When City of Melbourne planners considered raising minimum sizes for apartments in 2015, local architect Michael Roper – owner-occupier of a 24sq m apartment in the historic 1936 modernist inner suburban building 'Cairo' – suggested that rigid standards failed to take account of the diversity of individual buildings and amenities. His intervention in the policymaking debate proposed: 'an effective peer-review process, whereby trained design professionals assess the quality and liveability of multi-residential developments on a case-by-case basis'. Roper had a 10sq m private garden amid other apartment gardens, access to a rooftop terrace, and copious surrounding public gardens. Inspired by London living, Best Overend designed this block of 28 'minimal' one-bedroom and studio apartments with 'maximum comfort' in mind: a rooftop space for socialising, a communal dining room, two communal laundries, a shop (now defunct) and eight garages. Installing a foldout bed and internal curtain to divide and hide according to activities, Roper had found it perfectly adequate eighty years after Cairo was built.[67]

Such examples appear dotted round global cities. A shared garden, making maximum use of high ceilings, and a fold-away bed explain how a NYC owner-occupier couple made a 242sq ft (22.5sq m) apartment a comfortable home.[68] Figure 3.8 shows how an architecture firm converted another NYC studio into a one-bedroom loft apartment by inserting a central wood station – with an internal kitchen, bathroom, storage and mezzanine bedroom above – to effectively divide the space into three components.[69]

Many micro-apartment dwellers are professional singles under 30 years of age. Adaptable and movable furniture, built-in storage, fold-down tables and beds, and mezzanine bed spaces where there are high ceilings can make micro-apartment living feasible. Generally, micro-apartment dwellers have access to numerous common facilities: laundry, parking spaces and bike rack, gym, game room, storage and an

Figure 3.8   East Village Studio NYC (Jordan Parnass Digital Architecture)

Source: Photographer Frank Oudeman (Brooklyn)

outdoor or roof space. Furthermore, the ULI study indicated a recent movement to create many small meeting and leisure spaces throughout US micro-apartment blocks and increasing permission to have pets.[70]

Following MPF Research data, in the decade between 2002–2003 and 2012–2013, US studio and one-bedroom apartments rose from 41 per cent to almost 51 per cent of total apartment completions, significantly accounting for a reduction in the total average apartment size as three-bedroom apartments increased in size! Still, small micro-apartments were a tiny proportion (3 per cent) of total 2012–2013 deliveries. While micro-apartment dwellers tended to move on quicker than tenants of other apartments, ULI researchers found that more than one-third of those surveyed had showed interest in purchasing one. Some have flexible floor plans, utility components and walls so adjacent micro-apartments can be rearranged and merged to make a larger apartment.[71]

'Small spaces come in a myriad of styles, united only by size,' concludes architect Bruce Hayden. By way of examples, architect Gary Chang's 330sq ft (30.7sq m) 'transformer' apartment in Hong Kong and

Christian Schallert's 24sq m apartment in Barcelona show great inventiveness in making a tiny space multi-functional.[72] Micro-apartments might make CBD infill easier. They certainly suit specific age groups and demographic types, but residents depend on access to common facilities and services within their block, and proximity to even greater amenity within a highly urban environment, where their overall environmental impact is a matter for speculation.

CONCLUSION

Harvard Professor of Economics Edward Glaeser, who waves the flag of a contemporary version of the discredited trickle-down effect, iterates a popular forecast of expanding and unending urbanism while fellow US journalist David Owen, argues that we should all live like residents of Manhattan.[73] However, Lewis Mumford's conclusion was far more pessimistic. Based on experience of the half century before his *The City in History* was published in 1961 and heralding current deep-green analyses pointing to the apocalypse of unabated climate change, Mumford suggested that 'metropolitan civilization contains within itself the explosive forces that will wipe out all traces of its existence'. In short:

> Those who believe that there are no alternatives to the present proliferation of metropolitan tissue perhaps overlook too easily the historic outcome of such a concentration of urban power: they forget that this has repeatedly marked the last stage in the classic cycle of civilization, before its complete disruption and downfall.[74]

Indeed, forecasts of food and water shortages, mass migrations, climatic uncertainties and rises in 'natural disasters' in lieu of climate change all conspire to interrupt and frustrate the optimistic tone of Glaeser's *Triumph of the City*. Even he remarks on the strange paradox that 'in much of coastal America, home prices are dramatically higher than construction costs'.[75] To add to the illogic between drivers of market preferences and hard reality, it is precisely coastal regions that are prone to the effects of global climate change, such as rises in sea levels, tsunamis and hurricanes.[76] Here the economic and environmental dysfunctions of capitalist 'progress' clash. Furthermore, in his massive *Millennium*, Oxford scholar Felipe Fernández-Armesto forecasts that 'cities will wither' as people make use of networked technologies sited in smaller village-like towns facilitating intimate face-to-face contact: 'Today's cities are in part the products of functions which technological progress is gradually eliminating.'[77]

While the apartment does not owe its existence to the megalopolis, many urban dwellers do live in apartments. Despite all the reforms and experiments with different models over the last two centuries, the apartment as a generic type retains its original sub-types, highlighted in poorly designed and windowless micro-apartments with few environmentally friendly features versus larger middle-class apartments and monstrous penthouses where over-consumption proliferates. Contradictions born of poverty and prosperity, sprawl and towers, commercial standardisation and innovations at the margins characterise all capitalist societies.

The rest of this book uses this point of flux – as capitalism unapologetically furthers its thrust deeper and wider than ever before, even as harbingers of post-capitalism spring up in all quarters to call for, and bear news of, relief – to explore new forms of living, which might be urban, peri-urban or rural, that include both detached and attached residences and, most significantly, address the environmental perils that challenge the future of every city on Earth today. A key concern is the potential for each of us individually and collectively to act as 'sustainability citizens', embedding the structures, systems and behaviour we need to make the places we live in socially just and environmentally sustainable.[78] The next chapter, then, focuses on the area we seem to have most control over – our home as a nest, its interior design, functions and potential achievements in fostering and enabling sustainability.

4

Apartment Household Practices and Affordability

During the twentieth century, housing became a key sector and driver of capitalist economies. Owner-occupied homes emerged as a particular form of private property, a status symbol of personal income, worth and credit in a world where other forms of differentiation and identity were becoming vaguer and less significant. Household space had a price and residential dwellings defined private boundaries. This privacy is distinctive of the contemporary urban home: 'For most of human history, houses have not been private spaces, nor have they had, within them, more private spaces belonging to specific residents, nor spaces used by all the residents in turn for entirely private functions.'[1] In the past, sharing was more the norm.

Today many urban apartments are made from brick, concrete and steel and necessitate lifts and balconies. Similarly, the interior components and design of a contemporary apartment can heighten the unsustainability of its residents. Growth in access to a plethora of household fittings, furniture and appliances, the recent explosion of digital information and communications technologies, and the shrinking size of households has resulted in duplicated facilities and services, especially if an urban apartment block is considered as the unit of analysis. Furthermore, as a divided building with distinct ownership of its separate parts, the apartment block fragments potential communities.

This final chapter in Part I will complete the discussion arguing for changes in how we build and live in dwellings in cities. I point towards living in smaller spaces, modest consumption and sharing resources. Although householders of other types of dwellings are referred to, the focus is the urban apartment, the planned urban environments that offer apartment dwellers' services and amenity, and the environmental sustainability of apartment residents' practices. Every device and item of, say, soft furnishings, brought into the apartment is ultimately sourced from Earth, fashioned by so many hands, stored and retailed, before being used. Subsequently, appliances and items are frequently tossed out without being fully used or appreciated to end up in landfill. Buying less, using everything longer or sharing its use and handing on, for re-use or recycling, are the best household practices.

Relevant changes in housing and households, and in the rise of the apartment, were surveyed in Chapter 2 and Chapter 3, respectively. This chapter journeys into the interior world of apartments, and dwellers' practices within and beyond their apartment homes in terms of sustainability. I discuss the fatal attraction of domestic technology and household consumption and consider cleverly designed and used self-contained spaces, along with practical principles for more sustainable apartment living. The chapter concludes that resident engagement to drive innovation in urban planning and developments is needed to improve affordability, sustainability and sociality. Such neighbourhood-based and community-led improvements are, of course, foci of the rest of the book.

DWELLINGS AND DWELLERS

Dwelling in apartments reflects general trends in housing towards over-consumption as a result of reduced sharing, the plethora of high tech devices, long-distance travel and unnecessary purchases by those on above average incomes.

'It's mine' and the technological turn

The spread of gas lamps, electricity and, later, central heating altered ways that residents occupied home spaces. Once members of households had congregated around the service of a candle or gas lamp, fire, stove or radio but, during the twentieth century, as apartments came to typify modern life, members of households became more atomised in separate rooms and alienated in private activities.[2] This set the stage for personal mobile digital technologies, whose owners communicate most in 'Internetworks' that leap from kin and place-based relationships to interest-based and peer communities. Added to planned obsolescence pressuring residents to purchase new versions of even quite functional equipment, low levels of sharing for re-use, waste generation, and individuation within households results in overconsumption of floor space and services such as heating and cooling.

In contrast, added to greater affordability and operating efficiencies, studies have found that a small dwelling occupied by at least two full-time residents can encourage environmentally friendly practices through sharing their living, socialising and relaxation spaces, storage and equipment. For instance, while research into all kinds of dwellings being built in London in the mid-2000s indicated that the average occupant of a one-bedroom flat had 15sq m of 'habitable' area compared with 10sq m for members of other kinds of dwellings, apartments with more household members clearly had comparatively more *shared* space, goods, services, skills and knowledge.[3] Certainly even two-member households, compared with single households, occupying a similar space halves the per capita environmental cost of an apartment built of concrete and steel and high in 'embodied' energy and, similarly, significantly reduces operating costs for energy, maintenance and replacements.

During the twentieth century, technological advances diminished hard household labour, focusing such work overwhelmingly on women.[4] Cleanliness, including tidiness, became a core value as relationships between germs, dirt, mould and health became apparent. Even as equipment and appliances supplanted the paid servant and were promoted as saving time as well as effort, housework still tended to fill a housewife's day; perversely, washing machines and dishwashers actually had residents washing themselves, their houses and everything in them more as the century wore on. Studies suggest that by the start of the Second World War 'middle-class housewives equipped with the latest in labour-saving technologies actually spent more time on housework than their mothers had at the turn of the century'.[5]

These kinds of studies only confirmed pre-existing suspicions and active resistance to mechanising homely duties on the basis of cost, and questions around whether 'mod-cons' really saved time, were well designed for everyday use and were of sufficient quality. Awareness of environmental limits in the last few decades has heightened such cynicism of technology.

Holistic analyses of urban lifestyles: culture, consciousness and income

Critiques of research and rating tools that concentrate on making buildings more sustainable suggest that household members' practices and their consumption of clothing and food, and waste generation, must be included in sustainability assessments (as discussed in Chapter 3).

Holistic consumption analyses take a broad approach to householders' consumption. Excessive carbon-emitting travel in large powerful cars or air flights must be accounted for alongside the environmental costs of dwellings. Life outside home uses resources and energy so, if we are to better evaluate, understand and improve householders' practices, the focus must be lifestyles rather than simply housing or household practices.

Significant demographic studies have explored the sources and cultures of residential sustainability practices. One found that household practices of Australian migrants from non-Anglo-Saxon backgrounds were more sustainable than the daily lifestyles of either those born in Australia or migrants from the United Kingdom (UK) and North West Europe. The former, compared with the latter, shared more and consumed less, lived in smaller spaces, were characterised by a higher proportion of apartment dwellers, and used and owned fewer cars. The same study revealed that women, lower income earners and seniors were more likely to engage in sustainable practices than men, affluent households and young people.[6]

Most interestingly, a high consciousness of and concern about the significance of environmental challenges and climate change did not necessarily translate into more sustainable practices:

In the survey of 1,465 Illawarra households, 426 reported having a rainwater tank. These households were more likely to have solar power, compost, use grey water, and regularly grow their own fruit and vegetables. Contrary to this engagement in pro-environmental behaviours, this group was also more likely to own four-wheel drives, clothes dryers, dishwashers, computers, separate freezers, air conditioning and heaters. The results showed no statistical difference in the way household water was used. Tank households were not more likely than others to undertake water saving practices.[7]

Choices decide how urban services and buildings are used in everyday practices. Apartment dwellers might have no option but to use mains water and pubic sewerage systems – rather than collect, store and use water on site and have water- and energy-efficient grey-water systems – but they can follow sustainable household practices, such as flushing the toilet only as necessary. Apartment dwellers might be able to use more public transport and walk and cycle more, but flying in planes proves seriously negative for energy budgets and is commonplace amongst urban dwellers.

A study of residents of inner and outer areas of Detroit showed that higher-income households tended to have bigger and more powerful cars that consumed more fuel than lighter small cars, and that those on higher incomes tended to live in low-density suburbs, travelling much more frequently than households in compact inner areas of the city. In short, higher income households tended to contribute more carbon – and other pollutant – emissions than lower-income households.[8]

SMALL

Regardless of the impacts of income and lifestyle, a seemingly simple, immediate and easy way to limit consumption is to live in a smaller space, which automatically reduces space for 'stuff'. However, reducing consumption involves more than space. Taking clothing as an example, it's true that a small apartment will mean limiting purchases. Still, it is best if clothes are made of natural materials, grown sustainably not too far away, and can be laundered at low temperatures. Second-hand clothing is ideal. Using air and the sun to dry clothes is preferable to a drying machine. Where councils or apartment associations ban clotheslines, inviting unsustainable practices, clothes horses can be still be used discreetly.[9]

Unfortunately, in terms of apartments, 'small' still tends to be associated with poor quality and poor environmental sustainability. A City of Melbourne review of apartments constructed between 2006 and 2012 – more than half with just one bedroom and rental stock – found that all those in residential towers 16–41 storeys high ranked either 'poor' or merely 'average' in terms of adequate private and community space, storage and utilities, ventilation, light and layout, whereas 60 per cent of low-rise (buildings of five or fewer storeys) rated as 'good'. The review showed that car spaces had greater priority than residents' pedestrian and diverse life cycle needs! This was mainly due to council regulations and market drivers.[10]

The City of Melbourne review found that apartments were generally constructed with high embodied energy materials, such as concrete and glass, failed to observe good passive solar design principles to appropriately capture sunlight and adequately protect against the sun's heat, and neglected to install appliances for collecting solar energy and water for residents to use.[11] Given that Melbourne has won awards as the world's most liveable city, such trends gave city planners reason to pause.

If faults in such buildings are due to 'poor design', studies in both Australia and the UK show that 'good design' does not refer to any widely agreed upon criteria or values, let alone an established language for broad public discourse.[12] Meanwhile, surveys and interviews with apartment residents in the Melbourne study confirmed the need for more attention to accessing daylight, space design, natural ventilation, noise minimisation, and improvements to energy and resource efficiency performance.[13]

Digging into the detail of the growth in the average size of new dwellings in Australia, the City of Melbourne review referred to research indicating that, between 2008 and 2010, one-bedroom apartments had diminished in floor size by more than 15 per cent to an average of 44sq m and, similarly, two-bedroom apartments by 13 per cent to 67sq m. This size is below comparable recommended minimum sizes in cities such as London and Sydney. Furthermore, the City of Melbourne found that investors had bought 85 per cent of the apartments studied; in short most apartment dwellers had next-to-no say not only in how their dwellings were built but also in how they might make sustainability improvements.[14]

A UK study has shown a similar trend in London and, moreover, how averages conceal great discrepancies: despite the average internal size of a one-bedroom flat being 47sq m, a London bed-sit (studio) of 22sq m and one-bedroom apartment of 38sq m represented almost one-quarter of apartments in their respective buildings, which researchers estimated could 'form a very significant portion of overall output', especially given that prices per square metre were more cost effective for smaller than for larger abodes.[15] In global cities, commercial fare is highly conditioned by investors' rental prospects rather than residents' needs. Although I argue for small-footprint living in a small space, it is a fact that tiny, poorly designed apartments put residents off and tend to prove socially unsustainable; cramped residents in dingy apartments often rent extra space for storage and to work and determinedly aspire to 'bigger and better' in their next abode.

Before discussing well-designed small apartments, we pause to look at some key rooms that comprise floor plans and how styles in interior design assist and hinder in developing environmentally sustainable practices within apartments.

FLOOR PLANS AND ROOM FASHIONS

Floor plans spatially organise distinct activities room by room. Household practices naturally succumb to fashions adopted by commercial developers, such as the growth in rooms for leisure, and unnecessary duplication, as in the en-suite bathroom for each and every bedroom, and small kitchen spaces that encourage eating out or take-away food. How rooms are clustered following certain styles, also limit practices within apartments.

The bathroom

Those rooms that we associate most with nudity and privacy – bedrooms and bathrooms – are relatively recent developments for what were quite public activities just a few centuries ago. Gradually, curtains were used to secrete sleepers and bathers, and enclosed toilets were erected.[16] Only the spread of piped water in the twentieth century enabled a congregation of appliances related to personal washing in the bathroom.[17] Even then, the toilet was always prone to separation from the bath, shower and, later, the wasteful spa bath.

Finally, bedrooms and bathrooms have become private spaces from shared use including use one at a time, to belonging to one person, and often remaining vacant. The growth of the en-suite meant bathrooms and bedrooms joined in personal luxury, and many two-bedroom flats with two bathrooms readily duplicate not only appliances, plumbing, electricity and other built components but items such as shower curtains, toothpastes and shampoos. Today a field of study of everyday practices, situating sustainability practices such as bathing and showering in a social context, has evolved from the work of researchers such as Elizabeth Shove and the UK Sustainable Practices Research Group. However, by the mid-2010s there still seemed to be few substantial studies specifically on apartment practices.[18]

The kitchen

Government and commercial pressures focused on the kitchen which, by the nineteenth century and at least in middle-class homes, had become a clearly demarcated room for cooking and for which specially designed furniture and fittings and manuals evolved.[19] At the end of the

First World War, the Weimar Republic gave local councils the responsibility for creating affordable, social (public) housing. Subsequently, German cities featured standard apartments with minimum standard building regulations for size, windows and ventilation, which would prompt standard designs not only for dining and living rooms but also for kitchens – such as the innovative compact Egri-Küche and Frankfurt kitchens.[20] Such innovations spread and especially influenced other apartment developments worldwide – in Europe, the UK, North America, Australia and New Zealand.

Indeed, the 'rational' kitchen in the city apartment typified the modernist characteristics of manufacture, standardisation, masculinity, professionalism and functionality:

The introduction of labour-saving devices made the kitchen more of a laboratory or a workshop than a social centre and its size – at least in Europe – was correspondingly reduced. In America, though, the battery of new kitchen equipment – giant iceboxes, huge dishwashers, waste-disposal units, food mixers, automatic washing machines – was considered a matter of national pride.[21]

If washing, toileting and sleeping spaces have grown to unnecessarily generous proportions in many contemporary apartments, as a rule of thumb minimisation of kitchen spaces and maximisation of kitchen devices work against sustainability practices. Devices such as the electric kettle and toaster are notoriously high energy users. The most holistically sustainable practices centre on preparing meals simply, from fresh and local ingredients, and composting food waste, demanding more than the short kitchen wall in many apartments which, instead, seems to assume that most food eaten in an apartment will be purchased at least semi-prepared and simply microwaved. In short, many apartment kitchens have shrunk to a simple appendage of nearby hospitality services and supermarkets.

Floor plans and apartment styles

The 'upstairs–downstairs' stereotype of separated public and private spaces in eighteenth and nineteenth century dwellings endures yet Flanders suggests that many British homes had diverse floor plans and variously inhabited their residential spaces. Thus classes, genders and ages might either intensely cohabit and engage, or stand their distance as a segregated, and internally contradictory, unity.[22] Today, the typical layout of contemporary double-storey dwellings places private bed and bathroom spaces upstairs and public entry, living and eating spaces on the lower floor – even when the reverse would be more functional, provide better views and privacy, and result in better sustainability practices. Furthermore, built-in fittings and furniture mean little flexibility and adaptability in space use.

By the 1950s, 'open plan' became a convention that endures today. Open plan created a sense of space, light and airiness, allowing for flexibility and personalisation, and was often complemented by higher ceilings. Double-height ceilings, made fashionable by Corbusier, became especially functional in loft or studio apartments where mezzanines with beds and studies would proliferate. Through simultaneous rather than connected developments, the centrality of the fireplace gave way to the television. While the television altered the arrangement of living areas, it could easily dominate a small apartment and showed up certain failings of open plan. At the same time, television shows exposed viewers to diverse influences of how they might live differently – especially raising expectations of affluence.[23]

Meanwhile, modern apartments became environmentally expensive in embodied energy; the taller the building, the greater need for multiple lifts and massive energy expended in construction. Although steel and glass overtook concrete and wood as materials of function and style, a diversity of past styles and futuristic designs can co-exist in any apartment. Furthermore, fashions and new technologies have prompted more regular renovations, gutting and complete refits. Curtains, floor coverings and furniture became plasticised in various ways along with screen printing and glues in wood products. Plastic, in particular, has become a ubiquitous environmental hazard just as inks and glues have become pollutants endangering health, with all impacts likely to be exaggerated by warmer conditions driven by climate change.

Finally, in the last few decades, the green apartment became a niche fashion, often more in form than substance – unless the floor plan was modest, the apartment oriented and insulated appropriately, and complemented by minimal adequate sustainability technology. Instead, the commercial 'green' apartment tended to evolve within a conventional, environmentally unfriendly, spacious style with technology as the major add-on, and was often more expensive than the norm. One view of 'smart' automations such as 'intelligent blinds' is that they not only save, but even rob, residents of consciously and conscientiously managing their homes to perform more sustainably. Being aware of the weather and having an apartment designed and amenable to screening out unwanted sun, blocking out cold, ventilating through opening windows and vents – through active rather than automated means – not only enhances an appreciation of seasons, weather and nature more generally, but also forces the resident to think about and act responsibly over sustainable practices.

Contemporary spacious layouts reflect the fact that, as apartments (and dwellings more generally) have assumed the significance of an asset, the gravity of decision-making on style, size and 'mod-cons' centres on marketability advice in a system that aims for capital growth and gives status to luxury. Despite purchasers' personal preferences, they are apt to buy what is commonly considered most re-saleable, a perspective supported by often critical valuations made by mortgage providers. Sustainability researchers have found that developers tend to assume 'space and place' are what 'the market wants' even as post-occupancy evaluations and user-driven processes point more in the directions of functionality, affordability and sustainability.[24] Investors often follow developers' leads. London residents record most dissatisfaction with lack of kitchen space, areas for children or youth to play and socialise, and to fit in all their 'stuff'.[25] Once space is restricted, only clever design and diverse, affordable market options can address such complaints. Small spaces must be beautifully designed.

CLEVERLY DESIGNED SMALL SPACES: EXAMPLES

With respect to small spaces, internationally renowned designer Terence Conran insists on planning for flexibility, creatively considering many possibilities, addressing limits associated with the inherited structure and, most importantly, the imperative of holistic design.[26] Illustrating his arguments with plans of small apartments – three included here – Conran indicates the importance of storage space even as 'stuff' is minimised. Accordingly, the external walls of the Hong Kong apartment shown in Figure 4.1 are used for storage, releasing most of the interior for activities and functions. The Paris apartment (Figure 4.2) optimises high ceilings to create storage holes and recesses. All three apartments minimise on bed space, in distinctive ways, and can be readily heated and cooled.

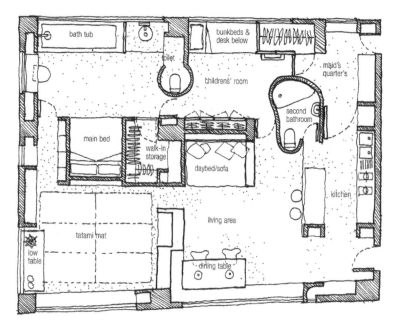

Figure 4.1   Floor plan Hong Kong apartment, 93sq m

Source: Terrance Conran, *Small Spaces: Inspiring Ideas and Creative Solutions*, London: Conran Octopus, 2001, p. 67

The 93sq m Hong Kong apartment offers economies of scale, a homely feel and intriguing features for a household of five (parents, two children and a maid). Each resident benefits from privacy in recessed bed spaces, just as the entire apartment offers distinct spaces for various activities by different members. Such recesses can contain personalised shelving, decorations, pictures and posters. The curved bathroom walls offer softness, associations with nature and economise on space. Tatami mats are strong cultural symbols in a minimalist setting of modernist features, such as stainless steel. All windows are covered with panes of acid etched glass to allow in light and block out depressing urban views.[27]

According to Conran, the redesigned nineteenth-century London basement apartment of 49sq m (Figure 4.3) benefited from gutting the previous kitchen to create a bedroom, placing a kitchen along a wall in the open-plan living and eating room, removing a bath for storage and wardrobe space, and opening the office–library in two directions for light and circulation. Note the flexibility here: the bedroom and study could be reversed for other needs. Great environmental efficiencies lie in

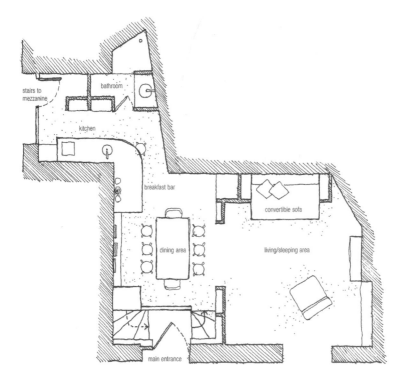

Figure 4.2 Floor plan Paris apartment, 36sq m

Source: Terrance Conran, *Small Spaces: Inspiring Ideas and Creative Solutions*, London: Conran Octopus, 2001, p. 142

its thick walls: apparently, it can all be kept warm by a bathroom heater! It has a tiny terrace for views, light and use as an outdoor room.[28]

The odd external shape of the 36sq m Paris apartment, a small open mezzanine area with a mattress for guests, and removal of certain doors have all allowed for views throughout resulting in a deceptive sense of spaciousness. As in many studio apartments efficiencies have been made by allowing the open living area to revert to the main sleeping space at night while a tiny basement area offers wardrobe space. In this case, downsizing space radically cut down the possessions the owner had expected to keep. Critically, taking out wall dividers allowed natural light to flow in from the double-height entrance.[29]

These are designs of small dwelling spaces to accommodate everyday activities. The Hong Kong apartment has separate spaces for adults and children to eat but common meals can be had Japanese-style on

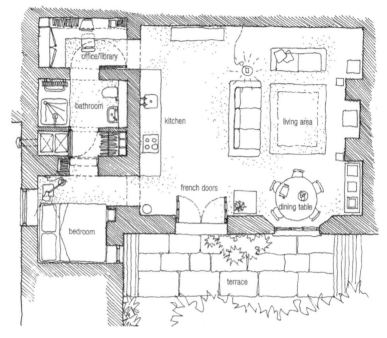

Figure 4.3   Floor plan London basement apartment, 49sq m

Source: Terrance Conran, *Small Spaces: Inspiring Ideas and Creative Solutions*, London: Conran Octopus, 2001, p. 93

the tatami mat. With flexible plans, such apartments can be inhabited differently for a diversity of purposes, minimising needs for environmentally expensive renovation when new tenants or owners move in or occupants grow up or grow old.

CLEVERLY DESIGNED SMALL DWELLINGS: PRINCIPLES

Ideally, residential dwellings need to either accommodate or be located so they offer access to spaces for sleeping, dressing, cooking and eating, washing, relaxing, studying or working, socialising and playing. Such activities require various external services to the dwelling and easily accessible fittings, furniture and equipment, storage and external space. Doors and windows allow for fresh air and sunlight. Construction materials, layout and ceiling height all impact on flexibility and liveability. As such, space and spaciousness rely on good design for the basic and special needs, techniques and practices of householders to occupy their space.[30]

Architect Sarah Susanka, born in the UK but based in the United States (US), has written numbers of books on 'not so big' houses that explore and offer hints on living in smaller spaces. They include ideas such as creating a wide window seat to function as a sofa, daybed or overnight guest-bed with roomy drawers underneath and shelving in the side walls: 'The window seat is treated as a little room.' She explores opening spaces by replacing walls with waist-height counters and, conversely, dividing rooms with two-metre high furniture or fittings; under-stair and other handy storage areas; small circulation spaces opening to other rooms that also function as serious storage areas, say with recessed cabinets. Susanka emphasises natural materials and the importance of aspect or views inside and out.[31]

Max Jacobson and his colleagues have identified 10 principles for 'patterning' a home. These principles are most useful to employ as a dwelling is designed rather than as an existing dwelling is re-inhabited. Even so, they can guide thinking about and creating solutions for retrofitting, renovating or forming additions to existing apartments. The 10 principles have been adapted and rephrased as questions as follows:

1. Could the natural and artificially built environments be more reflected, expressed or integrated into the dwelling?
2. What roles do, or could, each room – including balconies, courtyards and adjacent gardens – play for everyday activities, both spatially and functionally?
3. Do the roof and ceilings provide a feeling of shelter, protection and comfort?
4. Are the rooms open enough to light yet shielded from the sun's cycles?
5. Is there harmony in comparative proportions of rooms, furniture, windows, walls, floor space and doors?
6. Does the composite structure welcome and draw you through the house?
7. Is there an appropriate mix of private and common spaces; for privacy and quietness; for enjoying others company, say for eating and preparing meals?

8. Does it feel safe and secure observing external environments from protected spots?
9. How many places, say a bay or porthole window, or an external sliding floor-to-ceiling window-door, allow you to look over and enjoy the immediate environment?
10. How do the dwelling's materials affect residents: giving the hand texture, the eye colour, the heart space and comfort, and the head confidence that the home is secure and will endure?[32]

Most significantly these design guidelines do not require over-consumption, technology for technology's sake, the reproduction of fashions, or apathetic and uncritical acceptance of commercial fare. Moreover, they complement environmental efficiency while human needs remain central.

Such principles reveal the significance of home as a haven. Humans are central within a seamless stretch of contexts, from a womb-like bed(room), to apartment, to block, to public greenspace, other accessible and servicing buildings and infrastructure, that is, from the immediately personal to the intimacy of the household, from encouraging activity in public spaces to welcoming visitors and household members home, all the while being completely reliant on the external world as any unborn child is within its mother. This sense of the real connections in our daily activities reflect recent urban planning and architectural sustainability efforts in apartment buildings which see the block as a community and its neighbourhood as a reservoir of services.

SUSTAINABILITY, MARKET AND AFFORDABILITY

Once residential sustainability techniques were disseminated and demonstrated, as a plethora of 'sustainable' materials and technologies were produced, and as energy costs and concerns about the level of carbon emissions increased, theoretical life-cycle analyses and other research on sustainability-focused new builds and retrofits have come to show economic benefits.[33] Thus, added to co-benefits in the areas of health and comfort, environmentally sustainable residential building seems to be the way of the future.[34] But, is this how industry players, such as developers and builders, see it? Is this how it appears to house purchasers? Will these built sustainability advances be decisive for sustainability practices by householders?

Commercial fare and householder practices

The construction of an environmentally sustainable apartment building relies on the level of expertise of a developer and project manager orchestrating many different contributors in a complicated collaboration on a well-designed project abiding by government regulations and succumbing to commercial limitations centring on cost. The array of professional tasks include: cleverly locating and siting the block, and each apartment within it; sensible interior, exterior and landscape design; using sustainably sourced materials with appropriate construction methods; sustainability advice and close supervision by professionals and tradespeople, such as engineers, builders, carpenters, tilers, plumbers and electricians. Many regulatory requirements incorporate sustainability tools that rate qualities such as thermal performance and energy efficiencies of materials and appliances.

The independent US Green Building Council developed a building rating system, Leadership in Energy and Environmental Design (LEED), accrediting professionals accordingly with industry buy-in creating LEED as the primary reference point for the sustainability of buildings. This rating system has been taken up right across the world, in Europe, Asia and Latin America. However, a 2011 review noted specific challenges in the apartment sector, where:

> owners and operators opt instead for a minimum threshold of sustainability necessary to obtain LEED certification, ostensibly for marketing purposes. In addition, the siting decisions and capital expenditures associated with green apartment living suggest that this particular type of niche housing is more suited to upper-income households. This particular inequity sparks outcries of social injustice, especially as the populations that could most benefit from the savings inherent within green housing are low-income.[35]

Moreover, another US study points out that LEED for Neighbourhood Development ratings relegate only a few percentage points to affordability and most accredited professionals suspect that developers decide not to risk losing profits or tarnishing such projects by highlighting accessibility to low-income earners.[36] Furthermore, green building codes pay relatively little attention to size even though smaller apartments are key to householders practising sustainability.

Generally, apartments are built to economise on premium land at a high cost and in short supply. Moreover, as double-glazed windows, solar panels and hot water services, materials with high insulation properties, renewable or used materials, and energy efficient white goods now attract wider than niche markets, they are less expensive inclusions. Still, they often remain costlier than conventional options, and tradespeople can level hefty extra charges for working with unconventional choices. Savings could be made by minimising apartment sizes, through clever design, integrating collective infrastructure and storage, and by bulk purchases. However, sustainability features increase the time professionals spend on the job and collaboration takes time, both translating into greater costs. In short, despite the growing affordability of sustainable housing, commercial barriers remain considerable.

Both commercial and financial barriers include adversity to innovation or alternatives (see Chapter 9). For instance, many Australian mortgage lenders have tended to baulk at studio apartments less than 40sq m, especially if considered superfluous to market demand.[37] A specific challenge relates to residential and industry cultures putting a premium on offering greater space, or following fashions, say in conventional eave-less building styles even where such eaves are essential to protect walls and windows from harsh sun.

The knowledge, skills, needs and practices of householders can optimise, or make a mockery of, the ideal sustainability functions of their apartment. For instance, a clothes line might exist in the ceiling of their laundry, or the balcony might easily hide a clothes horse for drying, but, instead, new owner-occupiers, landlords or tenants might install an energy-guzzling clothes dryer. A fan might offer basic cooling and opening windows make for natural ventilation but both options are neglected and an energy-guzzling air conditioner installed. The next owner or renter inherits such superfluity. Professional advice on energy- and water-efficient practices are more freely available today than yesterday, but cultural and personal habits can be as significant barriers to change as lack of sustainability knowledge and skills.

Sustainability: flexibility and adaptability

Built-in, or even accidental, 'flexibility' and 'adaptability' of apartments enhances sustainability practices and dwelling performance. Ideally, apartments cater for the needs of inhabitants, and their visitors, transitioning through life's cycle from babies to seniors. Indeed, many building standards for new dwellings in global cities now include door and hall space for mobility aids, sloping bathroom floors without lips and edges for easy and safe movement, at least one bedroom on the ground floor of duplexes, and lifts and ramps instead of, or alongside, stairs. Apartment blocks can offer adaptability through diverse floor plans within and between units. Common spaces, too, need to accommodate all ages and stages to make everyday practices more sustainable.

Similarly, environmental sustainability criteria with respect to ideal heating and cooling ranges for maintaining internal temperatures, and ventilation, need to take account of levels of comfort necessary for maintaining good health. Air conditioning and heating have attracted special attention, with the focus on minimising use of both. Apartment dwellers can draw on traditional techniques to minimise the effects of heat waves, such as heading for the coolest place in the dwelling to retreat to and sleep in. Householders need to prioritise such space for those members especially sensitive, and vulnerable, to the impacts of heat stress.

Density in compact cities maximises opportunities for working at home or proximity to work. While work at home rarely parallels pre-industrial work–home spaces, during the twenty-first century we have seen increases in households with at least one member working from home. Work spaces can be provided by tidy cabinets opened and closed at will or located in mid-floor dens or lofts. Coworking in an apartment block space is a very useful option. Indeed, a range of options for working, gardening, child-minding, meeting and eating together can complement small apartment living in major ways. Because common facilities are used by multiple people in multiple ways up to, say 18 hours a day, they economise on space and equipment and optimise on neighbourly communal contact. Thus, attached dwellings in well-serviced precincts could become a natural home for cohousing, as discussed in Chapter 5.

Following the twenty-first century wave of suburban estates based on a cynical master-planned 'community' model,[38] and a tradition of certain shared spaces and facilities in apartment blocks, a small number of contemporary architects and developers have been exploring ways to satisfy market demand for both sustainability and community in apartments. Constructing and selling eco-communities is the main topic of Chapter 8. It suffices to point out here that mainstream developments promoted as high in sustainability and community features can be low performers due to overconsumption and relative cost, even commanding an above-average price on resale due to undersupply.

How sustainable?

Jaded by 'the poor quality of housing stock in Britain … plonked down with no regard for place or any kind of context' and by 'the dinosaur attitude of developers who were more interested in getting a return for investment in land than in making neighbourhoods that are decent places to live', presenter of BBC Channel 4 program *Grand Designs* Kevin McCloud ventured into green social housing. Significantly, after several years' experience as a developer, he concluded that while it was 'easy to build an eco house': 'What is really hard is to convince people to change their lives and live more sustainably.'[39] Everyday lives are constrained not only by costs but compulsion to live in a general merry-go-round of unsustainable practices – well-illustrated in a study of the Beddington Zero Energy Development (BedZED).

BedZED (2002) is 100 mainly apartment dwellings with 100 workspaces, communal facilities and amenities, built in south London by a well-established affordable housing association. Although a top-down market-oriented development, developer knowledge and skills gained in BedZED have been transferred to social housing more generally, contributing to the initial UK policy goal of zero carbon new homes by 2016 and the 2007 UK Code for Sustainable Homes (a standard for rating and certifying the sustainability performance of new dwellings). BedZED won the Royal Institute of British Architects 2001 Housing Design Award for sustainability and informed the One Planet Living approach of its initiator and collaborator BioRegional.

A 2009 evaluation of BedZED referred to the Global Footprint Network calculation that, if equity ruled, each and every inhabitant of Earth would need to live off 1.8 global hectares (gha) of productive land – thus equating to a 'one planet' lifestyle (likely to shrink to 1.2 gha by 2050). Applying this approach, BedZED residents had an average ecological footprint of 2.6 planets and, even a highly motivated BedZED resident in the ideal circumstances would live a 1.7 planet lifestyle. The study pointed out that 'residents cannot lead one planet lifestyles in a relatively small demonstration project like BedZED' mainly 'because the minute they step off site they are participating in the "three planet" higher impact world and using the facilities we all share, such as the health service, roads, shops and government services'.[40]

Such post-occupancy monitoring of sustainable housing developments is often neglected or ad hoc. Meanwhile, residents' practices and collective or organisational management varies, to produce different outcomes than the optimums indicated by ideal sustainability forecasts pre-occupancy. In practice, monitoring has many technical and practical difficulties, such as 'monitoring fatigue'. Furthermore, while monitoring can have a positive social effect, pressuring sustainable behaviour, there is the risk that residents slacken off good practices when not observed or subject to reporting. Interestingly, a thesis examining data from 16 international sustainable community settlements revealed that European cases tended to be more studious, and followed up on poor sustainability performance, while it was characteristic of US examples to gloss over any weaknesses exposed.[41] Many other questions can be raised, such as how much a greater occupancy rate might alter sustainability performance. The 100 BedZED dwellings were occupied by just 220 residents in 2014.[42]

How affordable?

Two other cases illustrate points associated with affordability. The designers of a block of 24 one- and two-bedroom apartments, The Commons, located 6km from Melbourne's central business district (CBD), incorporated small dwelling size as a sustainability criterion along with several key goals to achieve zero carbon through: both efficient energy use and solar energy generation in situ; sustainable construction and material use, including zero waste in demolition and construction through reuse and recycling; sustainable transport through public transit proximity, accommodating bikes, and not providing car parks to encourage walking and car sharing; sustainable water use through water collection, storage and onsite-use, and gardens and landscape designed to absorb and slow run-off with minimal householder water use through efficiency-based practices and devices; and – given that two-thirds of the average Victorian's ecological footprint derives from their food and other goods and services consumed – a rooftop garden was created with 46 raised vegetable garden boxes, bee hives and green purchasing facilitated by bulk green contracts and composting. Other community amenity included a cafe and artist studios.

While a two-bedroom The Commons apartment of 72sq m sold mid-2014 for A$605,000 when the median comparable unit price was A$485,000,[43] its developers stated that they intended to make subsequent projects 'affordable'. In 2016, significantly 'more spacious' apartments in their neighbouring development integrated a caveat on each title to require owners to limit resale prices to equal (or less than) their purchase price plus the average growth in house prices for the suburb, for the initial twenty years of the apartment's life.[44] The developer economised by limiting apartments to one bathroom and no laundry (centralising shared access to laundry facilities on the rooftop). Moreover, given that promotion of The Commons resulted in a long waiting list of interested customers, financing, real estate and advertising costs were markedly reduced. Nevertheless, these apartments, and those in another more expansive development planned in a suburb several kilometres distant, were expected to sell for a similar price to those at The Commons. Affordability remains questionable in these developments partly because the model, arguably, makes first owners bear the costs of the affordability caveat. Only post-occupancy evaluations will prove real sustainability gains.[45]

A final example shows similar sustainability and affordability challenges in a development in Issaqhah, a suburb east of Seattle in Washington State (US). The 10-townhouse transit-oriented zHome project was initiated to achieve zero-net energy use, 'at least cost' and specifically as a model for similar market initiatives. An interdisciplinary professional design process incorporated principles such as durability, maintainability and flexibility, minimising noise and maximising healthy conditions, such as sunlight and natural ventilation in dwellings. Because the design process did not include them, residents became the 'wild card'; various assumptions about lifestyle preferences were made on their behalf and technologies installed for them to monitor and modify their behaviour.

A ground source heat pump system feeds in under concrete slab and bamboo floors. Separate solar panels provide energy for each townhouse and for shared community facilities. Water and waste systems are similarly environmentally sensitive and 'equally' shared. Cars are housed on the margins, with extra parking and electric charging facilities in an adjacent street. The 'solar courtyard' and other communal green spaces, edible gardens and green walls (soil-free vertical gardens often watered by automatic drip irrigation) are maximised. The development has functioned as an education centre. Despite its sustainability features, the project cost over US$3 million, relied on free land, and was developed without resident input, which risked jeopardising compliance.[46]

If conventional fare and innovative market players face massive challenges in meeting ideal levels of sustainability and breach affordability targets, another layer of complexity is in city and environmental planning where, interestingly, grassroots activity is becoming vibrant.

NEIGHBOURHOOD PLANNING MATTERS

Neighbourhood has been, and always will be, a significant factor in living sustainably, especially if human practices come to mimic ecological diversity in unity, layers, niches and ecotones. First, I discuss global cities moving to address environmental and social sustainability by de-prioritising the car, increasing green and open spaces and planning for connectedness in neighbourhood precincts. Second, I show how planning encouraged sustainable practices in Edo (Japan), which urbanised in the seventeenth century on a compact model of multiple easily replicated cell-like districts with waterways and bridges used for transport and travel.

Car space, open space and green space

Many council planning guidelines fly in the face of sustainability principles, say by insisting on space for cars but not for storing bikes in apartment blocks and public spaces. Planning application and approval processes often prove unfriendly and unwieldy for individual applicants while at a general level appearing too lax, as in the case of the City of Melbourne, where the population is expected to rise from 4.3m (2014) to 7.7m in 2051.[47] A 2015 study of six global cities with high-density, high-rise inner-city dwellings showed that – in contrast to Hong Kong, New York City (NYC), Seoul, Tokyo and Vancouver – apartment block developments in Melbourne were proceeding without effective controls to density, height or proximity to other towers and little regulation of apartment quality, such as light (windows) and air. Furthermore, Melburnian developers did not pay bonuses used by other city councils to establish, improve and maintain open space facilities for residents. Instead Melbourne's apartment dwellers enjoyed a fraction of such space available in the comparison cities.[48]

To illustrate the implications of planning guidelines, the 2015 study proposed a hypothetical set of apartment developments centring on a dense CBD block, to reveal that Melbourne's policies demanded four to nine times the amount of space for cars than Vancouver, NYC or Hong Kong. Meanwhile, hypothetical residents in the Melbournian block would have to make do with a tiny 0.1sq m green or open space per capita compared with the World Health Organisation (WHO) 9sq m standard for green space per capita. While those in the other three cities would get 11 to 30 times the Melbourne average, they too fell far short of the WHO minimum standard.[49] In contrast, London boasts 27sq m and Amsterdam 87.5sq m green and open space per capita. As city populations rise, the pressures on competing uses for space increase, so planning skills and power are crucial to create and maintain quality amenity for residents.

To address these challenges, one mid-2016 plan for the polluted and noisy Catalan capital Barcelona – currently offering an average of 6.6sq m green and open space per capita (centrally located Eixample residents must make do with 1.85sq m) – envisaged slicing the city into superblocks (*superilles*) impenetrable by vehicular traffic unless travelling slowly and specifically for local purposes. Thus, locally, pedestrians, bicyclists and public transport would become dominant, bike paths would be extended to three times their current length, with more than half of the streets now monopolised by mechanical vehicles re-appropriated for environmentally friendly mobility and green and open spaces. Such superblocks would become stronger internally networked neighbourhood communities.[50]

A similar set of strategies recommended by Arup, to ban cars from the centre and greatly expand greenery on top of, among and around city buildings, has been adopted as urban policy in Spain's capital Madrid. These policies were developed to counteract the impacts of pollution, the growing numbers and intensity of heat waves, generalised drought and flash flooding resulting from climate change. Greenery absorbs and retains rain while preventing buildings, and their inhabitants, from heating up so much.[51] In 2009, Toronto authorities introduced regulations to ensure that all future industrial and residential buildings had green roofs and, in 2015, Paris authorities passed legislation requiring all new construction in the commercial zone to install green roofs and/or solar panels.[52]

From Edo to Tokyo

The superblocks proposed for Barcelona hark back to traditional planning in cities such as Edo, where Tokyo now stands. Furthermore, some traditional Japanese cultural mores continue to enhance urban living today. Centuries ago, crowded lower Edo had 1700 districts, each housing around 300 residents, and some 69,000 inhabitants per sq km. Each square district had a central main road, secured main gates at each end and, internally, were administered by five upper-class families selected from around one-quarter of the residents who were small property-owning artisans and merchants. Many districts were characterised by an industry, such as shoe-making or carpentry, and its associated culture. Property-less artisans and merchants rented overcrowded row houses from upper-class landlords – accessing shared toilets, baths and a well on an adjacent street. Japan's modernisation in the second half of the nineteenth century more or less eradicated these communities and their homes, a task completed by the 1923 earthquake and Second World War bombing.[53]

Multi-storey apartment buildings typified reconstruction in the centre and suburban areas of Tokyo, the world's most populous city. Yet Evelyn Schultz refers to numerous 'small neighbourhoods in which the elements and structures of the pre-modern era have survived', having parallels with intentionally mixed-use revitalisation and privately owned public spaces integrating residential, commercial and green spaces in North America. A recent longing for prioritising the 'slow life' – walking, eating local food, sustainability, cultural traditions, community and neighbourhood – are building blocks of what Schulz calls the 'collective living' of small-scale mixed-use urban redevelopments.[54] Similarly, Hildner points to sustainability benefits of Japanese culture: adept at living in small spaces and nurturing traditional concepts, such as likening a 'short useful life' with 'wood construction and ideas of religious purity and renovation', both reducing embodied and operating energy and materials.[55]

Planning for dense settlements

A 'compact city' means more than developing density through apartment building encompassing proximity to essential services, daily work and infrastructure. Improving designs for density and green spaces, many contemporary planning proposals focus on 'new urbanist' principles of transit-oriented development, where evenly spread infrastructure and services support neighbourhood precincts and local economies, as in Edo. A 'smart city', using multiple innovations in information and communication technology for systemic efficiencies, is often considered complementary to the development of a compact city.

However, the greening of our cities is far from a high-tech top-down story as guerrilla gardening and other forms of occupying public spaces, such as hand-knits for poles and seats, and hospitality and eco-tourist ventures promote green spaces and activities. The recent growth in participatory planning offers models for greater residential input into decisions made by local authorities, who are increasingly responsible for complex urban developments. Nurturing neighbourhoods and their communities, implementing mixed-use buildings and zones, and encouraging socio-cultural diversity and mix are key aspects of operationalising and assessing appropriate models for future cities, incorporating the best of planning in the past with greater democracy for the future.

Social media offers means for residents to access all kinds of information about activities, goods and services available locally. While claims of sharing economy and platform cooperativism advocates often exaggerate the potential of novel technology, provided they remain accessible to all, digital technologies can enhance the knowledge and skills of many individual and collective activities. For instance, supported by universities and others – for the purpose of collective resistance – the San Francisco Bay anti-eviction online mapping project collects and presents visual and narrative data recording residential dispossession through gentrification, homelessness and eviction and the privatisation of public spaces as a result of contemporary capitalist developments.[56]

CONCLUSION

This chapter discussed challenges relating to the demand and supply of smaller apartments if living in smaller spaces is to prove genuinely, holistically, environmentally sustainable. A small apartment needs to be well-designed for flexibility and adaptability and to either provide for two or more occupants, or nest in a building where householders can share, say, laundry, social and work facilities, and garden and other green spaces. Could not a community of apartment-block neighbours recreate the household sharing of yesteryear? Multi-unit apartment blocks can include shared space by economising on individual dwelling sizes, and shared facilities with equipment offer more than any small dwelling can hold while saving on purchase, energy and other running costs. If cars are marginalised, the block needs to be well-located to infrastructure with residents close to transport, parks and other open space with opportunities for community gardening, play, walking and bike riding.

In many cities, so few mainstream commercial developers offer community-based sustainable apartment options that such innovative developments often end up being unaffordable simply as a function of niche market forces. However, Part II discusses a range of community-based sustainable developments that offer, often more affordable, alternatives, such as: sustainability-focused cohousing settlements, ecovillages, cooperative housing, joint households and collectives of tiny houses. These developments have been characterised by their non-commercial and innovative nature, their victorious struggles with planners and other regulators, and their discreet disregard of authorities as they bent or broke rules that might otherwise shackle their efforts to establish a sustainable and affordable way forward for human habitation on Earth.

PART II

Eco-cohousing and Ecovillages

From Sharing a House
to Eco-cohousing

Part II of *Small Is Necessary* discusses efforts towards creating eco-communities, neighbourhoods of dwellings of the kind that might allow and encourage practices that are sufficiently sustainable to enable us to live within Earth's regenerative limits. This chapter moves through a range of collaborative housing arrangements from sharing houses and land to cohousing, specifically eco-cohousing. Chapter 6 examines ecovillages. Part II examines the functioning of eco-communities as collectives of households and as spaces for nurturing, caring, socialising and sharing, along with their environmental attributes and limitations.

This chapter aims to convey the lived experience of co-habiting in eco-sustainable ways by intentional sharing, and introduces themes in activist and scholarly discourse on cohousing. Held over for Part III are discussions of specific characteristics, potential, enablers and drivers of eco-cohousing and ecovillages that suggest further ways of achieving more sustainable futures through community-supported agriculture, community-based energy distribution and localised sharing economies. We start with small changes, namely co-owning houses or the land on which houses stand with a few unrelated people, and move on through increasingly significant changes to living circumstances pointing towards full eco-communities.

SHARING HOUSES AND SMALL LAND PARCELS

Avail. 1 July. One big bedroom and one small bedroom in share household of 20-something creatives (two females, one male). Big room, lots of light, okay for couple. Bond = one month's rent. Split bills. No smoking. Vegetarian. Tiny permaculture-inspired garden. 3 km to uni and arts college. Close to train station. Text Wendy – 0356 894 352

There is an unsettled temporariness about shared rental housing, especially when joining various strangers in an established household for an indeterminate period and without much formality beyond defining what one will pay and general protocol associated with storing, preparing and eating food, having guests and noise. Most of us have had this experience, typically as a tertiary student, working away from home, or between more permanent living arrangements. While some report great group household experiences – including meeting a life-long friend or partner, or fun parties and conversations – joint households can be insecure, frustrating and lonely experiences, putting up with unkept rules and irritating habits.

When people hear that you live in collective living, experiences of joint households are often alluded to: What about conflicts? How do you share the housework? There is even greater suspicion when you admit that you have bought into such an arrangement, especially if you mention the term 'intentional community', often interpreted as 'cult'. In fact, 'intentional' relates to the aspirational nature of the ideals and purposes of a collective living arrangement, one that involves a level of commitment and clarity unseen in more casual joint households.[1] Here, a transparent and responsible approach aims to shield householders from arbitrariness, impermanence and neurotic behaviour. Expectations are spelled out and agreed to, there are clear processes for resolving conflicts, and clearly drawn boundaries between personal and collective space and decisions – strong advances on conventional living with relatives where negative family cultures can be deeply entrenched and psychologically hazardous.

Co-owning a house

Many of the challenges found in more expansive and intensive forms of collective living are raised in a handbook by three middle-aged women who bought a house under a 'tenancy in common' arrangement in Pittsburgh (Pennsylvania) and contentedly lived together in it for more than ten years. *My House Our House: Living Far Better for Far Less in a Cooperative Household* describes how Karen, Louise and Jean decided that this might be a good option, found their house, entered co-financing and legal co-ownership arrangements, and worked out which rooms were for personal space and for whom.

My House Our House spells out successful approaches for tolerance and flexibility, 'drawing lines' and interdependence more generally. 'We've had more fun doing household tasks than we ever did before,' they write. From the start, 'if something needed doing, it got done ... by someone'. Their legally binding cooperative household general partnership agreement defines their partnership and its term ('until dissolved by mutual agreement'); details responsibilities related to mortgage, maintenance and operating expenses; outlines conditions of withdrawal, and options for the death of one of the partners; and summarises processes for addressing failures to fulfil obligations, and irresolvable differences more generally.[2]

In another example, media consultant Carmel Shute bought a large apartment with two others in an inner suburb of Melbourne (Victoria) when she was in her mid-30s, sharing it for 21 years with her co-owners and, when they were elsewhere, with tenants.[3] She has described it as 'one of the best decisions of my life'. Interestingly, the history of her apartment block, Summerland Mansions (Figure 5.1), dovetails with characteristics of the early history of cohousing in Denmark, which essentially started as serviced apartments.

Figure 5.1   Summerland Mansions, St Kilda (Melbourne, Australia)

Source: Heritage Victoria

In the early 1920s, Summerland Mansions replaced a stately home built in the early 1850s on the first Crown Land sold in an inner suburb named after the purchaser's schooner (St Kilda). Built for gentry – the rent was around double the basic wage at the time – Summerland Mansions was the first European-style apartment block built in an inner suburb now renowned for high-density apartment living. The front wall abutted the street, with shops on the ground floor and servants' quarters at the back, with separate access. Each apartment was roomy (175–200sq m) with remarkable urban and seaside views, a screened porch, a glazed and fly-screened sleep-out and balcony. Residents only had kitchenettes because they were expected to dine downstairs in the public dining room cum restaurant, 'a terribly progressive idea for the 1920s in Australia'. The communally shared rooftop was for leisure and drying clothes.

However, by the early 1940s, Summerland Mansions featured in a Melbourne University student study of slum living conditions. Still, by the late 1980s – when Shute and her two co-owners bought their apartment – the building had been sensitively renovated even if left bereft of shared facilities and services. Over the next two decades, some of Shute's co-owners sold their share to another person or arranged for a mutually agreed-on tenant as they moved for work or relationships. The apartment was an attractive gathering place for political and creative meetings. St Kilda was perfectly located, with parks, the sea and proximity to Melbourne's central business district (CBD) and local facilities.

These details on Summerland Mansions highlight widespread urban characteristics and trends that prompted the cohousing movement. Through the first half of the twentieth century, singles had found affordable rental accommodation by informally sharing or submitting to management in boarding houses, serviced apartments or owners of houses who rented out one or two rooms. While broadly seen as 'non-traditional' (the increasingly *nuclear* family was the norm, or ideal, owner-occupier) sharing space, facilities or dining together was commonplace. Urban market forces impacted on such arrangements, with rents going up when house prices and demand was high. Yet living close to secure work and places to socialise was a big drawcard and sharing made this option more affordable.

These co-owning cases were not driven by environmental rationale but by their affordability, and various reasons associated with sociality and support. Still they had flow-on effects in terms of economising on space and other household resources. Much of Karen, Louise and Jean's chapter on moving in together centres on cutting all the 'stuff' from three households – including five vacuum cleaners and eight couches – into one co-owned space.

Sharing a 'single-dwelling' lot

Concerns to be more environmentally sustainable, increasingly unaffordable housing, reduced social housing and limited residential land have contributed to a rise in both secondary dwellings – aka accessory dwelling units (ADU), illegal in certain places, such as Toronto – and three-or-four dwelling developments where connectedness is celebrated along with privacy. This trend, characteristic of the twenty-first century, is another step towards cohousing.

Well before contemporary environmentalists and urban planners recognised the benefits of dual occupancy and infill developments for compact and sustainable cities, renowned United States (US) ecologist Howard T. Odum established an ADU alongside his house in Gainsville (Florida) for future use by his adult children or carers for him and his wife. Similarly seeking 'resilience', Odum's daughter Mary and husband Dugan subsequently met building requirements for a dwelling of more than 2200sq ft (204sq m) on their 1.25acre lot by constructing a two-storey building for a household on each level.

Moreover, Mary and Dugan approached co-habitation along permaculture, adaptability and environmental principles. Although renting out the other floor, they intentionally developed 'symbiosis' between their households. Intergenerational households provide complementary caring services and supplementary sharing opportunities, including eating together, passing on food, security, social networks and, of course, economic benefits in shared utility and water bills. One of the strongest reasons Mary gave for compact collective living was resisting pressures for economic growth built in by mortgage debts.[4]

Even though infill development is applauded in planning circles, and progressive cities have paid attention to planning and building regulations to permit the division of existing buildings into two dwellings or building again on initially single-dwelling sites, such proposals face many hurdles. Commercial construction sectors tend to divide into firms focusing on a building type, such as detached buildings in suburban estates or medium-rise apartment blocks. Supply dictates demand. Legal and financial structures conform to commercial practices. Few builders develop a name in niche markets, such as two to three dwellings co-located for easy co-habitation with both linkages and privacy taken into account. As a result, small multi-household developments for interested kin and friends are 'under-catered for' despite demographic changes in cities that make such developments sensible and in demand.[5]

Reviews of Sydney and the Australian state of New South Wales more generally suggest that approvals for multi-dwelling sites are more likely in suburbs than the inner city. Even so, careful design is necessary to account for the National Construction Code and state and local planning regulations, which cover sizes of building envelopes, proportions of lots used for buildings, requisite car spaces, distances of buildings from boundaries, limits on sizes of secondary dwellings, and prohibition of triple occupancy. McGee and Wynne (2015) suggest that municipal planners should create particular permits with limits associated with 'a precinct-scale assessment of needs', giving apartments first priority and second preference to what they refer to as 'small-scale cohousing' (really just a few collocated residences) over single dwellings on one title. They point out that simple subdivision producing two titles has led to perverse outcomes: inflating house prices and inappropriate, profit-driven, developments that do not deliver savings for either the environment, home buyers or tenants.[6]

A holistically successful example of the type of development proposed has centred on adding two dwellings to a quarter-acre (1011sq m) rural town block with a pre-established 1970s brick veneer. Initially, the new owner improved the sustainability of her ideally situated north-facing house in Castlemaine (Central Victoria) by fully insulating wall and roof cavities, adding double glazing, and solar electricity and hot water. Through simple redesign involving a few walls, she maximised occupancy to three active residents. She established an edible front garden and, to collect rain off the roof, water tanks sheltered from the sun by the house.

The first addition, 'done on a shoestring budget' of A$70,000, was for the owner's adult son. This 50sq m detached self-contained dwelling with a mezzanine bed space was constructed mainly from recycled and upcycled materials, with power, water and sewerage connected to the original house. Its cost was covered by subdividing the block further – for one of Australia's first hyper-insulated, triple-glazed PassivHaus-accredited residential buildings. Airtight and ventilated through a healthy heat-recovery system, this 40sq m dwelling has been designed for comfortable internal temperatures, rarely requiring extra heating or cooling.

This homely cluster now shares common use of a chicken pen, and driveway. Good neighbourliness is achieved by incidental contact, mutual support when required and maintaining the privacy of householders. Not only is this development in accord with best-practice urban consolidation but also incorporates sustainability features with affordability.[7]

Another example in Melbourne's outer suburbs is a 'micro' farm – winner of neighbouring Darebin and Banyule Councils' Sustainability Awards (2012) – where families and friends took down fences between their houses to grow a non-commercial sustainability hub: orchards, some fruit of which is preserved; goats whose milk is turned into yoghurt and cheese; vegetable gardens irrigated from roof-water-storage tanks; egg-producing chooks and ducks; and bees for honey. Produce made on site has included beer, soap, bread, chocolate, tomato sauce and conserves. Participants only work for money part-time so they can be rostered on activities at Hibi Farm, doing childcare, and preparing collective meals. In one month in 2012 they produced 90kg of vegetables. Excess is shared locally with friends and family. In 2012, 'the hood' comprised five houses with various households – two couples and one child, a single adult and a couple, a couple with a baby, and two households with a couple and two children – and a network of involved friends in the immediate locale.[8]

Sharing homes, land and work

Having attended a Quaker cooperative farm school, and happily living at Pioneer Valley Cohousing Community in Amherst (Massachusetts) that she had co-founded, in mid-2012 Rebecca Reid and her husband Michael made a brave decision for a couple in their 60s. They and a younger family left cohousing for condominium ownership of a 'two-family house with nine acres and two barns' in Leverett (Massachusetts). It took 18 months for 'kindred spirits' (another young family) to purchase a small property over the road with whom they established a successful partnership to progress their farm in a permaculture direction.

Six adults and three children now live and work together. They share food and meals, respectfully maintain houses with open doors, perform caring services and optimise bulk buys. They are financially independent households but their farm is effectively a collective enterprise. They aim for collective sufficiency, self-provisioning as much as possible within their intergenerational farm community, then bartering and sharing equipment, labour and materials with neighbouring farms and local businesses. In these ways they 'hope to create a web of interconnections that will be resilient in what may be difficult times to come'.[9]

Another case shows the importance of demonstration projects of environmental sustainability as a way of life, rather than simply technologies and techniques that can be purchased and retrofitted to mainstream capitalist society. Aprovecho, near Cottage Grove (Oregon), is a residential community which runs a non-profit sustainability educational organisation from a 16-hectare property bought in 1981 and owned as a land trust. In 2016, they taught courses such as organic gardening and permaculture, appropriate technology (simple efficient technologies for home or farming work), ecoforestry, watershed restoration, bee-keeping, ecological stewardship, food preserving, natural building and green design. Their community education was open to all, offered within a gift economy. They offered small grants matched to an Oregonian's personal savings to start a career based on Aprovecho's sustainability principles. Living where they train, Aprovecho attracted well-networked permanent residents, adding vibrancy to the Cottage Grove and South Willamette Valley communities, and maintaining strong relationships, including with local schools and two Oregon universities.[10]

In 2010, when Rosie Kirincic had been at Aprovecho for three years, sharing the space with several other trainers, she developed six guidelines to collective, consensus-based living (with examples), as follows. 'Create shareable spaces': Aprovecho trainers held meetings and shared some meals in an area below accommodation for course participants and some coworkers (an area regularly used as storage) and cooked together over summer in an outdoor kitchen. 'Value privacy': most full-timers had a personal cabin while those sharing space made sure they got private time by, and for, themselves. 'Define your mission': a clear vision helps distinguish priorities, values and clarifies differences. 'Meet face-to-face': a dedicated weekly meeting to listen and decide. 'Expect disagreements': non-violent communication techniques assist in processing and solving conflicts. 'Choose new members wisely': fresh enthusiasts can fizzle out fast leaving the collective with unfinished business.[11]

The growth of collective living

Greater access to universities encouraging youth from family homes, the rise of feminist and environmental movements, and a drift to experimentation and non-conventional lifestyles in the late 1960s and 1970s, made the emergence of house sharing and other kinds of collective living more visible. Developing non-hierarchical cooperative governance, such households differed from conventional ones, just as intentional communities developed various formal forms of co-ownership of collective property.

The principles of such governance developed on a long history of popular resistance, mutual support and solidarity later embedded, say, in the Occupy movement, through consensual decision-making, sharing and free exchange, inclusiveness and commoning.[12] This progressive political culture of collective living attracted many (and repelled others). Even though formal legal models of collective ownership have developed, they flout certain accepted norms of capitalist societies, namely private property ownership and management.

COHOUSING

'Cohousing' is purposively co-located and connected neighbour-hoods of multiple households, each household with a private dwelling but sharing, with their neighbours, specific common spaces, typically a common kitchen and dining area; resources, such as laundries and gardens; and activities, such as preparing and eating meals collectively. Cohousing developed in the late 1960s in Scandinavia, especially with the Danish movement of *bofællskab* or 'living communities', the Swedish *kollectivhaus* and, a little later in the Netherlands, *Centraal Wonen*. Such models inspired projects in Northern Europe, such as Germany (*nach-barschaftliches wohnen*). During the late 1980s, cohousing emerged in North America and Australia, appearing a few years later in the United Kingdom (UK), New Zealand and Japan.[13] Cohousing settlements have formal, legal, community governance arrangements covering rules for entry and exit, shared access, maintenance, fees and other sets of mutual obligations and expectations. Many US projects were based on home ownership whereas, right from their beginnings, European projects tended to incorporate social-housing tenants.

Invisible scope of 'cohousing'

Worldwide there are difficulties with collecting reliable data on cohousing and collective living more generally because national housing statistics have not been 'grainy' enough, and policymakers not interested enough, to include them. Another problem with counting cases of collective living is lack of consistency in defining distinct types. For instance, certain cohousing projects in the UK Cohousing Network directory appear in the Confederation of Co-operative Housing directory of over 1000 projects in England and Wales with a 'cooperative' legal status. However, cooperative housing covers a large range of styles and types of housing and tenancy arrangements, such as student and social housing where residents exercise more control than in the past over the management, if not administration, of their housing block. However, the vast majority are not as intentional or communal as cohousing proper. Conversely, not all cohousing is formalised as a legal cooperative.

We know that, in the 2010s, around 1.5 per cent of Danish stock was cohousing – the highest national percentage.[14] In contrast, just 20 established projects appeared in the online directory of the UK Cohousing Network in mid-2016, with 50 more listed as on the drawing board, demonstrating the upsurge of interest in cohousing this decade. The established-project list indicated diversity, many retrofitted self-contained units within a mansion or similar large building, along with the first UK new-build (Springhill Cohousing in Stroud), initiated in the early 2000s. The UK network defined cohousing loosely as a community comprised of 8–40 households, noting a recent trend away from privately owned cohousing to rental, social and affordable housing – such as the first cross-tenure project, Threshold Centre in Dorset – and even the option of collective ownership.[15]

Diggers and Dreamers Publishers have produced a range of reviews and directories of UK collective living over several decades, with an historical and radical emphasis, recently highlighting cohousing as a small and special type. In contrast, European cohousing researchers, such as the Chairman of Kollectivhus NU, Dick Urban Vestbro, tend to incorporate a range of collective living models into the term 'cohousing', though they carefully begin each work with definitional boundaries appropriate to its context and audience.[16] Lidewij Tummers, for instance, introduces a special issue of *Urban Research and Practice* on 'self-managed collaborative housing initiatives', which are regularly referred to as 'co-housing' throughout and loosely defined as 'initiatives where groups of residents collectively create living arrangements that are not easily available in the (local) housing market'.[17] In another work, Tummers points to the similarity of residents' attraction to cohousing despite cultural, policy and legal housing distinctions, so they seek 'collaboration during building and management' and desire 'to create a "nonanonymous" neighbourhood; nonspeculative, affordable housing; energy-efficiency buildings and a reduced ecological footprint'.[18]

In 2004, a German expert commission recommended enhancing and encouraging 'cooperative tenure', meaning arrangements such as buying a share to enable the perpetual lease of a cooperative dwelling. A few years later, following evidence that around 200,000 over-50-year-old Berliners were seriously attracted to 'independent community-oriented living', the government funded Stadtbau as an information clearing house on practical options and possibilities.[19] In the first half of the 2010s, Ache and Fedrowitz identified around 500 cohousing projects in Germany, half of them comprised of fewer than 30 residents and more than half constructed 2000–2010; still that figure included communes and ecovillages.[20] A similarly all-encompassing definition of German cohousing resulted in a calculation of '1000' by Droste.[21] The German case illustrates the difficulties, encountered worldwide, in collecting reliable data on cohousing, and collective living more generally.

To confuse a chequered history in which collective living mushroomed organically, underground, and in ad hoc ways in all kinds of places and styles, this century European (and UK) 'cooperative housing' is the new face of social (public) and affordable housing. It has become an example of co-production policies in state welfare and housing provision, and has attracted support from not-for-profit private organisations. Moreover, William-Olsson points out that most contemporary new rental stock in Sweden has been state-subsidised to some extent.[22] Such cooperative housing does not need to be intentionally designed or redesigned for neighbourhood interaction, nor does it highlight shared facilities. Indeed, often, 'private life is basically untouched'.[23]

For these reasons, such types of cooperative housing are ignored here, where concerted collective management of numerous households who share resources and activities is our main concern. Confusingly, certain projects – even radical income-sharing communes such as Commonground (Central Victoria, Australia) – adopt a cooperative legal form. In short, legal forms do not necessarily indicate the type or content of a community. This example shows why it is difficult to collect detailed data on various types of collaborative housing projects even though it is critical that such statistics are assembled.

Cohousing as a type of collective living

As a subset of collective living more generally, cohousing models stand at the mainstream end of a radical–conventional pole. Despite distinctions between national cultural, governmental and housing systems, cohousing models have commonly developed formal legal and planning status, fitted into conventional real estate markets and tenancy arrangements, and focused on physical design and construction as a neighbourhood community. As a Toronto cohousing group pointedly wrote: 'One thing Canopy wants to make clear is this is not some form of commune.'[24] Settled in contemporary, often urban, environments where residents live very much like other citizens in private dwellings, except that they share use of and responsibilities for additional collective facilities, many cohousing models do not overtly challenge capitalism.

In whatever form, as private owner-occupiers, private or social housing tenants, on leased or privately owned land, in leased or privately owned buildings, cohousing models tend to simply ameliorate the social alienation, gendered roles, economic inequities and affordability crises of contemporary society. Kim Stanley Robinson rejects cohousing projects as 'pocket utopias'. Lucy Sargisson has concluded that the US model, in particular, has been 'anti-radical' at source – enabling residents to 'live a new life without dropping out … comfortable with the values of mainstream culture but seeking a better way of life for their members'.[25]

Nevertheless, discussions of income, house size and value need to be tempered by an appreciation of the extent of differences between, and sometimes within, cohousing communities. For instance, in a study of three US cohousing communities, Shedd reports that an 'average resident' was approaching retirement, had 'considerable disposable income' and 'a large and expensive home'. However, the composite averages that Shedd calculated obscured significant differences between each community; the smallest community's average income was 40 per cent of the richest. The average size of houses in the middle-sized community was around 42 per cent of the richest and 37 per cent of the richest in value.[26]

Moreover, it is hard to ignore the self-empowerment and collective empowerment that is central to most cohousing. Surely a commitment to and experience of sharing collective facilities and spaces, equipment and activities – preparing and eating meals collectively and community gardening – enhance grassroots governance skills in ways that that could be applied for genuinely radical purposes? Furthermore, Australian

Graham Meltzer, who lives in the Findhorn (Scotland) community, has emphasised the benefits of more easily mainstreamed and up-scaled cohousing models – compared with informal and often hidden communes under the planning radar and even illegal under regular building regulations.[27]

Similarly, Kadriu has explained the evolution of 'co-housing' as an example of 'self-help' approaches that reappeared as a broader movement in the latter half of the 1960s – referred to by Harms as 'small-scale, self-sufficient, non-hierarchical and autonomous actions of free and independent self-governing people'. In an associated way, Knorr Siedow has described 1970s Berlin as 'self-help city'. Facing high rents and eager to break away from conventional suburban lifestyles, many younger people who had been living in shared households, some in squats, others in squalor, not only in European countries, but also throughout settler societies, decided on co-living in more permanent and affordable ways.[28]

Tummers (2015) makes a parallel observation, that the recent resurgence in Europe of 'co-housing' (in a broader meaning than our 'cohousing' is used here) was self-styled do it yourself (DIY). Perhaps doing it ourselves (DIO) would be more appropriate when talking about collaborative or collective ventures? Still, compared with other types of resident-led community and sustainability-seeking projects, like communes or ecovillages, cohousing has been more, on the one hand, subject to initiation, leadership and guidance by experts – such as architects, interior and landscape designers, and developers – in North America and, on the other hand, subject to support and even supervision by government agencies and not-for-profit organisations in European models. Certainly cohousing is an expression of mainstream 'sustainability citizenship', with discussions of sustainability within cohousing discourse centring on conventional light green triple-bottom-line approaches rather than dark green environmental or red solidarity criteria.[29]

Defining 'cohousing': cultural models

The formula developed by architects and cohousing developers Kathryn McCamant and Charles Durrett (2011) has had a strong influence on the major North American cohousing model, typical projects averaging 15–35 attached dwellings with a common house or clearly defined common space in one (or more) multi-unit building/s. McCamant and

Durrett list six key distinguishing characteristics of cohousing: participatory planning and design within a residential management model;
building and site design for residential interaction; private dwellings
alongside common shared facilities; resident management of social
and physical aspects of shared resources; non-hierarchical residential
management; non-income sharing, residents pay fees and dues to a
homeowner association (following a condominium arrangement).[30]
This narrow and culturally specific definition has certain limitations, for
instance, only the initial residents actually participate in built design.

Levels of participation and power-sharing between residents, professionals and developers vary considerably from project to project, as
do approaches to non-hierarchical governance. Architects have been
prominent in cohousing, just as sustainability experts and consultants
have been influential in designing and creating eco-cohousing. The roles
of such experts in cohousing is somewhat controversial. Many cohousing
communities benefit from their advice and skills but at other times such
experts seem to assume leadership and advocacy roles at odds with a
non-hierarchical approach (as detailed in Chapter 8).

Despite Charles Durrett protesting that, having coined 'co-housing',
he would like to retain control of its meaning and models, the term –
including minor spelling variations – has been used in much broader
and even ad hoc ways by activists, journalists and researchers. The 2015
definition of the Cohousing Association of the US accentuated social relationships, such as collective governance and shared values, the privacy
of dwellings and independent incomes. This is the 'social architecture' or
'social infrastructure' that Jarvis draws attention to, cohousing as 'a living
arrangement', which seems even closer to the Danish *bofœllskab* (living
communities) than Durrett's translation, and the definition he gives to,
'cohousing'.[31]

Referring in a negative way to 'intentional communities', McCamant
and Durrett have argued that cohousing is 'a "new" approach to housing
rather than a new way of life'.[32] However, the US association actually
classifies cohousing as a form of 'intentional community' and neither
refers to participatory design nor to a specific common house but,
instead, to 'shared space'.[33] Indeed, European cohousing researcher Dick
Urban Vestbro has pointed out that Swedish housing companies have
tended to create cohousing ('well functioning collaborative housing
development') without the participation of future residents and centres

his description on collective participation and shared spaces and facilities as core principles.[34]

Here, I adopt a more inclusive approach than Durrett, without dispensing with the need to work towards a clear definition. This enables us to cluster many social housing and not-for-profit initiatives in European models alongside the private-homeownership-based commercial North American model. Scandinavian examples are illustrative. The Danish cohousing model developed as a typically low-rise medium-density socially oriented model with a detached common house. In contrast, the Dutch model was very urbane and intimate, with several households sharing a kitchen and dining area. Despite its radical beginnings, government provision on this low-rise model was forthcoming and pragmatic. The Swedes went for substantial medium- to high-rise cohousing developments where common facilities might take up an entire floor connected to all levels and included professionalised services.[35]

One way to throw 'cohousing' into sharper relief is to compare it with other forms of collaborative living. For instance, cohousing appears essentially as a housing arrangement between neighbouring households when contrasted with more holistic ecovillages and communes that attend, to varying extents and in varying ways, to fulfilling basic needs (as discussed in later chapters).

Five contextual characteristics of cohousing

Before focusing on *eco*-co-housing, I make five observations about cohousing more generally. First, cohousing has drawn inspiration from collective models associated with the growth of capitalism and its critics, such as progressive utopian, feminist and worker projects. For instance, Chris Coates points to the sentiments, aims and models of cooperative housekeeping in the latter half of the nineteenth century, the Garden City movement of the early twentieth century and the *Reilly Plan* of 1945 as precursors of cohousing in the UK.[36] Similarly, Vestbro and Horelli highlight the evolution of cohousing to facilitate gender equality.[37]

Second, cohousing has gained support from municipal authorities in some regions and philanthropic organisations in others, with both government and not-for-profits increasingly attracted to the mutual care, welfare and affordability benefits of such housing, especially for seniors. If governments are to address the environmental, social and economic unsustainability of growing numbers of single-occupancy dwellings and the challenge of caring for seniors, then models such as cohousing offer numerous advantages. It is clear why policymakers, politicians and planners are now attracted to the model for its capacity to advance such state welfare concerns (as detailed in Chapter 7).[38]

Third, even without specific environmental aims, cohousing tends to have environmental co-benefits compared with stand-alone housing and households of a comparable price in a similar location. This is simply due to space, resources, services and amenities being shared, and the obvious potential to easily install off-grid, or efficient grid-connected, neighbourhood-based water and renewable energy systems.[39] Cohousing dwellings are generally compact because price and housing design take account of common areas to which all households have access. Cars are marginalised to boundaries, public transport and carpooling encouraged, and facilities for bicycles abound. Furthermore, there is room for productive community gardens to thrive in cohousing projects. The latter points are very relevant when one remembers that UK householders' food and travel produce more carbon emissions than the energy costs of their homes.[40] More environmentally sound design, materials and equipment can be purchased in bulk, potentially making a cohousing unit cheaper than a one-off house.

Fourth, affordability of cohousing is a vexed question. Meltzer's study, which spanned the mid-1990s to the mid-2000s, found that cohousing seemed 'no more affordable than regular housing, possibly less so'.[41] However, a third of his small sample were 'genuinely' affordable. Still, project affordability often relies on philanthropic or governmental assistance and work contributed by resident (and non-resident) volunteers, which is hard to cost or ignore in budgetary analyses. Many cohousing projects cost more because they are more complex and time-consuming, and deliver more benefits than living in separate dwellings. Moreover, in as much as costs derive from their niche market status, costs would fall if cohousing was in greater demand and supply. Indeed, since Meltzer's study there has been an improvement in affordability, reported in case studies below and, for instance, Mühlenviertel (Tübingen, Germany) where environmental building costs were reported as 'comparable to other projects' with the conclusion that 'a zero energy house can be affordably built'.[42]

Fifth, in the 2010s, 'cohousing' was flexibly used by media and residents to refer to a plethora of arrangements which, in reality, are distinct in terms of tenure, legal forms and building styles and designs. A series of terms emerged for the type I refer to as cohousing: 'co-housing', 'CoHousing' and 'collaborative housing'.[43] Consequently, UK activist-researcher Martin Field's characterisation seems most useful, inclusive as it is of the growing diversity of arrangements.[44] He refers to 'intentional neighbourhoods', a neat segue from the controversial nomination of cohousing as 'intentional communities', pointing, instead, to the built nature of cohousing.

Furthermore, Field's definition focuses on private dwellings and common facilities, especially for sharing meals, gardening and other outdoor activities; design and social concerns with balancing privacy and community related to the number of households and adults in each cohousing project; and, the significant level of autonomous collective initiative and management by residents, requiring formal rules between members and the development of legal partnerships. This level of resident participation in a sector traditionally dominated by commercial and state housing provision has resulted in both subversive and submissive responses, in short a dynamic struggle by residents to set reasonable terms as a collective client negotiating in their own interests with housing professionals, planners and financiers.

European diversity

The Institute for Creative Sustainability in Berlin (Germany) has produced a useful handbook on European 'CoHousing', its term for a range of multi-dwelling housing types where residents variously play roles as co-developers, co-designers and/or co-builders in projects where residential and garden spaces are shared and residents participate in the everyday ongoing management of their collective housing. The handbook refers to such projects as 'significant field research labs' – illustrative of innovative partnerships and collaborations between citizen–activist associations, housing professionals, not-for-profit organisations, and politicians and bureaucrats (planners and community development agencies) – and influential to the extent that they are nodes in data collection and advocacy networks that attract media and public interest. The authors emphasise that collective housing has gained greater traction from governments and not-for-profit welfare bodies to solve multiple challenges, from addressing housing and care needs of an aging population to responding in creative ways to increasingly unaffordable urban housing through harnessing the economies of scale obtained by constructing environmentally sustainable dwellings at a substantial building, or street block, scale.[45]

Furthermore, *CoHousing Cultures* presents case studies showing how the cultural, legal, governmental and financial structures distinguishing European countries has created a diversity of models relating to tenure, demographics, building style, size, purpose and outcome. Berlin has had a diminishing advantage, say over Vienna, due to accessible land and buildings and a culture of self-help and government housing policies; recently Vienna has developed collaborations involving housing associations, the construction sector and residents. The Swedish history of rental cohousing has spawned a 'second half of life' (from middle-age onwards) rather than a 'seniors' model. Meanwhile, Stockholm and Vienna are integrating cohousing models into social and public housing policies and programs.[46]

Indeed, across the board, local authorities seem most effective in advancing cohousing and are uniquely positioned to encourage and support integrated neighbourhood housing and community developments in co-located and complementary ways. The 250-metre length of Basel's Bärenfelserstrasse is an example, with more than 70 per cent of its multi-dwelling buildings under collective management, and a collectively managed neighbourhood meeting space enhancing local activities amongst a socially mixed residential community and multi-cultural street life. Here, and elsewhere in Basel, changes started during the 1970s, as the policies and finances of this particular Swiss canton government and private philanthropic bodies both supported grassroots pressure for open, accessible projects preserving old buildings, providing affordable collective housing and neighbourhood associations.[47]

THE ECO-EDGE OF COHOUSING

Cohousing, and collaborative housing more generally, always had the potential to offer environments that encouraged and enabled household and community sustainability. Yet the turn to eco-sustainability concerns has been a recent, and not always evident, development in cohousing so it is necessary to point out that the focus from here on is what I refer to as 'eco-cohousing', cohousing dedicated to environmentally sustainable aims and achievements. However, sometimes I drop the 'eco' prefix if, for instance, the communities or analysts in question do not use it.

Sharing by multiple households

Meltzer completed one of the first detailed studies of the environmental implications and efficiencies of a range of cohousing communities in the mid-2000s, examining 12 cases in detail – eight North American, one Japanese, two Australian and one in New Zealand. His study showed that 'the consumerist imperative that seems endemic in the West is significantly diffused in cohousing', especially in terms of sharing or gifting everyday goods, such as food, clothing and books, and small household devices. Items shed by residents included 75 per cent of lawnmowers, while the number of freezers, dryers and washers was reduced by 22, 29 and 26 per cent respectively. Yet, there was a growth, even if negligible (1–3 per cent), in resident dishwashers, televisions and refrigerators. However, he found variable savings for white goods.[48] Meltzer's study did not mention use of white goods, which, if modified, would impact on relative energy use and durability. Moreover, a report from a more recent eco-cohousing development in New Zealand, Earthsong Eco-Neighbourhood, had their 32 households successfully sharing just four washing machines and two lawnmowers.

Further research might usefully compare the quality, size and age of specific white goods in a set of cohousing communities with the average in their neighbourhood and account for the fact that most models of white goods are made for small householders' use, deteriorating quicker and causing maintenance costs when used by a lot of people. This concern was raised in a 2012 study of Ganas (Staten Island, New York City), an intentional community like a commune, sharing more than the cohousing norm: around 10 people inhabit each of seven Ganas households, compared, say, with Earthsong's average household of just over two people. The small household private dwelling formula of cohousing constrains the level of sharing of white goods in more communal models. Ganas often procures relatively high-quality white goods second-hand. (Use of hospitality equipment is expensive and rarified for communal households.) Ganas offers more opportunities to economise on space, amenity, goods, services and other resources than in Durrett's stereotype of the North American cohousing model. However, such a level of sharing presents distinctive requirements unmet by the market.[49]

Other contextual questions include comparing the level of cohousing residents' environmental practices compared with a national or local average. Based on residents' self-reported before-and-after practices, Meltzer's study suggested energy efficiency was enhanced broadly by 5–6 per cent and water conservation by an average 9 per cent yet, significantly, showed variable results between communities. Perhaps the most interesting finding in Meltzer's analysis was indications of a substantial growth in environmental practices related to air polluting toxic materials, general waste, and water and energy conservation after four years' residence compared with the first year of residency. This strongly suggests development of more environmentally friendly and efficient practices from conscious and unconscious collective behaviour change.[50]

In terms of built environments, the 12 Meltzer cases showed a density more than double that in the average suburb in Australia and United States at the time, consistent with a cohousing dwelling size around half the average size of new-builds in both countries. Similarly, cohousing was typified by attached dwellings when detached dwellings prevailed. When Meltzer conducted his study few cohousing neighbourhoods incorporated energy, water and waste technologies that were environmentally economic for multiple household use. Since then, the accessibility of such technologies and eco-cohousing have both spread.[51]

Following Meltzer's study, comparative work has tended to subject specific projects to rating schemes, such as 'one planet' approaches, all constrained by imposed assumptions, select proxies, foci and boundaries. This makes meta-comparative work very difficult. Similarly, Tummers points to a general problem in comparing cohousing and conventional households; national environmental ratings schemes are designed to evaluate single dwellings rather than multi-household complexes.[52] On their websites, many communities record, or include, results of environmental studies that are time and community specific and, therefore, not easily comparable across projects. Furthermore, certain studies question the highly variable environmental benefits of cohousing indicated by household comparisons, criticising general overconsumption typically associated with travel, and embodied and operating energy use related to unnecessary space in residences.[53]

Nevertheless, it is generally acknowledged that eco-cohousing has the potential for substantial eco-savings as a result of conscious environmental design, communal encouragement of sustainable habits, and as co-benefits flowing from wider social and community functions. Co-benefits include child-care and entertainment on-site rather than a drive away. Descriptions of a small suite of eco-cohousing projects successful in such ways follow. Many more, equally eligible, similarly impressive and multi-dimensional cohousing projects exist. Selection was based on diversity, complementarity and geographic representation.

Hockerton Housing Project[54]

Eco-cohousing has evolved from two drivers. First and most recently, broad trends in building standards to improve environmental sustainability. Second, longstanding and specific concerns of a minority of homeowners, tenants and building professionals in building construction and associated sectors to show that environmental sustainability can be enhanced by living in residential communities. An example of the latter is the tiny Hockerton Housing Project (HHP) in Nottinghamshire (UK), occupied since 1998. HHP is distinctive because of its use of earth-sheltering for biodiversity and aesthetic functions, which facilitated municipal authority permission to build outside the residential town zone. This self-built project mixes private dwellings and gardens with communal spaces and resources.

The mission of HHP is to 'bring sustainability to life'. Legally it is a cooperative with a constitution incorporating terms and conditions of planning agreements and land leases from municipal authorities. They have a 999-year lease on land on which dwellings and associated facilities stand, and a farm tenancy lease for the remaining property. Lease regulations and a series of other 'common sense' rules bind all members. They report that the cost of each dwelling was in the range of a similarly sized house built in the UK at the time. Their tour, event and consultancy firm is a not-for-profit trading cooperative that allows for non-resident membership and pays wages for non-voluntary work. The consultancy services self-builders, housing developers, professionals, researchers and planners on sustainable housing systems.

Each household works very part-time for the HHP firm and helps to co-maintain joint services, facilities and amenities. The five-household domestic arrangement centres on food self-provisioning; maintenance of collective services, including two wind turbines producing 11 kW and 13.6 kW solar photovoltaic (PV) panels; and land conservation and use. They have an orchard, vegetable gardens, an apiary, and keep chickens and sheep that assist in land management. They maintain a woodland, other vegetation and a large wildlife lake, where they fish carp.

Each household contributes to organic gardening and other tasks – such as running tours, events or acting as consultants – for around 600 recorded hours per year, averaging two hours per day in a six-day week. They gain no wage or community currency credit for this contribution but an in-kind benefit of an estimated 60 per cent of their food requirements; they also have considerable water and energy requirements met renewably and collectively, and remain fit! Like many other cohousing projects, they gain from shallow environmental efficiencies, such as carpooling. Unlike the sometimes onerous governance of eco-villages (discussed in Chapter 6), five households easily communicate and make joint decisions at meetings, often weekly, on a Friday about who will do what, and when. After 15 years – the UK average length of tenure – three households had changed hands without great challenges to governance processes.

HHP housing is ultra-durable clay brick outside and concrete internally, contributing to high thermal mass but without extraordinarily high embodied energy, has passive solar design and super-insulation of buildings and hot water tanks. Householders have efficient energy use practices. Compared with the national average, in the mid-2010s, energy costs were around 16 per cent (£1000p.a.) and material energy 25 per cent – despite dwellings being larger than the national average three-bedroom house (80sq m) and the energy costs of working onsite. They are water self-sufficient with a septic-pond system to deal with grey and black water waste, so effective that the water quality allows for bathing. Additionally, they pioneered use of wind energy locally and, after overcoming substantial initial opposition, installed a 255kW wind turbine to export power. The project has been independently assessed and, not surprisingly, has featured in showcase examples of low carbon housing.

Low impact living affordable community[55]

Inspired by HHP, Lancaster CoHousing and Findhorn communities, the Low Impact Living Affordable Community ('Lilac') in Bramley (Leeds, UK), stands out as accessible for those on low incomes and a model for affordability. In the first half of 2013, residents moved into this eco-cohousing project comprising 12 apartments, eight houses and a two-storey common house on a 1.5-acre (0.6-hectare), L-shaped lot. Efficient renewable energy sources included grid-connected solar PV panels, currently cross-subsiding communal energy and water bills, a mechanical ventilation and heat recovery system to complement the solar passive dwelling design, and highly efficient gas boilers. The dwellings and common house – with its food cooperative, guest quarters, shared laundry (no private washing machines), kitchen and dining facilities, multi-purpose room and workshop – were constructed out of a lime-rendered, locally made straw bale and timber sheeting. Over time, straw bale absorbs rather than emits carbon dioxide so, in comparison to the average UK home, Lilac homes make considerable savings in carbon emission.

'UK's first affordable, low impact cohousing neighbourhood' benefited financially from municipal authority and UK government agencies for their land purchase, experimentation with building materials, and decontamination. Nevertheless, Lilac has been a solidly grass-roots initiative aiming to contribute to post-carbon urban solutions. As indicated in the term 'low impact living', the founders took a holistic approach, the collective governance and management of a cohousing model and community agreements appropriately complementing physical details such as environmentally sound building features. In 2015, they had 10 car spaces, room for 40 bicycles and a neighbourhood of 35 adults and 12 children.

Transport is just one area where Lilac community agreements guide resident practices and relationships in accessing and maintaining shared resources. Lilac's pioneering shared-ownership equity-based leaseholder Mutual Home Ownership Society model, which achieves affordability for members into the future, would seem a carrot for compliance on sustainability restraints (see Chapter 7). Paul Chatterton has emphasised that holism works against the grain of conventional society; Lilac has counteracted this by focusing, in a glocal way, on 'post-carbon value change, mutualism and economic justice, and cooperative self-governance'.

Pioneer Valley Cohousing[56]

Quite a few architects and sustainability professionals have co-initiated, and become resident-members, in eco-cohousing projects. Mary Kraus and Laura Fitch (Kraus Fitch Architects) have consulted for a few dozen cohousing projects, with special foci on conservation, sustainability and environmental design, and reside in the appropriately named Pioneer Valley Cohousing (1994), an early North American East Coast neighbourhood established in Amherst (Massachusetts). This is a 32-household neighbourhood clustered on 25 per cent of a 23-acre site, leaving the remainder for nature conservation. The buildings are super-insulated and oriented to maximise passive solar benefits. The building materials were chosen on the basis of producing healthy interiors and ecological sustainability.

Kraus and Fitch see environmental features as evolving from built and communal characteristics, so process and interdisciplinary holism are central to their approach. Fundamental questions include choice of site and weighing up the social potential and limits of infill and renovation. They facilitate participatory design workshops, including one on 'eco-programming', to identify goals, values and parameters (including cost limitations) and the functionality and amenity required. Working from this big picture, they drill down to realise requirements in room-by-room details, fixtures and appliances. They consider a staged approach to maximise meeting needs and cost limitations.

They aim for a customised design centring on a 'cosy' and 'homely' common house and 'pedestrian neighbourhoods' (Figure 5.2). They advocate for 'small' dwellings and centralising heating and cooling,

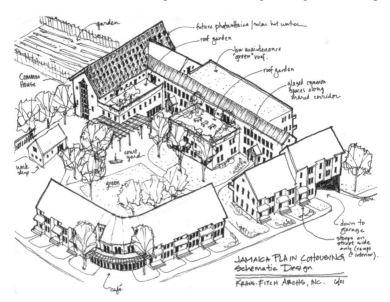

Figure 5.2 Early schematic design rendering for Jamaica Plain Cohousing

Source: Laura Fitch, architect (Amherst, Massachusetts)

provided they are the most efficient options. Among other examples of sharing at Pioneer Valley, Mary Kraus cites the 'frugal luxury' of neighbours co-owning an old red Porsche. Car sharing, car borrowing, offering lifts, purchasing on behalf of others and community-based activities all economise on transport. The monetary savings made by the Kraus household dispensing with one car was equivalent to the cost of their solar PV system. Some residents of Pioneer Valley Cohousing co-own a coworking building, with office equipment, that they share with the rest of the community.

Mary Kraus advocates for Community Supported Agriculture (CSA) either on site, as with the Ithaca Eco-village (New York) and Cobb Hill Cohousing (Hartland, Vermont), or through bulk subscription between local organic farmers and the community in question, as has occurred with urban Cambridge Cohousing (Massachusetts). By the early 2000s, Pioneer Valley Cohousing had an arrangement with Northeast Cooperatives that included wholesale prices and delivery of food for common house meals and two-thirds of all households. A dairy farmer delivered bulk fresh milk. Local organic beef, cut to order, was bought in bulk. Pioneer Valley has facilitated sharing of all kinds of second-hand goods and equipment using a 'Take it or Leave it' area. Similarly, Kraus suggests 'convenient facilities for recycling and composting'. Common spaces are designed to be accessible and fully functional for public events, not just residents, so sharing extends beyond the cohousing community.

Christie Walk[57]

Few cohousing, let alone eco-cohousing, projects exist in a city centre. Christie Walk did so purposively, as 'a practical prototype for the ecological development of our cities', a cell of an eco-city. Construction in central Adelaide, the capital of South Australia, was completed late 2006 on 2 hectares of infill land. The 27 dwellings are: four townhouses and a block of six apartments, both three storeys high; four detached cottages; and a five-storey block of 13 apartments with a communal space for meeting, dining, a library and toilets. The cohousing project started with 15 housing cooperative members, then used different legal entities to fulfil various functions, and benefited from one member making the deposit on an urban land lot that was relatively cheap at the time. With low-interest loans and some sweat equity, the end cost was comparable with that for the median Adelaide house at the time.

The sustainability features of Christie Walk include: passive solar design; no active heating or cooling infrastructure; building with sustainable materials, including straw bale and aerated concrete; paving with demolition materials; solar hot water systems and a communal array of solar PV; rainwater collection, storage and onsite use (but not for drinking or bathing); and, a small productive food garden. The dwellings are projected to last a century, four times the life-span of the average Australian dwelling. As a transport-oriented purposively sustainable development, the council permitted a 50 per cent reduction in car space on the margins. It is widely reported that the communal atmosphere and eco-cohousing objectives inspire a strong ethic of sustainability practices amongst residents.

L'Espoir, Brussels[58]

Many European models benefit from government grants because they improve the environmental sustainability of neighbourhoods – and the city more generally – through integrating residents who have disabilities, economic or social disadvantages, offering work opportunities or spaces, some even co-developing or embedding themselves in innovative districts. Some models are equally socially and environmentally progressive, such as L'Espoir, a subsidised multicultural eco-cohousing project in Brussels for 14 low-income families, or approximately 80 residents. L'Espoir has numerous environmental features, with passive design and thermal solar energy, a green roof and wood construction. Residents organise street activities and open their community garden to neighbours outside L'Espoir. While it has been observed that it stands out like a jewel in low-quality public housing – with as much potential to inspire jealousy as constructive aspiration – a valid rebuttal is that this circumstance says more about the context than substance of this eco-cohousing project.

Munksøgård, Denmark[59]

In the cradle of cohousing – in the mid 2000s, Lietaert estimated that 50,000 Danes resided in cohousing – the case of Munksøgård (Trekroner, near Roskilde, 35km from Copenhagen) illustrates a turn to smaller dwellings and larger common spaces than earlier models. Completed in 2001, around 240 residents live in 100 dwellings, in five clusters, supported by four work teams. An intergenerational settlement, the clusters support distinct tenancy arrangements and management: 20 owner-occupier apartments, 20 apartments comprise a private cooperative, 20 apartments are rented to families, 20 apartments are rented to youth and 20 rented to seniors. The resulting demographic is balanced into one-third young families, one-third middle-aged (45–60-year-olds) and one-third over 60 years of age.

Constructed by a commercial developer and contractor, sustainability features include a permaculture design site; a community grey and black water system; a community wood-heating system; solar hot water; car sharing, including electric and hybrid cars using renewable energy; farm buildings refurbished as workshops; certain buildings insulated by green and locally supplied mussel shell roofs that slow rain run-off; re-use of organic materials and recycling systems; composting toilets and urine separated, collected, cleaned and stored for use in a large irrigated organic garden onsite, managed by resident elders.

CONCLUSION

Cohousing is neighbourhood-based collective living where each household occupies a private domain, often a discrete apartment or house, while using and managing shared space – and a range of other resources – and engaging in collective activities, such as preparing and eating meals together. Internationally, cohousing comprises a variety of cultural characteristics, tenancy arrangements, housing and planning styles. There has been a strong emphasis on grassroots initiatives, autonomy and collective management. However, professions such as architects, and more recently sustainability experts, have been influential in inspiring and supporting cohousing groups, some selecting them as ideal living arrangements for themselves and using them as demonstration projects.

In an uneven way across national borders, governments – especially municipal authorities and state agencies responsible for housing, sustainability and welfare – have been active stakeholders in, not just regulators of, cohousing. Such authorities and agencies have funded or given in-kind (land or building) grants and played roles in selecting residents and administering rental tenancies. Philanthropic bodies and commercial interests have been engaged in various and numerous ways in cohousing developments, again sometimes active in overall management and administration. While such partnerships can limit the autonomy of a cohousing project, they can make them more readily achievable, visible and open. Needless to say, no government agency or not-for-profit organisation can make cohousing a success. The driving force remains residents. Bresson and Denèfle emphasise 'three core concepts: sharing, environmental awareness and citizen participation'.[60]

Sometimes 'cohousing' has been used to refer to comparatively small projects, such as three or four collocated private dwellings with some interdependence, sharing and collective sufficiency between their households, including common space. Even though, in this chapter, I referred to the tiny (five-household) HHP, I would prefer to limit 'cohousing' to upwards of, say eight, discrete and connected households. HHP is exceptional due to its environmental features and capacity for extension, its unusual level of integration and variety of mutually supportive activities for such a small project. Moreover, account needs to be taken of the sizes of households and their capacity to comprise a 'living community' (*bofaelleskab*). The terms 'community' or 'neighbour-hood' remain defining characteristics of collaborative housing. Meltzer suggests a range of 20–40 households or 50–100 household members.

There are references by residents and authors to cohousing as an element of ecovillages, the topic of the next chapter. Instead, I argue that cohousing proper is no more (or less) a building block for ecovillages in general than a step is for a stairway, or a curated 'pocket neighbourhood' is for cohousing.[61] Indeed, Vestbro defines cohousing and ecovillages as 'separate phenomenon'.[62] Cohousing can be created relatively easily within current planning, financial and residential structures and need have no higher level of environmental characteristics than building and planning codes require. This is not to understate the massive effort and frustrations of pioneering residents in achieving certain cohousing developments. However, cohousing is collaborative living within private property and market norms, with residents relying on their own incomes and able to purchase and sell relatively easily out of this housing form through the real estate market.

As such, many run-of-the-mill cohousing projects do not reflect the level of interest in sustainability in this book, which is why the focus of this chapter became *eco-cohousing*. In contrast, the ecovillage movement explored in the next chapter has had very strong grassroots sources and a level of idealism and intentionality absent from cohousing proper. It suffices here to suggest that, in a politico-sustainability context, cohousing as a generic concept and practice might be described as 'shallow' or 'light green' and ecovillages 'deep green'. The sustainability of Earth has been a central concern for ecovillagers who have often experimented with breaking down private property and income barriers to achieve equality and communality.

6

Ecovillages:
Sustainability and System Change

The ecovillage movement has been driven by a grassroots urge to address environmental crises across the planet in very immediate, practical and everyday ways. Typical pioneers of ecovillages have decided that we need to completely change our lifestyles and our relationship with nature to live sustainably in the twenty-first century. Paul Wimbush, co-founder of Lammas ecovillage in Wales, insists that 'there's a basic underlying problem in the capitalist system that we've got at the moment in that it is based on infinite growth of a finite resource' and, with respect to climate change, 'no amount of tweaking corporate capitalism is going to create a solution'.[1] As the name suggests, the idea of an 'ecovillage' joins select characteristics of traditional villages as connected place-based communities and highly localised economies, with strong environmentally concerned practices to heal, and adapt to the limits of, Earth.

Two chapters comprise Part II, the previous chapter on cohousing and associated models, and this one on ecovillages. Although recent eco-cohousing projects have incorporated environmental features, generically cohousing simply focuses on clusters of housing with householders intentionally connected by sharing certain spaces and facilities for everyday living. Ecovillages extend beyond these concerns to involve more onsite production, collective sufficiency and educational outreach to non-members. Ecovillages have always been broader in scope and idealistic in their mission than cohousing. Cohousing essentially transforms the built and socio-cultural nature of housing. In contrast, ecovillages are characterised by holistic – collective, material, bioregional and personal – transformations integrated variously and to differing extents.

As a result of their holistic and transformative aims, ecovillages are very much works-in-progress that tend to be more experimental, diverse and ambitious than cohousing. The international Global Ecovillage Network (GEN) has promoted various definitions of an 'ecovillage' since GEN formed, in 1995, in distinctively regional ways to encompass pre-existing ecovillages and encourage more. Today, the network defines ecovillages as 'intentional or traditional communities, consciously designed through participatory processes to regenerate their environments', commonly characterised by 'low-impact, high-quality lifestyles' and 'a holistic regenerative development model that is adapted to local contexts'.[2]

Many outstanding ecovillages and associated themes are held over for analysis in later chapters. Beyond geographic and cultural distinctions, many forms of collaborative housing, including ecovillages, have had particular drivers and potential trajectories that prove significant in imagining housing and settlement futures, the focus of Part III. Part III is structured by the drivers-cum-strategic foci for collaborative housing: government, market and grassroots communities. Developments associated with government intervention with financial and in-kind support are discussed in Chapter 7. Those analysed in Chapter 8 have been market- and private-property-driven. Chapter 9 examines environmentally focused communities that aimed for autonomy from state and market.

Meanwhile, this chapter describes and analyses some of the typical internal workings and environmental aims and achievements of ecovillages by detailing four cases. I aim to show how and why ecovillages might transform housing production and distribution to address afford-ability, accessibility and environmental challenges in one stroke. These analyses are bookended by a brief introduction to the scope of ecovillages worldwide and summary remarks regarding significant themes on the ecovillage as a concept, in theory, and practice.

SCOPE OF ECOVILLAGES

Here I make a general distinction between ecovillages and cohousing, framing ecovillages as broader, deeper, larger and more radical experi-ments than cohousing models. Similarly, for analytical clarity, I deal with cohousing and ecovillages in separate chapters, by imposing a distinct terminology. In the field, inconsistent nomenclature by communities, legal, planning and political authorities leads to confusion. There are examples of what I term 'cohousing' that are called 'ecovillages' by their own residents, such as Westwyck in Melbourne (Australia) and BedZED in London (UK).[3] Vagaries multiply because the intentions and visions that drive many projects take years to fulfil; the GEN website includes planned or starting, as well as tried-true-and-tested, communities and even educational projects promoting and supporting ecovillage life.[4] Litfin explains this apparent distraction with education by arguing that more ecovillages have morphed out of existing sympathetic and energetic communities influenced by advocates and opportunistic learning than have grown like oases in deserts or lights on hills.[5] Examples of the former include Indigenous and permaculture-inspired communities.

Besides autochthonous development of ecovillages, the umbrella GEN body has made concerted efforts to spread the model. There are thousands of ecovillages and associated learning centres as works-in-progress across the world; GEN coordinates the activities of six regional networks to claim around 10,000 ecovillages in its orbit. While some ecovillages or ecovillage-type developments prefer to grow organically without formal connections to the network, GEN includes some 2000 Sarvodaya villages in Sri Lanka transforming towards an international ecovillage model, an active Senegalese network of ecovillages and a Pan-African Ecovillage Development Programme, representatives of which led the GEN contingent to a United Nations Framework Convention on Climate Change COP22 (22nd Conference of the Parties) event in Marrakech.[6] However, the focus here is on the United Kingdom (UK), North America, Europe, Australia and New Zealand.

In terms of size, a few ecovillages in the Global North have thousands of members, though many support fewer than one hundred. Some aspire to greater numbers of members, others imagine scaling up through inspiring multiple developments of various sizes. Indeed, ecovillages such as Twin Oaks (Virginia, Washington) seem to reach an optimum size and readily spawn smaller offshoot communities – such as Acorn (of course) – with whom the originators maintain economic and cultural relationships.

Viennese researcher Iris Kunze emphasises that ecovillages have had a much greater influence than their number in the Global North suggests, because such models are innovative and creative by nature, due to the ways that they address collective sufficiency. Moreover, many residents stay for only several years but continue ecovillage practices and advocacy. Furthermore, most ecovillages are open to visitors, many formally functioning as educational centres with thousands of visitors per annum. Andreas and Wagner point out that the German Advisory Council on Global Change is just one example of observers and analysts who acknowledge that ecovillages are 'pioneers of change'.[7]

Internally, ecovillages naturally subdivide into affinity and interest-based groups, and their governance models often incorporate small, semi-autonomous working groups enabling a level of delegation and specialisation. At the same time everyone is encouraged to participate in as many different types of activities as they can, so skills and knowledge can be widely shared. Consequently, the governance and everyday working of many ecovillages departs from hierarchical traditional village life. Sieben Linden 'has no police', writes one of its residents, 'neither is it a typical village with a church, influential farmers, or an elite group of local personalities'. Furthermore, an expert on intentional communities, Bill Metcalf, points out that, during the 2010s, ecovillages have been 'rapidly increasing' and, while some are religious, 'the vast majority are secular'.[8]

Ecovillage residents select, settle into, and rotate, roles within task-focused groups and more administrative or managerial positions, operationalising decisions made in consensual forums similar to general assemblies in Occupy and other such movements. Those most relevant to our study, which concentrates on outward-looking ecovillages of the Global North, have readily accessible and informative websites with detail on legal, governance and ecological arrangements and practices and contacts with whom to follow-up. They are transparent, generous and inviting to seriously interested visitors and guests, but often streamline outreach activities through regular open days and formal public tours.

Ecovillages stand out from other intentional communities in as much as they identify with extensive networks of variable and energetic projects dedicated to both healing Earth and living more communally and, consequently, highlight whole-of-life sustainability. At the same time their characteristics and core concerns can be quite distinctive, depending on their cultural and ecological contexts, regional planning and legal regulations, and the collective skills and material resources of members. For this reason, this chapter describes the variety and commonalities of four impressive ecovillages before discussing some more trends, characteristics and debates in general literature on ecovillages.

LAMMAS: RURAL LOW IMPACT LIVING

Lammas's core group formed 'around a campfire at a summer festival'. Subsequently, they would co-dream a tight community of household-based farms and self-built dwellings, incorporating locals and visitors by including common paths through their 'village' and a dedicated visitor educational centre. Their initial plan for Tir y Gafel in Glandwr, Pembrokeshire (West Wales) was for a circle of 20 dwellings around a central ecovillage green. In 2009, they gained planning permission for a smaller number of households and, by the end of 2016, had nine dwellings (one shown in Figure 6.1) all with active plots fulfilling ambitious targets tied to the Welsh One Planet Development policy.[9] Thus they became an, albeit small, ecovillage.

Figure 6.1　Exterior of a Lammas dwelling

Source: Simon Dale, photographer

Low impact living

Although a grassroots initiative, the growth of Lammas was partly determined by the Pembrokeshire County Council's low impact development policy and, subsequently, by the Welsh 'One Planet Development' policy, both regulating low impact communities today. Low impact developments aim to create a relatively seamless inhabitation of land and water with as minimal disturbance to the local natural landscape as possible, along with practices that minimise both material use and activities that lead to carbon emissions. Based on varying levels of collective sufficiency, self-management, and environmental and social values, low impact living is pursued through approaches such as permaculture and a do-it-ourselves mutual support. In short, the scope of low impact developments moves well beyond housing to embrace livelihoods. Low impact developers have become known as 'lidders'.

In the case of the Tir y Gafel site, regeneration would mean a 'huge transition from pasture to a mosaic of different ecosystems'. The land had been heavily degraded through grazing sheep. The complexity of processes to achieve a transition, and its heart-warming results, is indicated in a quote from just one detail in Lammas's 2015 monitoring report for authorities:

> The millpond continues to be managed for biodiversity and wildlife through a policy of maintaining water levels, regulating algal blooms and cultivating an attitude of appreciation and conservation. Earthworks were undertaken … to slow down the rate the millpond silts up. Barley straw was used to prevent the build-up of filamentous algae. The millpond continues to support a healthy population of trout as well as supporting a range of breeding waterfowl. The millpond hosts a large population of breeding toads and is a valuable feeding ground for bats. Otters have also been sighted using the millpond.[10]

When coined by Simon Fairlie, in 1996, 'low impact development' had already emerged as informal, even illegal, 'low impact communities' in the UK. In contrast, the initiators of Lammas aimed to formalise their community and gain planning approval for their model to enable others to follow suit. Their engagement with authorities dragged out for more than one thousand days, and their proposal amounted to one thousand pages, given revisions after repeated consultations and knockbacks. Finally, they gained planning approval on appeal, in August 2009, for their development on around 31 hectares of degraded south-facing pastureland with some woodland and springs.

Fortunately, Lammas had been offered an extended option to buy this land, sited in an area long favoured for alternative living experiments. Still, neighbours initially reacted with a mix of ire and support. Committed members stood the test of time as their detailed dwelling and plot plans for 2 hectares were shared, along with planning application expenses, including a permaculture consultant. Lammas has made detailed reports on lessons from the planning approval process; co-founder Wimbush attributed challenges more to 'politics within the council' than to planners. However, Jones outlines a complex tango in which state authorities and academic studies were influential in shifting planning ordinances to cater for low impact developments. Lammas was just one of many low impact communities that sustained cat-and-mouse struggles with authorities, including standout Brithdir Mawr, also in Pembokeshire, and protests against threats of demolition before low impact development came into force.[11]

The cooperative association that Lammas formed followed what has become an ecovillage status quo: consensual decision-making with a fall-back to voting or some other resolution-based process in the case of any stalemate, an elected and accountable executive committee of directors, along with small teams working on specific issues. Consistent with co-founder Wimbush's preference for 'self-reliance' over 'self-sufficiency' as a descriptor for Lammas's position in a trade-based society, they would decide on a market-oriented model of member entry and exit to the community via purchase and sale, a service charge to members for areas held in common and an unusually casual approach to members' engagement in governance.[12]

One Planet Development

During the first half of the 2010s, the Welsh One Planet Development policy had limited application, mainly in rural areas, because of stringent requirements for associated developments to be substantially supported by 'land-based livelihoods within five years' (75 per cent sufficiency in basic household needs or £3000 per adult); wholly supported by renewable energy and water collected onsite; living in zero-carbon housing with respect to embodied and operating energy – mainly using local, recycled and renewable natural construction materials; all of which would contribute to the essential aim of a 'one planet' ecological footprint of 2.4 hectares per capita, or 1.8 global hectares (gha). Wimbush has identified the biggest challenge as generating from their land produce worth around £80,000, comparing that to the previous farmer who gained around £3000 per annum and neighbouring farmers who gain subsidies for farming their land. Adding value to excess produce has proved the main means to successfully achieve niche trading outside their ecovillage economy.[13]

The One Planet Development calculations applicable to Lammas estimate the household domestic ecological footprints of applicants using a Stockholm Environment Institute tool. While the calculator uses much financial data, the results are generated in global hectares per capita. A 'global hectare' is 'a biologically productive hectare with world average biological productivity for a given year', the unit of account used to measure ecological footprints and biocapacity. Therefore, the global hectare is a standard that varies through time to account for different levels of production and productivity, and requires modification for applications to specific types of productive land. A measure of biologically productive land and water, it incorporates impacts of both consumption and waste on the regenerative capacity of Earth.[14]

The ecological footprint covers both carbon and non-carbon footprints. Globally, carbon emissions became the greatest, and fastest growing, share of total impacts during the 50 years between 1961 and 2011. The carbon footprint is incorporated into the ecological footprint through the amount of biologically productive area necessary for absorbing emitted carbon dioxide (CO_2 and other greenhouse gases measured as a CO_2 equivalent). An initial carbon evaluation (2009) concluded that regeneration through permaculture farming and woodland management would enable a positive carbon sequestration rate of around 120 tonnes CO_2 per annum, whereas Lammas's site had, in its depleted state, emitted an estimated negative of seven tonnes of CO_2 per annum. At the same time, the land would provide substantially for the inhabitants' basic needs and cut carbon emissions attributable to their lifestyles to less than one-quarter of those associated with previous practices.[15]

Lammas: achievements

The Lammas 2015 annual report showed that they were living well within a one planet footprint, shrinking to an 0.8 planet footprint from a 1.36 planet footprint in 2010.[16] In short, through sustainable practices in their work, play, homes and travel, residents reduced their impact to around one-third of the Welsh average. This achievement required neither 'smart' technologies nor total retreat from advanced technologies, such as the Internet. They simply minimised their use of many things, including machinery, water and energy. They car-shared and strove for self-reliance in food.

While it is unclear as yet how low impact living will be applied in cities such as Cardiff and Aberystwyth, the significance of low impact living was strengthened by the end of 2016, when the Welsh government confirmed broader applications of ecological footprint measures to monitor achievements under the Well-Being of Future Generations Act and with respect to the 2050 target to reduce Welsh people's ecological footprints to a one planet lifestyle.[17]

Being a lidder sounds like 'hard work' but Wimbush casts the experience in different terms:

> it doesn't feel like work because ... you're coming from a place of freedom with it, so I get up when I want...

> ... it doesn't feel like work coz we play hard and ... it's not like we work for a number of hours for money.

> You're playing for the love of the land and the love of growing food and then you're going to reap the rewards.[18]

Compared with other British residents who are subject to power blackouts or water supply being cut off, Wimbush has pointed out that off-grid living empowers lidders:

> here, in the house, I know exactly where the electricity comes from when I turn on the light, and exactly where the water goes when I pull the plug out of the sink, and so all the kind of solutions, all the support systems, are micro. They're kind of homemade and I can tweak them and mend them.[19]

Furthermore, the cost of establishing a dwelling (Figure 6.2) and plot at Tir y Gafel ecovillage has been estimated at around £40,000 to £65,000, with resale values expected to remain low because of the responsibilities and challenges attendant to the associated lifestyle. By comparison, a local town house plot of just 0.1 acre was marketed in 2009 for £130,000, whereas a 5-acre lot and share in Lammas woodland cost only £35,000. In short, entering into and living at this ecovillage is highly affordable.[20]

LOS ANGELES ECO-VILLAGE:
URBAN, DIVERSE AND WORKING CLASS

Los Angeles Eco-Village (LAEV) began on New Year's Day 1993 after civil unrest, urban fires and riots subsequent to the Rodney King verdict (1992). These protests redirected the attention of a group of 20

Figure 6.2   Interior of a Lammas dwelling

Source: Simon Dale, photographer

visionaries set on building a US$25m 'state-of-the-art eco-development that might have taken decades to develop' on 11 acres of city-owned landfill several miles away. Instead, as co-founder Lois Arkin recounts, the unrest prompted them to retrofit environmental sustainability and ground cooperation and community in the diverse, disrupted and damaged working-class neighbourhood that had been her home for more than a decade.

This leap of faith was economically rational: damage from several earthquakes during 1992 as well as the civil unrest had sent real-estate prices down, making the purchase of degraded apartments in this area more feasible than other options they had considered. LAEV activists – many of them artists, who would apply artistic skills to spread sustainability practices – began on the street, getting to know their neighbours better, in order to inform and lay the groundwork for realising the eco-communal housing and neighbourhood activism that has remained central to their very urban ecovillage ever since.

By the mid-2010s, LAEV intentional community had around 40 committed members and a similar number of active participants assisting in a range of ecovillage activities. Managing 50 apartment dwellings, they were immediately accessible to 500 neighbourhood residents, predominantly on low incomes and from around 15 ethnic backgrounds. In short, LAEV acted as an outreach hub, for locals especially, to learn about urban community-oriented sustainability as a way of the future:

> The space includes cooperative affordable housing, native landscape, on-site food growth, micro social enterprises, a community land trust, pedestrian-friendly streetscape, bike-friendly amenities, and a host of democratic community-building activities. To visit is to not only feel the history of community transformation, but also be inspired about what a more liveable L.A. can exemplify.[21]

Formal LAEV structure: networked institutions

As is typical of many ecovillages, the complex activities, scope and range of responsibilities that comprise LAEV are managed through an integrated web of legally distinct institutions, each with specific aims and organisers. In the 1990s, the Cooperative Resources and Services Project (CRSP) – established in 1980 as a not-for-profit community development organisation and the seedbed for LAEV – bought two apartment buildings. In 2011, the Beverly-Vermont Community Land Trust (BVCLT) and the CRSP purchased yet another apartment building. Existing renters were offered the option of remaining in their homes irrespective of whether they decided to become active in LAEV or not.[22]

Instead of conventional banking, funds from CRSP's Ecological Community Revolving Loan Fund – supported by US$2m credit from friends and other donors, most of whom had been repaid by 2014 – enabled the property purchases and rehabilitation of dilapidated, damaged apartments and environmental retrofits. By the mid-2010s, most LAEV members lived in one of two adjacent apartment buildings on land owned by the BVCLT – donated to the CLT by the CRSP in 2012 – with the buildings owned and governed by another not-for-profit, limited-equity housing cooperative Urban Soil/Tierra Urbana (USTA). Members of the CRSP, the BVCLP and the USTA comprised the LAEV Intentional Community. Renters' payments covered building costs and the ownership models were designed to protect the land and buildings from re-entering the speculative real-estate market.[23]

Urban dwellers: transport and food

While conveniently located to public transport, LAEV operates over two blocks in East Hollywood close to 'one of Los Angeles most auto congested traffic corridors, Vermont Avenue'. LAEV members have driven a movement away from automobiles in their neighbourhood and beyond by encouraging reduced car usage, offering a discount of hundreds of dollars per annum to renters without cars, renovating garages into work and business spaces, promoting and supporting bike use (such as through the LA County Bicycle Coalition), a LAEV member establishing a vibrant repairing Bicycle Kitchen, installing arty SLOW DOWN signs on street posts and campaigning to eradicate all through traffic in their neighbourhood. As such, they lay groundwork for Mayor Villaraigosa (2005–2013) to champion a 2011 Los Angeles' Bicycle Master Plan to establish 1680 miles of interconnected bikeways (40 miles per annum) and advise all agencies to promote bike programs and education.[24]

Encouraging walking and cycling is significant to reduce car and air travel to reverse climate change. For instance, a 2006 environmental audit of the well-established Scottish Findhorn ecovillage community and business showed that even though both the total travel and the overall ecological footprint of Findhorn residents were half the Scottish average, alarmingly, Findhorn residents' air travel was around double the average Scottish level per capita. Findhorn residents made significant savings in terms of car, but not air, travel. A study of the well-known Beddington Zero Energy Development (BedZED) in London showed similar results and advised guilty residents to reduce or eliminate air travel. To avoid regular commuting, many LAEV members have found work close to home.[25]

Furthermore, such studies indicate considerable environmental savings from self-provisioning in food, a tall order in a global city. LAEV have established a food cooperative in their main apartment lobby where residents and locals can order fresh organic vegetable and fruit boxes delivered from local farms on a weekly basis. Locals can join the cooperative to buy cheap bulk dry foods by paying a nonmonetary fee working in the cooperative around 20 hours per annum. The LAEV blog is replete with news on the dozens of small garden beds and fruit trees that they co-developed throughout their neighbourhood with the aim of greater locally produced food sufficiency. Many LAEV members and their neighbours belong to the Arroyo Seco Network of Time Banks where they contribute work by the hour credited by another kind of work done by another member for an hour – a system that can facilitate sharing the product of growing, preparing and cooking food locally and collectively.[26]

The ecovillage has implemented programs to improve the environmental efficiency of apartments through water and energy saving appliances, use of solar energy, drought-resistant landscaping and rain gardens, and by connecting pipes to divert grey water to community gardens (requiring householders to watch what goes into their waste water, such as keeping to biodegradable detergents). Erstwhile waste, along with material mined from local landfill, is reused as construction materials, recycled or composted in bins or holes in LAEV food-producing gardens, of which there were 24, along with 100 fruit trees, in 2011.[27]

Core values

After an international tour of ecovillages, Litfin suggested using a four-pronged approach to their analysis, combining ecology and economics, and community and consciousness ('E2C2').[28] Litfin associates spirituality and religiosity, through 'consciousness', to environmental respect. But, is there a necessary and straightforward link between either spirituality and sustainability, or consciousness and commitment? For instance, as discussed in previous chapters, studies show that consciousness of environmental imperatives for change does not necessarily inform more sustainable behaviour in practice.

Furthermore, from her E2C2 perspective, Litfin was surprised that the determinedly secular LAEV 'was also the most religiously diverse community I visited'. By highlighting 'consciousness' and weighing its definition down as the driver of practices, Litfin assumed that the secularity of LAEV would lead to the 'lowest common denominator'. If, instead, one acknowledges that secular environments are tolerant and protect diversity – giving no particular set of beliefs privilege in communal rituals and decision-making – LAEV's religious diversity is understandable.[29] Sustainability motivation and commitment in practice can be driven by simple scientific understandings and strong socio-environmental values and are, arguably, easier to apply collectively than in an individual household.[30] This point is made by LAEV core values, listed in Box 6.1, that members have committed to since 2001.

Box 6.1   Los Angeles Eco-Village Core Values

1. Celebrate & include joy in all our endeavors
2. Take responsibility for each other & the planet through local environmental & social action
3. Learn from nature and live ecologically
4. Build a dynamic community through diversity & cooperation, giving & forgiving
5. Inspire compassionate, nurturing, & respectful relationships
6. Create balanced opportunities for individual participation & collective stewardship
7. Engage our neighbors and broader community in mutual dialog to learn, act and teach

Source: Los Angeles Eco-Village, 'About', 2015 – http://laecovillage.org/home/about-2/

In terms of cultural diversity, impressed by the community's self-reliant 'DIY ethic', a Chicana who lived there from 2008 to 2011 recalled LAEV as 'an important site where a racially integrated group experiments with life beyond the usual story for many of us who grew up in marginalized communities'. She described LAEV's approach as a complete reversal of mainstream aspirations – 'rising above poverty, we are expected to embrace status-oriented consumerism' – while LAEV taught voluntary collective simplicity instead.[31]

CLOUGHJORDAN ECOVILLAGE: SMART AND SLOW

Cloughjordan Ecovillage (Tipperary, Ireland) has a distinctly twenty-first century, eco-smart and market-oriented character: 'We have over 100 residents living in high-performance green homes, over 20,000 newly planted trees and Ireland's largest renewable energy district heating system.' The heating system was partly funded by a European Union (EU) sustainable energy program. Infrastructure, such as fibre-optic cabling for high-speed broadband, was completed in 2008 and construction of permanent dwellings in 2009, a decade after the ecovillage's initiators had started discussing their ambitions for it.[32]

Ninety minutes from Dublin by car – train services are limited – the ecovillage has been lauded for revitalising a rural settlement. Drawing on two twenty-first-century movements associated with sustainability,

Cloughjordan Ecovillage seems like a subtle mix of 'smart' and 'slow'. According to the metrics of environmental consultant Vince Carragher, by late 2015 the average resident was already achieving an ecological footprint of 2gha (one-third of the Irish average of 5.5gha) and heading for a one planet lifestyle of 1.7gha. Framed as low carbon lifestyles as much as low impact living, Cloughjordan member-residents had already built more than 55 of an expected 130 dwellings (including 16 work–live units) by 2016.[33]

Establishment[34]

As with Lammas, the founders of Cloughjordan Ecovillage advertised successfully for appropriate land. Consequently, a 27-hectare greenfield site spreading from just north of the main town street out into the countryside was purchased in 2005. Six years beforehand, they had established a company, Sustainable Projects Ireland Limited (SPIL), registered as an educational charity. SPIL became a vehicle to establish the ecovillage, certain associated organisations, and has operated as a not-for-profit cooperative.

Especially given that many members had come from Dublin, once they identified an appropriate site in 2002, it was imperative that community member-cum-developers first worked on becoming part of the existing social and geographic environment of the prospective Cloughjordan Ecovillage. They invited considerable input from the around 500 pre-existing village residents of Cloughjordan (Cloghjordan), a town established in the mid-seventeenth century in an area inhabited by humans for several millennia. A year-long consultation included schoolchildren creatively involved in modelling the ecovillage.

Planning permission from the local authorities took another few years to accomplish, in stages, starting with the master plan before the land purchase was completed. The ultimate plan included a relatively dense residential area, woodlands to be augmented with tree plantings by residents, 12 acres reserved for community-based farming, along with individual plots meaning that food production and biodiversity were twin principles (see Figure 6.3 for the masterplan for their land use). Even though local authorities rejected the community's bid for a reed bed and wetland system for black and grey water, subsequently their drainage system successfully dealt with precipitation that caused local flooding outside the ecovillage.

Figure 6.3   Masterplan sketch of Cloughjordan Ecovillage

Source: Sustainable Projects Ireland

Residential obligations

Each member has to abide by standards set out in a long *Village Ecological Charter* with environmental rating targets and approved methods for developing dwellings, other built environment features, and management of natural zones. For instance, water-use targets are 60 per cent of the national average per capita. Technical specifications for buildings – energy use, air-tightness, passive solar design, ventilation and insulation – are more stringent than with current building standards. In 2013, even though amounting to just 0.0015 per cent of all dwellings in Ireland, Cloughjordan Ecovillage dwellings represented 6.25 per cent of all A-rated dwellings and 2.5 per cent of B-rated ones, and scored very strongly in building energy ratings compared with other Irish homes.[35]

However, sustainable practices rely on much more than a green eco-smart home. Carragher's calculations show that common transport accounts for one-third of the average residents' ecological footprint – car travel (19 per cent) and air travel (15 per cent). In this study, indicator scores varied by a factor of 10 'for all consumption categories', which proves just how important personal practices are over and above the eco-standards of homes. In addition to travel, food transport and packaging burdens ecological footprints. In the mid-2010s, beyond individual efforts and access to Cloughjordan Community Farm produce, adult residents of Cloughjordan Ecovillage would sign on to an average of two hours per week voluntary community work (*meitheal*) on communal ecovillage spaces, such as community gardens producing vegetables and fruits – generally attending to gardens adjacent to their homes.[36]

Community-supported agriculture

Residents of the ecovillage can elect to join others, including non-ecovillage locals, as members, of the Cloughjordan Community Farm. Horses plough the member-owned and operated biodynamic Cloughjordan Community Farm (Figure 6.4), which traverses 5 hectares of ecovillage and a further 12 hectares located 2km away. This community-supported agriculture (CSA) farm started in the latter half of 2008, with members becoming guarantors for an €80,000 loan from a German ethical bank. Fifty members pay a regular subscription to ensure wages for farm workers and to cover lease of the land. Low-income members pay less and gain more while children are free. Members have input into the management of the CSA and associated activities, volunteering as coordinators and workers, especially for planting and harvesting. The farm benefits from work by Willing Workers on Organic Farms (WWOOFers) and, in 2016, was calling for applications for one-year EU-funded youth volunteers. In return, live-in volunteers

Figure 6.4 Cloughjordan Community Farm: Hard at work ploughing

Source: Davie Philip, photographer

are accommodated by members – or at CSA expense at the inexpensive ecovillage eco-hostel, which has more than 30 beds – and are often fed by rostered members.

CSA members pick up produce such as vegetables, milk, eggs, honey, apple juice and grains on the basis of their needs, and can dry, freeze or preserve surplus. Meat produce is accessed independently. Some grain goes to the local bakery and farm animals, and milk is distributed to cheese-makers. One study of the CSA during 2010–2011 reported on a governance and management restructure in response to disappointing levels of produce on the farm and financial straits; appropriately redesigned, roles and responsibilities showed a capacity to analyse and creatively revise this CSA to more appropriately satisfy members' aims.[37]

Cloughjordan Village, governance and affordability

Alongside environmental sustainability learning initiatives using the ecovillage as a demonstration site and space, members have developed many local businesses beyond the farm, including a wood-fired bakery, a book café, several sustainability consultancy services, the first community-operated FabLab in Ireland, and have attracted national offices of relevant sustainability organisations to relocate to Cloughjordan town.

Much has been made by certain authors about the specialness of the Cloughjordan Ecovillage governance structure, but it replicates many features found in other ecovillages. In short, non-hierarchical work planning and monitoring teams develop on permanent (or temporary) bases to address specific continuous (or one-off) responsibilities yet remain answerable to the whole body, which is coordinated by elected representatives with regular meetings for all members. This is the most common ecovillage model, where a modified form of consensual decision-making operates, that is, consensus is sought through a process of proposal, discussion involving deep listening and engagement, scoping and reframing the issues at hand, and proceeding at the point when there is an outcome formed that all can live with.[38]

In contrast to Lammas and LAEV, Cloughjordan Ecovillage presents definite hurdles in terms of affordability. In October 2016, estimates of building costs were €800–1500 per sq m. Prices ranged from €32,340 to €38,340 for apartment sites (on a 999-year lease), and €50,620 to €94,340 for detached house sites inclusive of a Community Development Charge for the benefit of a fully serviced site (including a cheap heating source). Sites are owned outright with the caveat that re-sale is limited to a member of SPIL.[39] In late 2016 there was a 170sq m semi-detached four-bedroom, two-bathroom ecovillage house that had been completed in 2012 for sale for €195,000.[40] Hemp seems to have been used extensively, and timber framing, self-building, owner-building, and cooperative building all deliver some economies but Cloughjordan Ecovillage is certainly not as affordable as others considered in this chapter.

LIVE, WORK AND PLAY: DANCING RABBIT ECOVILLAGE, MISSOURI

In 1993, some Stanford University students in California set their sights on establishing a post-petroleum off-grid 'eco-town' of some 500–1000 residents. Subsequently, they met regularly to discuss the realisation of an ecovillage of individuals and fluid self-organising smaller communities. By 1995, many had joined a shared household within a multi-house community, which enabled greater interaction and progress. It became apparent that Californian planning laws and land prices effectively prohibited establishing the ecovillage there, so a desktop search for a promised land ensued. In August 1996, those still keen rode off to physically search for, and finally settle, temporarily, at an established community already known to them, Sandhill in Scotland County (north-east Missouri).

Community land trust

Using a community land trust (CLT) model, early in October 1997, the community now known as Dancing Rabbit Ecovillage (DRE) finalised the purchase of a US$190,000 property in the vicinity of Sandhill – 113 hectares of depleted farmland with a couple of farm buildings. Subsequently, they reserved around 5 per cent for dwellings, a common house and other facilities, 36 hectares are reserved for food production and sustainable forestry and 65 hectares has become part of a funded US Conservation Reserve Program. Their mission is deeply ecological – as indicated by an aerial view of their ecovillage in Figure 6.5 – their approach experimental and their sustainability practices broadly community-based. In 2014 its population was around 75 mainly adult member-residents, a dozen or so children and several non-member residents (such as those on work-exchange).[41]

Figure 6.5   Dancing Rabbit Ecovillage: An aerial view

Source: Jim Barmore, photographer

The CLT model enables every member to lease plots, but they must seek ecovillage approval to build a dwelling, develop gardens or farm. These plots can be sold on to any prospective buyers who, however, must be pre-approved members. By the mid-2010s, there were around 25 small, mainly self-built, dwellings and further community buildings and other facilities. Members have no buy-in charge, low leasing rates (circa US$300 per annum in 2016 for dwelling plots) and memberships are a progressive 2 per cent of any level of income.[42]

DRE has an outward focus through their educational Centre for Sustainable and Cooperative Culture, which has been attracting some 1000 visitors per annum, many staying for weeks at a time. They produce webinars, on 'low carbon, high quality' lifestyles, that are easily accessible worldwide. Furthermore, partly due to their proximity to Sandhill and Red Earth Farms, they have administered the international Fellowship of Intentional Community and its publishing arm.[43]

Governance and culture

Members are expected to be active on committees and the structure includes a board of directors and village council featuring consensus decision-making. Two distinctive foci of DRE are an explicit stand on encouraging population degrowth and a determinedly feminist ethos. Sustainability guidelines include voluntary population control and shared responsibilities for children, which fulfil feminist approaches. Many secular sustainability-oriented ecovillages make a concerted effort to open all roles, learning opportunities and responsibilities to every member irrespective of gender or other characteristics. Sharing skills and empowerment for women are explicitly advocated. A feminist ethos and practice is seen to be of strong benefit, releasing males from stereotypical limitations and expectations as much as women, as males participate in childcare and nurturing roles.[44]

Perhaps the achievements in these directions are best expressed in the words of one DRE resident – they call themselves 'Rabbits' – contemplating impending parenthood:

Whether it's a boy or a girl (or however they choose to identify later in life), we will teach them the basic necessities that our education system does not (in addition to going to school, of course). They'll know how to grow organic fruits, vegetables, and herbs; how to navigate without GPS; how to source and filter water; how to craft basic shelters; and how to limit their personal impact on both the environment and other people and cultures by recycling, repairing, and reusing as much as possible. They'll know how to defend themselves as well, without the gaudy pride and trendiness that has become synonymous with guns and violence nowadays.[45]

Strict sustainability practices

Several covenants bind all Rabbits to sustainable practices along specific sustainability guidelines focusing on renewable energy and material use. No personal motorised vehicles can be used or kept there; the ecovillage has a car cooperative using energy-efficient vehicles, biodiesel and solar energy, and car-pooling with member contributions covering costs proportional to use. Fossil fuels cannot be used either in vehicles or for heating or cooling spaces or water, or for refrigeration. Only sustainable energy is generated onsite and any imports of energy must be offset by communal energy exports.

Many DRE households do not have a kitchen in their dwelling; instead they share preparation and eating of meals in a food cooperative and common house kitchen. Similarly, a Rabbit is likely to launder in one of just a few washing machines in a general cooperative. Besides an assembly room, the community's common house has offices and a library, showers and sinks, and a room for children to play in.[46] Organic standards are observed, organic materials are composted onsite from household waste, and humanure is used. Recycled materials are reclaimed, timber must be second-hand and locally grown or certified as sustainably harvested, and paper must be made from re-used materials or sustainably regenerating resources. Purchase of necessary goods and services is limited to non-exploitative or 'the most socially progressive source'.

There is minimal husbanding of domesticated ruminant animals producing methane.[47]

As mentioned, Rabbits live on a fraction of their land, leaving the rest for farming, including orchards and gardens, woodland under ecoforestry and 65 hectares under a remunerative federal Conservation Reserve Program contract to control erosion and conserve wildlife. They have regenerated the land with local indigenous plants, such as 8 hectares of native prairie grasses and thousands of trees, to encourage wildlife habitat and restore the landscape to its precolonial eco-diversity. No mean feat, this continuous work-in-progress requires sharing and developing special knowledge and skills. In February 2017, for instance, the Rutledge Fire Department assisted in managing a burn of approximately 25 hectares of grasslands to encourage local ecological regeneration. The fire brigade brought crucial equipment and tools vital to managing a fire subject to windy conditions.[48]

Carbon footprint

DRE uses the US average as a yardstick for assessing the progress of its socio-material structure and culture for environmental sustainability. In 2013, the average US emission per capita per annum was around 20 metric tons of CO_2-e (Table 6.1). An average Rabbit's energy use within the home was less than 20 per cent the US average. Moreover, the community wholly relied on generating its own renewable (solar and wind) energy and exports through a community-wide solar electricity cooperative. So, even with the embodied energy of its energy-generating equipment included, the ecovillage had an almost zero electricity footprint in 2013. Food sustainability is notoriously hard to measure, but DRE residents calculate that their consumption generates only 50–70 per cent of the carbon emissions of an average US resident. By minimising car usage, in 2013, the average DRE resident used around 11 per cent of the US average for local transport. Harking back to the discussion regarding Findhorn and BedZED in the LAEV section, where DRE members fell down was long-distance travel – consuming 90 per cent of the US average level of emissions due to long car trips and air travel.[49]

Table 6.1 DRE average carbon footprint compared with the US average (CO_2-e metric tonnes)

Sector	Rabbit average	US resident average
Electricity	0.02	2.87
Transport, local	0.31	2.90
Heating and cooking	0.35	2.23
Goods	1.04	2.30
Food	2.10	3.00
Services	1.76	2.52
Travel	2.58	2.86
Other	1.90	1.90
Waste	−0.63	−0.60
TOTAL	9.43	19.98

Source: Data drawn from Tony Sirna, 'How Dancing Rabbit Ecovillage's footprint compares to America's footprint' in Cutting Our Carbon Footprint at DRE site, accessed 28 June 2017

Four Rabbits have summarised their approach in the following inter-connected points:

Basically we do as much as we can to reduce our impact on the earth.

We do this, not only by making serious changes in our daily lives but also by working together to create a new culture.

A culture that supports and encourages its members to live more consciously...

... that encourages experimentation and that offers lots of opportunities for creativity, compassion and connection.[50]

ON THE 'ECOVILLAGE'

The four ecovillages sketched here have received acclaim in independent environmental sustainability analyses and evaluations. The Lammas ecovillage made the 2014 'Top 10' *Guardian* list of eco-homes – selected with specialist advice from authorities such as the UK Green Building Council and the BREEAM building development standard agency. Furthermore, Lammas attracted a £346,935 award from the Department of Energy and Climate Change (late 2009) to build their Community Hub. Besides fame throughout Ireland – winning the National Green Award for Ireland's greenest community every year from 2012 to 2014 – Cloughjordan Ecovillage was a gold medal winner at the 2013 International Awards for Liveable Communities (the 'Green Oscars') supported by the UN Environmental Program. Ecovillage researcher Litfin has referred to LAEV as 'Eden', behind the 'unremarkable' façades of its urban apartment blocks, and lauds its 'huge ripple effect'. Furthermore, DRE featured in a 2005 episode of a US reality TV show, '30 Days', which aired internationally and followed ordinary people learning how to live at DRE.[51]

Nevertheless, all of these ecovillages faltered at some time or another. The decisive move interstate saw several participants withdraw from DRE and, soon after their land purchase, conflicts and departures shrank the group to just four members in 1998. Yet, by 1999, its population started a long upward swing to 75 in 2014.[52] Perhaps the Sandhill connection was crucial to its survival. It is hard not to remark, too, that DRE remains far from having the great number of members anticipated by its founders. Lammas endured a lengthy and tortuous planning process, and had to overcome an uncomfortable anti-Lammas campaign by certain locals.[53] LAEV is not the type of urban environment that many people feel comfortable about raising children in, but the ecovillage has lived with and accepted this detraction while continuing to work with numbers of families in the local area.[54] In 2007, Cloughjordan found it critically necessary to substantially revise its governance system.[55] In reality, challenges are endemic even to successful, complex and novel collaborative communities.

Size

There are many well-known ecovillages that are larger or smaller than those presented here. Populations rise and fall as different residents enter and exit. In the more substantial range, Crystal Waters (Australia) had a population of more than 200 residents in 2016; Sieben Linden (Germany) had 140 in 2017 (aiming for around 300); Ecovillage at Ithaca (New York) had more than 175 in 2016; Svanholm (Denmark) had 150 in 2015; and Findhorn (Scotland) had more than 210 members, 120 coworkers (many living onsite) with 200 local residents regularly involved in mid-June 2017. Most ecovillages' informative websites include legal and historical detail on their formal association, planning, finances and governance. This detail is often sufficient, for those interested, to shortlist ones with attractive features for the purposes of a tour.[56]

Diversity

Ecovillages in general have been criticised for not being sufficiently diverse and, contradictorily, for not representing their immediate locality enough, in terms of age, culture, and educational and income levels.[57] That certain ecovillages are primarily made up of migrants, a greater proportion of professionals, or speakers of one particular language is hardly surprising. Do such characteristics make these experimental socio-material laboratories failures? How far do any such characteristics invalidate what their participants set out to do which, most commonly, is to show that other, more environmentally sustainable and socially satisfying, ways of living are possible?

All the ecovillages considered here were started by tiny groups of people, many who met as activists. Three of the four ecovillages were established in 'new lands' by non-locals and even LAEV members already living in Los Angeles started by spending time and effort engaging directly with their immediate neighbours so both felt informed and comfortable as they established their collaborative living experiment. All these communities are not just locally, but also globally, active, especially in educational work. Equally they have striven to root themselves in their built and natural environments by applying ecologically sound principles.

Sustainability

The ecovillages discussed here were selected for examination partly on the basis of their post-occupancy results, what environmental savings householders are really making, not merely the potential pre-occupancy building standard potential of dwellings that regular ratings systems measure, or prospective targets made when communities form. In a review of studies of the carbon footprints per capita of residents in 16 intentional communities, Daley found that, on average, their impact was one-third of local, regional or national comparison averages, with Sieben Linden around one-quarter of the German average.[58]

Using a life-cycle assessment of energy used in three US ecovillages – Ecovillage at Ithaca (New York), Earthaven (Black Mountain, North Carolina) and Sirius (Shutesbury, Massachusetts) – Jesse Sherry has calculated that, if all US households reduced their energy consumption to the average level of those ecovillages, it would save the US more than one billion tons of CO_2 emissions per annum. Based on results from all three ecovillages, the average resident wasted much less than the average US resident, as the following proportions show: paper (16 per cent); glass (13 per cent); metals (15 per cent); plastics (11 per cent); rubber, leather and textiles (57 per cent); wood (4 per cent); yard trimmings (5 per cent); food scraps (3 per cent); other (25 per cent). Sherry attributes the ecovillages' achievements to both 'fostering community and restoring nature'.[59]

Real-world living laboratories

Ecovillages are not micro-societies, nor is a sustainable planet likely to evolve simply from scaling up ecovillages. Many ecovillages have put into practice ideas for doing all kinds of things differently and are accurately described as experimental socio-material 'living laboratories' for sustainable futures.[60] They are, in effect, laboratories of participatory action research and, as such, have even been referred to as 'communities of practice'.[61] They have led innovations in techniques, technologies and relationships for sustainable living. Most importantly, they provide experiential opportunities for a range of short and long-term visitors to observe and engage and live with their residents – to learn what it really feels like to live in alternative ways. The significance of offering such opportunities cannot be underestimated: unless vast numbers of people reduce their ecological footprints, we will experience rising global climate temperatures and natural re-balancing dynamics that might well pose conditions that make human life on Earth impossible.

To nest themselves in their environments, ecovillages have challenged planning and legal options, policy directions and regulations, and many have successfully co-developed models that are readily transferrable for adoption elsewhere. DRE highlights the planning barriers negatively, its founders simply moving interstate to specifically avoid planning limits. LAEV took on the urban planning authority status quo by deterring and tempering the behaviour of car drivers in their area, campaigning for bicycles to be taken seriously as a transport mode in Los Angeles more generally as well as successfully protesting against an inappropriate school development that was proposed opposite their buildings by constructively finding a better alternative local site. Lammas and other such communities have proactively acted as constructive test cases bringing planners, advocates and proposers of such eco-communities together either to change or create additional legislation and provide professionals with models to more easily incorporate, zone and create standards for such communities. These kinds of topics are discussed further in the next chapter.

Many ecovillagers are bent on creating a seemingly impossible synergy between market and ecological dynamics. This is a trapeze act that guidelines such as the Welsh 'One Planet Development' policy might seem to avoid – through an orientation around self-provisioning and material ecological footprint metrics – but the calculations on which the land per capita use are based incorporate simply indicative monetary (price-oriented) units.[62] Still, the Lammas approach is clearly based on 'use values' (qualities and measures that are quality-specific), rather than 'exchange values', where the price is the only or predominant value considered – so many decisions by ecovillage practitioners are relatively free of a market framework.

Cloughjordan is the most market-oriented of the four ecovillages discussed and the least affordable. The implications of integration with mainstream markets is the main theme in Chapter 8 whereas Chapter 9 centres on groups, such as squatters, who have continued to challenge the deep structures of ownership and private property rights as cultural, political, and economic barriers to achieving collective sustainability and stewardship of nature. In the following three chapters, coursing our way through this maelstrom of powerful and energetic community-based, state and market actors, we weave three distinct future directions for collaborative and sustainable housing, such as ecovillages.

PART III

Futures: Scaling Up, Shared Landscapes, Shared Livelihoods

'Will You Dance with Us?' Governments and Collaborative Housing

Three drivers and trajectories characterise the future of collaborative housing, such as eco-cohousing, ecovillages, collectively managed ('self-managed') social housing and self-build collectives. The state, the market and grassroots communities play together in complex partnerships that tend to be dominated by a particular actor, especially at distinct stages of their development.

This initial chapter of Part III is concerned with government interventions that provide crucial financial or in-kind support for collaborative housing with shallow environmental benefits that arise coincidentally with sharing and for deeper environmentally oriented collaborative housing, 'eco-collaborative housing'. Chapter 8 will analyse a suite of substantially pre-planned market- and private-property-driven community-oriented eco-cohousing projects into which householders buy. In contrast, grassroots eco-collaborative communities examined in Chapter 9 have developed with substantial autonomy from governments and the market, with the community housing group firmly in the driving seat.

OVERTURES BETWEEN CITIZEN GROUPS AND GOVERNMENTS

For cynical and logical reasons, governments and their housing, planning and welfare agencies have become interested in collaborative housing. Ironically, from a neoliberal perspective where individuals are expected to cater as much as possible for themselves, the solidarity and sharing of community-driven models offer social welfare solutions to meet mundane needs. Community initiatives save government money by supplying inexpensive ways to address numerous contemporary challenges, such as improving the sustainability of the built environment; enhancing sustainability practices of householders; creating more liveable neighbourhoods; embedding climate-responsive design; providing affordable private and social housing options; supporting 'aging-in-place' and offering community-based low-level care by volunteers for those with any kinds of special needs; and fulfilling neighbourhood mix, inclusion and integration policies.[1] Today state policy interest in senior cohousing is a worldwide trend.

Such policy agendas refer to models developed well before neoliberal approaches were applied in the 1980s. Since the 1960s and 1970s, community-driven initiatives in a range of cities and rural areas have sought government planning, financial or in-kind support for housing and household types that are co-produced by prospective residents and relevant experts, and subsequently co-managed by their community of residents who share amenities, facilities and spaces.[2] However, as in the case of certain low impact communities in the United Kingdom (UK), more socially and environmentally radical initiatives have existed 'under the radar' or neglected by authorities, their exposure risking forced abandonment or deconstruction.

Citizen groups wanting to pursue collaborative housing have faced considerable planning, building and financial barriers, even in countries such as Germany where government support is long-established. Collaborative housing models integrate a plethora of players, and their plans and proposals are complex and multidimensional. Falling outside the eligibility criteria and principles of both planning and financial models for houses and households, many collaborative housing projects have relied on state financial agencies or state-guaranteed financing in the early years of their development. Projects with multiple dwellings require massive investments up-front, well before residents move in, which complicates financial arrangements for lenders and borrowers. Thus, groups look to governments to guarantee, partly fund or otherwise support such arrangements.

Furthermore, issues of scale in governmental responsibility and power can frustrate progress; while community-based projects face local authorities to plead their case, many planning, zoning and building regulations are based on national and provincial standards or guidelines. Local authorities might make case-by-case exceptions for, or supplementary planning and building regulations to embrace, more collaborative housing options but, frequently, financial institutions of national or international scale remain resistant to applications that, from a market-based perspective, appear marginal, with additional and hard to quantify levels of risk.

Until specific schemes were set up in certain regions, garnering government support often required strong advocacy skills, specialist knowledge, time and effort so only activists driven by passion and conviction won the day. Other citizens squatted disused public sites or private buildings of historic significance, protesting for both their preservation and affordable housing. Without occupation, other citizens have stridently argued for keeping public property for social purposes and environmental benefits rather than watch its sale to private developers, destroying public heritage for private profits. Ideally, negotiated settlements ensued, involving, for example, government permission to use land for socially advantageous housing for a peppercorn rental, the granting of land, or land sales considerably below market rates and allowing time for communities to arrange finance.

European governments, in particular, rationalised sponsorship to communities for performing conservation, cultural and outreach services, and providing facilities and spaces open to the wider public. Most recently, collaborative housing projects have been identified as ways for governments to fulfil affordable eco-housing policies. In short, governments responding to community-driven demands have led to government-enabled, government-supported and, finally, even government-driven projects. Thus, this chapter examines a range of initiatives that recognise citizens' rights to affordable, sustainable and community-based housing and to environmentally sustainable districts and neighbourhoods developed in public–private partnerships incorporating affordable eco-cohousing.

First, I discuss how governments started supporting intentional communities and Scandinavian governments assisted the development of cohousing types of collaborative housing from the 1980s. Second, I outline the kinds of collaborative housing that current structures prohibit or make difficult to achieve, as such delaying – often completely putting off – groups realising such visions. Third, I identify certain building and planning breakthroughs, as well as financial models suitable for international uptake in locally, regionally and nationally modified and adapted forms. Fourth, focusing on the present, I refer to supportive networks and umbrella organisations for collaborative housing that governments would do well to finance for a range of public benefits. A

short conclusion features a table indicating typical drivers of collaborative housing efforts that, among other functions, makes sense of the way
Part III is structured.

CRADLES OF COLLABORATIVE HOUSING

For millennia intentional communities evolved to pursue philosophical,
religious and political aims and to avoid persecution. Many coincidentally integrated sustainability principles in the form of simple living
and collective sufficiency, either for doctrinal or pragmatic reasons
because, despite private institutional and voluntary donations, many
were essentially self-supporting. However, with the revolutionary
ferment of the second half of the nineteenth century and cooperative
ventures in a range of sectors, certain governments began to support
utopian settlements. Historian Bill Metcalf refers to efforts by the state
'in Australia in the 1890s, New Zealand in the 1970s, and Palestine/Israel
for much of this century'.[3]

Indeed, up to 2 per cent of Israel's population still live in kibbutzim,
collective communities typically based on agriculture, although only
around one-third are still income-sharing. After a decline, since the
1980s kibbutzim have experienced a range of reforms, adaptations
and resurgence of interest from young parents wishing to live in more
affordable, rural and community-oriented ways. Kibbutzim are not
dealt with here due to their religious and state specificity, which hinders
transference and, therefore, relevance to this study. In contrast, Metcalf
contends that intentional communities flourishing in the last half
century have tended to be secular, even if utopian to the extent that
they frequently pursue environmental sustainability in their everyday
practices.[4]

Given that this chapter refers to a range of models in various regions, it
is important to iterate that certain legal terms for distinct kinds of collaborative housing, ownership and sharing arrangements have developed
in particular municipal and national contexts, sometimes confusingly
bearing similar names across jurisdictions where regulations, practices
and technicalities differ markedly. As discussed in Chapter 5 regarding
the scope of cohousing, 'housing cooperative' refers to many different
kinds of relationships and housing tenures. Indeed, in one article
Vestbro understandably rules 'cooperative housing' out of discussions of
'alternative ways of living and building with shared facilities' altogether.

Yet, a cooperative legal form has been used for diverse projects stretching from state- and market-oriented models of governance, and from social housing and cohousing through to communes, including the intentional community Commonground that, in the mid-1990s, Bill Metcalf nominated as the most radical case presented in his classic Australian collection.[5]

Irrespective of distinct legal terms, this book aims to be specific regarding essential types of housing and households (see glossary). Furthermore, for reasons of space, generic legal models, along with differences and complexities between jurisdictions, are ignored because the primary barriers to collaborative housing involve planning and financing. Appendix 1 includes a select list of legal references and links for interested readers.

Short descriptions of outstanding state support in three co-located countries follow. They indicate how social movements informed the demand for cohousing and how important government support has been to enable, and impede or deter, interested citizens to realise their dreams for collaborative housing.

Denmark: the cradle of cohousing

The initial development of government-supported 'cohousing' in Denmark during the 1980s was secular and social in its orientation and purposes. Many proponents were attracted by its emancipatory opportunities, especially for gender roles and collective organisation of households. Rather than wrangle privately with a partner over household duties, a formal and collaborative approach to domestic chores and caring tasks promised greater responsibility and accountability. Furthermore, sharing child-care and playing spaces had potential for more efficient co-parenting, and parental support for singles, sole parents and couples alike.

Thus, architect-crafted collaborative living of the cohousing type found today in North America evolved through discussions in Denmark in the 1960s and took root there in the 1970s. By 1982, 22 Danish owner-occupied cohousing projects had been established. Professional support from the 'live together' (SAMBO) association (1978–) and national Cooperative Housing Association Law (1981) facilitated financial backing through state-sponsored loans. Banks perceived pre-sales an advantage. In recent decades, cohousing complexes show reduced household dwelling sizes in favour of increases in collective facilities – making them more compact, sustainable and affordable.[6]

Estimates of the proportion of Danes living in such housing settle around 5 per cent, the greatest proportion in any country in the mid-2010s. Danish seniors' 'collective housing' accommodates just over 1 per cent of Danes more than 50 years old. In 2010, there were around 350 units with 5–156 dwellings (15–30 dwellings on average) supplemented by 140 or so similar units of intergenerational communities that conscientiously integrated seniors.

Kähler has referred to the eco-cohousing of Munksøgård (Roskilde) as a 'very good compromise' between these two models. There seniors are housed together in one 20-dwelling cluster of an intergenerational settlement of five distinct clusters, each with their own common house. Munksøgård owner-occupiers, cooperative members and renters integrate activities across their separate neighbourhoods, and all support an organic farm.[7] Such well-established seniors' models are attractive to other governments in as much as they successfully address welfare and housing challenges associated with aging populations.

Sweden[8]

Vestbro's short history of Swedish collaborative housing starts in 1935, in Stockholm, with a privately developed, multi-storey block of 54 serviced apartments that he describes as a 'modernist collective' or 'functionalist cohousing'. A radical 1970s development with a similar 'cohouse' (Hässelby Family Hotel) had collective self-provisioning taking over services once supplied by workers. Later, a ground-breaking 'self-work model' in a renovated municipal housing company building in Stacken (Gothburg, 1979) was inspired by the Bo I Gemenskap (BiG, 'Live in Community', 1977–) 'working-together' model which, as in Denmark, responded to household re-organisation as more women worked outside home.

A spate of cohousing followed in Stockholm because, in 1980, the city started to take a serious interest in it – soliciting three public municipal housing companies to develop distinct models. Consequently, Kärnekull reports that between 1983 and 1993 more than 1000 apartments concentrated in 19 building complexes were characterised by affordability, central kitchen and dining areas, a range of rooms for working and playing, and municipal kindergartens. (Similarly, a Dutch cohousing agency facilitated partnerships with housing companies for tenanted cohousing during the 1980s though, after 2000, support diminished just to financing assistance.) Then, in the 1990s, the municipal housing company Färdknäppen became a prominent builder and owner of a Swedish version of seniors cohousing, the 'second half of life model' for those 40 years and over without dependent children.

Although a 2009 survey indicated that around 10 per cent of Swedes were attracted to cohousing, at that time, there were only about 45 cases on the self-work model and two-thirds were owned by municipal authorities. Vestbro identifies this kind of government backing as 'almost unique' to Sweden, in sharp contrast to the almost exclusively private cohousing model in North America. He explains the universally low uptake of cohousing, based as it is on equality, as mainly attributable to a patriarchal culture. Indeed, around 20 per cent of the self-work cohousing projects developed in the 1980s were, at a later date, 'de-collectivised'.

Despite the neoliberal trend for cash-strapped councils to pass housing provision more to market-based companies, public companies remain attractive to Swedish cohousing groups because, even though such companies need to make a profit, they are subject to political directives. Of course, housing companies such as Familjebostäder (Stockholm) offer assistance only where an incipient cohousing community is already proactive. Thus, government is best described as 'responsive'. Even so, Kärnekull reports that smaller groups have difficulty attracting support because larger groups are preferred by the housing companies, which have no competition given that private housing firms 'show no interest in collective buildings' and land is a prohibitive cost without financial support.

Typically, Swedish state-owned cohousing was vertical stacks in urban centres. By way of an example, Lietaert pointed to Stoplyckan (Linköping), with 184 apartments in 13 tall buildings housing more than 400 residents, and its efficient arrangement with public healthcare companies that co-rented shared spaces to work in, the residents enjoying them outside business hours. This critical mass enabled a multiplicity of group activities and legitimised the establishment of two adjacent childcare centres.

Germany

Especially due to the leadership of city municipalities such as Berlin, Tübingen, Freiburg and Hamburg, Germany has been a leader in practical legislative, financial and policy models for enabling a range of types of collaborative housing in response to strong community-based pressure. So much so that Droste has argued that the scale of realised projects and 'the emergence of entire co-housing neighbourhoods' indicates that municipalities need to consider mainstreaming this approach rather than leaving it a niche development. In fact, more progressive cities offer substantial pathways for collaborative housing models: Hamburg will sell land to groups at market prices but is prepared to delay the sale for up to, say, one year; Freiburg reserves 20 per cent of land for such housing.[9]

German state support for collaborative living has been seen as an affordable housing strategy. Yet, left-wing criticism pivots on rearguard action to expand as well as protect further incursions on low-income social housing. The associated criticism that collaborative housing is a gentrifying force is shallow given that gentrification is a function of market forces[10]; gentrification is a function of unmet demand, which would disappear if the demand were satiated. A more reasonable argument combines cohousing with demands for social housing as a matter of choice and in recognition of its various co-benefits.

Indeed, Droste confirms many co-benefits of collaborative housing, including that, as 'a part of strategic housing policies, it contributes to relieving some of the burdens of social-welfare provision'. The Chair of the German community housing association Forum Gemeinschaftliches Wohnen, Albrecht Göschel, has distinguished collaborative housing from family-based and service-based public approaches to seniors. As a form of self-help and mutual management, collaborative housing is essentially a case of 'alternative production of personal services' that offers a third, cooperative, way. Caring is not specific to cohousing for seniors and other philanthropic and government-assisted collaborative housing; many wholly self-funded cohousing projects are intentionally inclusive across abilities, ages and income, and share responsibilities for those with special needs. They also offer local, public, facilities as part of the vibrancy and space advantages of community-based settlement.[11]

Despite such benefits, German state progress has been patchy and inadequate – especially in collaborating with groups as co-generators. Tummers explains this in terms of the failure of the planning profession worldwide to include genuine processes of engagement in their suite of learned and applied skills: 'the position of inhabitants is often weak, despite legal consultation requirements' and, as such, the kinds of co-creation required by collaborative housing projects 'presents a serious challenge to the current top-down planning cultures'.[12]

Berlin's lead has been partly due to authorities building on a tradition of housing cooperatives since the nineteenth century, and the revitalisation of the 10 per cent of cooperatively owned housing stock by a twenty-first century model of active resident participation. Furthermore, between the mid-1980s and 2000, Berlin ran a *Wohnungspolitische Selbsthilfe* (self-build housing) program offering financial and institutional assistance to hundreds of self-managing groups, formalising and integrating squats and bottom-up collective housing initiatives that appeared aplenty with re-unification. As LaFond has said, 'the city became a fantastic field of play for alternative projects, which cemented the local Co-Housing culture'.[13]

PLANNING FRUSTRATIONS

Today, many observe how rigid planning forces United States (US) residents to conform to a single house or apartment structure, and how legal contracts and state policies make 'families' and 'family households' central, despite the fact that they are no longer the standard unit. Orsi et al. offer a shortlist of shared housing proposals in need, and receipt, of US government municipal authority support, confirming that 'density restrictions, minimum lot and home size requirements, outmoded permitting and fee structures, parking space requirements, and other zoning barriers prevent cities from benefiting from the range of shared housing models citizens may want to pursue'.[14] These statements apply to many other cities in Canada, Australia, the UK and New Zealand, even if the detail on hurdles vary from case to case.

Policies for Sharable Cities urged a relaxing of restrictions to developing accessory dwelling units (self-contained spaces within a dwelling or on a lot in addition to the main dwelling) and rental arrangements with nonrelated people that would allow more households or householders to jointly share space and other facilities and services. Similarly, allowing for the consolidation in clusters of micro-apartments, tiny houses, small alternative dwellings (such as container abodes) might create opportunities to maximise access to shared amenities contributing to environmental sustainability and affordability. Congratulating Amherst (Massachusetts) zoning ordinance allowing for collaborative housing as a model, and Canadian examples of approvals for ecovillages (both described further below), the report argued for city authorities to 'require or incentivize clustering housing around central courtyards' and 'the inclusion of common areas and common houses designed for shared activities' – as in the case of a development associated with the University of Minnesota.[15]

Other examples of frustrations to, and recommendations for, collaborative living abound. An Australian study of boarding houses and residential parks (where caravans and manufactured mobile homes are semi-permanently parked through rental or ownership of a lot) revealed that many, especially seniors, enjoyed living in such communities provided rules and management were fair, even-handed and responsive to residents' input. The study revealed younger residents supporting older ones, not just individual garden lots but also community gardens, and that a simple life could prove comfortable and enjoyable. Many interviewees mentioned the co-benefits of living as a community: 'Everyone sort of helps each other ... the lifestyle is absolutely fantastic'; 'so many of my neighbours have stepped in to help give me a hand'. Still, in other cases, exploitation and social and physical risks prevailed. A general insecurity related to the fact that many privately, and publicly, owned parks are eventually sold.[16] Significantly, one set of residents in a coastal New South Wales park threatened with closure commissioned an independent feasibility report for government to show how they might collectively buy and own, or lease, the park in a self-managed way. While unsuccessful in gaining necessary state support, they revealed unmet demand and social capacity.[17]

Squatters, those living on barges or other kinds of houseboats, and residents of all kinds of mobile dwellings on sites that regulators have allowed to be available for 'temporary use' or 'meanwhile use' (where land is vacant due to a long resale or pre-development process) could be catered for by legislation that would protect all parties. The rarely enacted British Empty Dwelling Management Order has potential use in this way, especially given that by the mid-2010s more than 240,000 households were living in overcrowded conditions while 600,000 dwellings were vacant.[18] The UK Commission for Architecture and the Built Environment, dissolved early in 2012, had campaigned for new, shorter, simpler and clearer sets of home-building and planning regulations, with separate processes for assessment.[19] Certainly new, complementary or supplementary codes are required to account for current needs, as in the short set of exemplary planning and financial breakthroughs that follow.

EUROPEAN PROGRESS

This section aims to show how government agencies have engaged in various ways with community groups to support the realisation of collaborative housing projects.

Germany

Privately owned dwellings and collective ownership of shared spaces characterise many *baugemeinschaften* ('community building partnerships' or 'building communities') in Germany and collective self-builds in the Netherlands. Some *baugemeinschaften* only operate collaboratively up until the build ends and have few common facilities. *Baugruppen* are self-administering building groups of owner-occupiers, who collectively buy land and collaboratively design, and sometimes labour on, a multi-household build (*baugruppe*), the architect being pivotal and saving the usual profit-margin. Levels of sharing are determined by each group, including sharing gardens that are accessible to the neighbourhood. Hamiduddin and Gallent suggest that the level of collective self-build activity in Germany is associated with the comparatively high proportion of small building firms and cooperative housing. Moreover, 'the power of speculative providers (especially over the land market) is curtained and group-build is given a chance to flourish'.[20]

Significantly, collaborative housing in Germany has been supported for decades by the federal German Development Bank (Kreditanstalt für Wiederaufbau, KfW) that not only finances collaborative housing ventures as a matter of course but also, in 2016, was offering hefty interest discounts of up to €75,000 per household for sustainability features.[21] These types of schemes have been used to assist projects such as the Klima Solar Haus (2009) the original multi-household passive house in Berlin, where an environmentally friendly communal lifestyle meets high environmental construction and energy-use standards.[22] There are other banks and foundations that support such ventures, such as Nürnberg's green UmweltBank, so financial constraints are limited to eligibility criteria and amounts available for borrowing.

Berlin

Since 1975, around 1000 developments collectively demonstrate that Berlin is the most active collaborative housing urban node in the world. The *Wohnungspolitische Selbsthilfe* program alone seems to have accounted for up to one-third of these initiatives. As such, Droste has referred to Berlin as a 'socio-spatial lab of urban development', replete with different kinds of collaborations that include architects as drivers, proactive government policies, and self-building community groups as developers – all with significant heterogeneity.[23]

Berlin's government has supported the Institute for Creative Sustainability (id22) (2002–), a not-for-profit organisation promoting 'CoHousing' cultures and post-growth initiatives such as community gardening, offering learning opportunities and an interactive website for promotion of projects, networking and sharing data.[24] CoHousing is id22's generic term for collaboratively designed and built housing spaces for multiple households that develop 'self-managed social architectures' to share activities and experiences, not just spaces and resources.[25]

Despite achievements in choice and access to collaborative housing models, the scramble for available land and support remains; generally municipal governments use 'design-based competitive bidding' and evidence of financial feasibility to decide sales of public land to citizen groups. *Selfmade City* presents various progressive collaborative housing and sustainable self-initiated projects in Berlin to identify key aspects as criteria for evaluating proposals to receive government support. Such criteria are useful indicators of sound CoHousing characteristics: neighbourhood and urban interaction; shared space, community and social foci; long-term affordability; open and green spaces; re-use and reactivation; hybrids; quality (re)densification; customised solutions for each generation; investment in ecological building; and future-oriented solutions and experimental models.[26]

Spreefeld, Berlin

The *baugruppe* cooperative housing model of Spreefeld (2011) on the River Spree in Berlin (Figure 7.1) has low- and middle-income resident-members who are, in effect, permanent tenants paying affordable staggered rent, say for 20 years, or until they leave and sell their share (estimated at around 50 per cent equity). They were actively involved in some construction, which focused on simple, straightforward, multi-use interior design. Three apartment blocks with 64 cohousing dwellings (25–150sq m) accommodate around 140 inhabitants, who benefit from sustainable energy-saving features of a passive house standard, generate renewable energy, electric-car-share and enjoy private and community spaces, such as a children's day-care centre; music, guest and carpentry rooms; and dozens of workspaces. At ground level, multi-functional rooms and outdoor spaces are accessible to the public. Communal living is an option in six cluster-apartments with 6–21 residents.[27]

Figure 7.1   Spreefeld: Three blocks of collaborative housing on the River Spree, Berlin

Source: Ute Zscharnt (Berlin), photographer

Despite the success of Spreefeld, Michael LaFond – architect and Spreefeld resident, and director of id22 – has made a generic complaint that 'local government is fairly slow, and not that creative'.[28] Droste agrees that the skills, concerns and programs for encouraging collaborative housing at a municipal level in Germany are patchy, discontinuous and questionable, especially regarding effective and streamlined inter-departmental collaboration.[29] In Berlin, the average dwelling price increased around 55 per cent between 2009 and 2015. Instead of simply selling public land off 'to the highest bidder', municipal readiness and prioritisation of collaborative endeavours in land-use decision-making could support more affordable housing.[30] However, as Tummers points out, engagement skills are not the planning profession's strong suit and groups complain of bureaucratic red tape and patronising, rather than co-generative, approaches.[31]

Tübingen: Mühlenviertel

Governments have a unique capacity to lease or sell public land at reasonable rates for collaborative housing purposes, and their agencies can orchestrate multi-stakeholder partnerships and give projects a formality to reassure financiers. Droste identifies Hamburg and North-Rhine Westphalia, along with Berlin, as proactive state governments. Moreover, Freiburg and Tübingen, both in Baden-Württemberg, have encouraged collective self-development for decades. Building on prior experience of encouraging innovative re-use in small-scale neighbourhood complexes, in 2003 Tübingen authorities developed an urban planning agency responsible for the conversion of the Mill District, Mühlenviertel (2007–2010), pitched as a model for replication elsewhere. Eliason points out that Tübingen housing had become prohibitively expensive by the mid-1990s, whereas the recent collaborative housing model achieved affordability and, despite taking longer, 'a quality of sustainable urbanism very difficult to come by' in mainstream developer-led processes. Tübingen's supervisory agency demonstrated a range of skills, orchestrating multiple actors to fulfil numerous social and sustainability objectives.[32]

The planning agency held a competition among citizens to name the district, encouraging variety and mixed uses. The agency led and arranged multiple *baugemeinschaften* for 250 apartments in 25 clusters with shared community spaces. Future residents, including seniors, participated in designing their dwellings. *Baugemeinschaften* offer experiential opportunities for residents to build skills in community and neighbourhood-making. It is a reliable model: 'banks gladly lend to them'. A set of ten zero-energy and 'energy plus' dwellings established by one *baugemeinschaft* surpassed a proposed 93 per cent coverage of primary energy needs to 103 per cent without high-tech or expensive options. Using wood construction materials, cellulose insulation and natural linoleum on floors, passive house dwellings were designed for energy efficiency using renewable wood, and geothermal and solar photovoltaic energy sources. Homeowners saved on construction costs, which were a reasonable €2000–2800 per square metre.[33]

Vrijburcht, Amsterdam

The Dutch government has had a history of funding and renting large *Centraal Wonen* (cohousing developments) since the 1970s. Many subdivide into clusters of 5–10 dwelling units, with substantial governance over membership and shared facilities, and access to larger spaces held in common for the whole development.[34] Owning 80 per cent of land in its jurisdiction, the City of Amsterdam is a powerful landlord, typically leasing tracts from one to 50 years. This unusual level of control over land use prevents a highly speculative market arising. Annual ground lease is paid but the leasehold is negotiable and can secure a mortgage, expanding opportunities for supporting collaborative living. For instance, in 2002, a site was leased for 50 years to a successful competing group proposing affordable housing with live-cum-work spaces. Designed in a participatory way with prospective residents, they worked with radical architect Hein de Haan (CASA Architects), who was already highly experienced in designing public and social housing. Subsequently, Vrijburcht became a collective self-build model of pride to Amsterdam authorities because of its size (52 dwellings) and location in a diverse mixed neighbourhood that features other, if smaller, collaborative housing projects.[35]

GLOBAL–LOCAL: ONE PLANET AND LOW IMPACT DEVELOPMENTS

Low impact communities and low impact developments (LIDs) aim to create laudable whole-of-life equilibrium with their productively used natural surrounds yet they face considerable planning and financial challenges.

Planning for low impact developments

As outlined in Chapter 6, Lammas ecovillage struggled with planners and planning legislation contributing to the evolution of the ground-breaking Welsh 'One Planet Development' (OPD) policy. By way of an example, the Undercroft house 'largely constructed from sustainable timber, stone and earth on the land and placed to maximise natural energy flows, such as solar gain' exemplifies a plethora of hurdles in the Lammas – and similar – applications. Despite the fact that its embodied energy exceeded government targets 'both in its construction and future-proofing possible effects and disruptions of climate change', Dale reports that 'the materials and construction techniques met considerable resistance from building regulations which operate under the strictures of industrial, global standardisation'.[36]

The OPD policy was instituted in 2011. Just 23 applications (including the nine from Lammas residents) had been successful by mid-2016, with five in process at 22 May 2017.[37] Moreover, in October 2016, a three-bedroom Lammas home featured on Kevin McCloud's Channel 4 series *Grand Designs*. A massive collective effort, the straw bale and timber home used only £27,000 worth of materials but cost an extra £5,000 to feed the 277 volunteers assisting in its build. McCloud endorsed it as 'how we could and should live' and referred to their accomplishment as 'a clarion call'.[38]

Indeed, the introductory context statement of the OPD practice notes, published alongside an ecological footprint template, spreadsheet and further advice for local authorities and applicants, reads:

> The Welsh Government's Sustainable Development Scheme, 'One Wales: One Planet' has an objective that, within the lifetime of a generation, Wales should use only its fair share of the earth's resources, with its ecological footprint reduced to the global average availability of resources of 1.88 global hectares per person (the global availability of resources in 2007). This is a very challenging but necessary target.[39]

Similarly, Paragraph 4.15.1 of the relevant technical advice note (2010) refers to the OPD as an application of LID, 'zero carbon in both construction and use' and a 'potentially exemplar type of sustainable development'. The notes outline requirements for 'robust evidence' and justification that a formally constituted community could collectively provision for its basic needs within five years of approval. Consent is conditional on a legally binding agreement focusing on a development-specific management plan, that includes several elements:

- *Business and Improvement plan* to identify whether there is a need to live on the site and establish the level of the inhabitants' requirements in terms of income, food energy and waste assimilation that can be obtained directly from the site

- *Ecological footprint analysis* of the development
- *Carbon analysis* of the development
- *Biodiversity and landscape assessment*
- *Community impact assessment* to identify potential impacts on the host community (both positive and negative) and provide a basis to identify and implement any mitigation measures that may be necessary
- *Transport assessment and travel plan* to identify the transport needs of the inhabitants and propose sustainable travel solutions.[40]

The practice notes duly spell out expectations in addressing each element, referring to OPD as beyond 'a physical development', 'a way of living differently', and laying out best practice for planners to effectively engage with and advise future applicants and assist in fostering 'understanding and trust'. Permaculture is identified as 'intrinsically site-based and focused on low environmental impacts'. There is due concern with assessments of the land as capable of supporting its prospective inhabitants and acceptance that mobile and canvas structures such as caravans and tents are, ecologically speaking, light-footed.[41]

In short, this legislation shows remarkable conceptual and practical advances in understanding the needs of future sustainability and the appropriate kinds of skills and approaches planners need to adopt. While a Welsh OPD does not need to be collaborative, unusually for planning codes, the policy acknowledges and accounts for them: three of five defined OPD types are majorly collaborative. Beyond singular self-sufficient households and agriculture-oriented enterprises that are self-provisioning, they identify small clusters of dwellings with a modicum of shared activities and facilities through to either small or large planned communities with 'economies of scale and cooperation' that involve substantial collaborative activities and facilities. All are self-provisioning but in more collective ways than the simpler stand-alone types. At the same time, a further category of 'loose networks' is recognised – associations between OPDs, say for cooperatively value-adding, sharing equipment or distribution. Inclusion of such a category is indicative of the policymakers' big-picture and long-term view and expectation that OPDs are outward-looking and inclusive.[42]

Simon Fairlie, who coined 'low impact development', has criticised the OPD policy for being 'so prescriptive', suggesting it 'actually makes it harder rather than easier for land-based LIDs to get permission'. Still, the OPD only applies in Wales. While Fairlie reports that 'most competent low impact smallholdings manage to acquire permission' even if on appeal, he suggests building a LID in England and, later, applying for permission. Indeed, Pickering has pointed out that Lammas was the exception, the 'first eco-village in Britain to be built legally, rather than requiring retrospective planning permission'. Fairlie explains the barriers to many attracted, but ultimately deterred, groups as first, the necessity of a loyal driver with boundless energy; second, that the mainstream application process is so arduous that 'it is hard to find people who will stay the course' (say, sitting it out for five years); third, the costs of conforming to bureaucratic details blows out the budget; fourth, in reality, the LID method is to make it up as you go, such as by obtaining at-hand, local, reusable material that might depart from the original plan but is appropriate.[43]

Financing low impact communities

A significant disadvantage of illegal and ad hoc construction is the inability to gain financing. Financial assistance is less necessary with the level of sweat equity common to LIDs, but obtaining fertile land in an increasingly expensive market and necessary processing of agricultural produce make funding a useful, even critically needed, option. Today, a few financial institutions operate in the UK that are prepared to assist with funding collaborative housing projects, such as the Dutch Triodos bank, the Ecology Building Society and the Co-operative Bank. Moreover, there are more financing models, such as communal fund rotating loans or individual private loans guaranteed by the community.

A community housing association or philanthropic organisation might grant funds or advance finance for land, say on the basis that they will own rental properties in the final development for low-income social housing. Half of the 14 dwellings of the eco-cohousing Threshold Centre in Gillingham (UK) – legally a company limited by shares – are owned by a local housing association under such an arrangement. Radical Routes, a secondary or umbrella cooperative of British housing cooperatives, functions to finance cooperative housing that is infused with social and environmental values.[44]

The not-for-profit Leeds housing cooperative Lilac (low impact living affordable community) (discussed in Chapter 5) adopted an equity-based share/leaseholder Mutual Home Ownership Society (MHOS) legal structure. The MHOS owns the property and structures via a long-term mortgage provided by Triodos. Every member-resident pays the MHOS a 10 per cent deposit based on the total of equity shares proportionate to income and built dwelling cost:

> Members of Lilac pay their housing costs through the purchase of equity units. Every member pays around 35% of their monthly net income, and the income from these payments pays off the mortgage that financed the land and development costs. In addition, Lilac has chosen to detach the value of the equity units from the property value, removing the possibility of speculative investment. Instead, the value of Lilac equity units is linked to earnings ensuring they remain affordable in perpetuity.

This model has similarities with community land trust (CLT) models, many of which operate in North America. CLTs tend to use a collective financing model and try to insulate subsequent member purchases from increases in market value. Lilac bought its site from the Leeds City Council at a market price but half the cost was deferred and they received significant funding to decontaminate the site and for a trial straw construction (from the UK Homes and Communities Agency). Significantly, Leeds had councillors proactive in promoting self-build and cohousing.[45]

FROM ENVIRONMENTAL LIVING ZONES TO TWENTY-FIRST CENTURY ECOVILLAGES

A number of collaborative housing initiatives have prompted specific planning legislation or new ways of engaging with citizens by planners that serve as models for transference or adaption. Certain exemplary initiatives follow.

Environmental Living Zone

Round the Bend Conservation Co-operative (RBCC) in Christmas Hills, Victoria (Australia), started in 1971. Thirty-two shareholders jointly purchased 326 acres (132 hectares) of land – in what has become the peri-urban fringe of the state capital, Melbourne – for the purpose of protecting and conserving its indigenous Box Ironbark woodland ecology by living there with minimal impact. RBCC states that conservation is 'what we do', cooperation is 'how we do it' and governance refers to the structure and process for achieving their land-management objectives. Some examples follow. No pets, such as dogs and cats, are allowed. Any planting outside a carefully defined kitchen garden associated with each house site must be indigenous plants of local provenance. When tree branches, leaves, bark and trunks fall they must be left to function variously, for instance, as native animal habitat, compost, and to create shadow for delicate indigenous plants to grow and flower. There are no fences. All dwellings (sited on the upper slopes of three ridges) must be built out of materials that minimise ecological and visual impact on the landscape. Resident full members perform many collaborative activities such as weed control and bushfire prevention. Furthermore, purchasing a site is comparatively cheap and self-built houses are especially affordable.[46]

In the 1960s, local environmental activists – some of whom would found RBCC – formed the Bend of Islands Conservation Association (BICA) to protect the area from flooding for a dam. Later, they campaigned for an environmental living zone with more than 100 properties, double the size of RBCC and including it, based on similar conservation principles. After a great deal of political lobbying their proposal was sanctioned, in 1976, under an interim development order (IDO) of the local planning authority. It took until 1982 for its formalisa-tion as the Bend of Islands Environmental Living Zone (ELZ) when the Victorian *Government Gazette* proclaimed incorporating the IDO within its planning ordinances. These special, low impact, planning provisions were reinstated and superseded by Schedule 2 to the Special Use Zone 2 Environmental Living: Bend of Islands in 1999. While state and local planning bureaucracy took ages to formalise the ELZ model, BICA and RBCC instituted environmental practices in the neighbourhood. Due to weak monitoring by local council and inadequate resourcing to follow up on contraventions to ELZ requirements, the bottom-up vigilance of BICA has been essential. This case suggests that many, especially peri-urban, local communities could work towards turning their areas into ELZs of various types but without bottom-up pressure there is unlikely to be either any formal or effective change.[47]

Eco-neighbourhood

A driver of the permaculture co-housing community Earthsong Eco-Neighbourhood (New Zealand), architect-resident Robin Allison has had a mission to see its principles extended and its learning applied in the local suburban township of Ranui (20km west of Auckland's central business district) and beyond.[48] Thus, Earthsong Stage 2 (2008) completed the total of 32 dwellings (including eco-apartments) and established a common house open to the public. Writing in 2004, just after Stage 1 was completed, Graham Meltzer referred to the 17 relatively small dwellings (averaging 92sq m) made from mudbrick excavated from the site and other materials with high sustainability and health qualities, as 'beautiful' in design, pleasurably 'organic' in character and judged the eco-technology applied to saving water, energy and waste as 'amongst the most comprehensive in cohousing and undoubtedly the best documented'.[49] An action research approach to reporting, reflection and action, and appreciation of being a community eco-neighbourhood shows the potential of such projects to contribute to creating sustainable settlements on Earth.

The Stage 1 development cost NZ$4.2m, with just over NZ$1m contributed by members, and 70 per cent by the private National Bank of New Zealand. A permaculture design for Earthsong Eco-Neighbourhood was retrofitted to the already sensitively designed Stage 1 development. Half of the land was reserved for communal gardening space with productive food plants, including orchards, and native bush subsequently under 'guardian' management by body corporate members. The Earthsong Common House built in Stage 2 functions as the Earthsong Centre, run by a charitable trust drawn from unit owners of the Earthsong Body Corporate and the broader community, with an extensive sustainability-oriented educational program centred on the eco-neighbourhood as a demonstration site.

Because the centre would progress the council's eco-city policy, its construction was supported by a NZ$300,000 interest-free loan from the Waitakere City Council in 2004 (repaid in 2009), and a grant worth over NZ$200,000 from the ASB Community Trust (now Foundation North). Another key financier was the not-for-profit developer firm 'Cohousing New Zealand Limited'. Shareholders are all full members of the eco-neighbourhood. These overlapping but distinct legal entities perform clear functions in delegating and sharing power, responsibilities and financial arrangements relating to the eco-neighbourhood and the wider community, including local government and other government agencies.

Twenty-first-century ecovillages: against, and with, government

Certain ecovillages have developed as appendages to, or in the womb of, traditional villages – revitalising the existing village and co-creating twenty-first-century ecovillages. As described in Chapter 6, Clough-jordan Ecovillage carried the village proper and planning authorities along with them. In contrast, developed under the radar of planning authorities, was the restoration of the abandoned Italian Torri Superiore village, close to the French Riviera, by an intentional community. While unimpeded by regulators and successful, its informality constrained financial opportunities.[50]

Another example of robust self-organisation, that defied the Italian government authorities' post-disaster plan after L'Aquila earthquake (2009), was Pescomaggiore ecovillage, initiated by residents who rejected relocation several kilometres away. Finding half of their town's buildings rendered 'unfit for use' – and the town's historic centre closed by the state – they spontaneously they set up their own temporary tent camp and set about developing their very own 'community resilience initiative', an autonomous ecovillage in the proximity of their severely damaged town. There, using horizontal governance, they created earthquake-proof straw and wood buildings with a mind to localising their economy.[51] Such initiatives are very difficult without government support.

British Columbian (Canadian) municipality authorities rezoned rural and agricultural areas to accommodate Yarrow Ecovillage and O.U.R. Ecovillage. Chilliwack City Council approved the first official 'ecovillage zone' in 2004, to permit development of 40 dwellings, a multi-purpose community building, organic farm, cottage industry, open public and commercial spaces, and an educational centre. The year before, planning authorities managing Shawnigan Lake (Vancouver Island) had rezoned land into a Comprehensive Development Zone for multiple dwellings, an organic farm, food production, ecological restoration and provision of education services. These kinds of zoning changes and developments take time.

Planning authorities often wince at collaborative housing applications because of a lack of precedents or special conditions attached each time. In contrast, Orsi et al. (2013) point to provisions in a zoning ordinance of

Amherst (Massachusetts, US) to accommodate cohousing communities, with their diverse mixes of individual and collective ownership, through an explicitly flexible 'Open Space Community Development' model that also permits complementary non-residential uses and encourages the inclusion of affordable dwellings through density bonuses. Such models enable planners to streamline processes using clear criteria for applicants to address.[52]

As with Cloughjordan, the advantage of such developments is that they revitalise small rural towns or city neighbourhoods. Thus, local authorities – and higher levels of government – avoid having to fund other revitalisation efforts, and infrastructural expenses in such areas benefit a greater population than was the case prior to the collaborative living and working developments.

One remarkable recent development has been the Schloss Templehof ecovillage in Germany. This community purchased an abandoned village in 2010, after zoning issues had been resolved with planning authorities to allow mixed-use developments, including farming, commercial and other working uses, re-use, renovation and extension of buildings. The 27 hectares of farmable land and 4 hectares of buildings could accommodate up to 200 residents – around 150 lived there in mid-late 2016 – developing a self-managed solidarity economy with many employed locally. Since mid-2014, with the first civil society assembly and a representative on the Kressberg village council, their progressive principles for governance are having wider influence. Later in 2014, a new state law allowed experimental buildings, so Templehof started by experimenting with an Earth Ship building.[53]

An example of an enclave urban post-industrial village is Westbeth Artists Housing and Community in New York City, which would not exist were it not for philanthropic support and funding from the US National Council for the Arts (now National Endowment for the Arts). An industrial conversion of 13 historical buildings in Manhattan's Far West Village – once the site of the famous Bell Laboratories (1898–1966) – since 1970, the complex has provided housing and workspaces for just under 400 artists of various kinds, and accommodates a variety of prominent art spaces and organisations. This integrated public-cum-private space has a years-long waiting list for eligible low-income applicants who pay an affordable rent way below market rates for the local area. In this instance, environmentally beneficial building conservation, artistic and urban equity and justice principles co-support one another in one of the world's best-known cities.[54]

Small steps

Finally, I suggest that planners start by making small steps towards more holistic collaborative developments. 'Pocket neighbourhood' approaches might be retrofitted to suburbs where residents want to enhance joint, or even public, use of spaces between dwellings. Pocket neighbourhoods include nineteenth-century pebble and stone rights of way for cars between streets of terraces which, if all stakeholders are in agreement, can be re-used by pedestrians, for children to play and for adults' leisure through bolsters or end gates fitted to eliminate car entry excepting, say, emergency vehicles.

Initiatives designed to satisfy an immediate neighbourhood purpose and, simultaneously, a model for broader planning changes have been called 'tactical urbanism', which applies a classic action-research method and result in a suite of initiatives such as road calming, intersection repair, quirky block improvements and popup spaces (including cafés, benches, parklets and park-mobiles).[55] If communities already work together, it is more feasible to apply other communal approaches, such as retrofitting a neighbourhood renewable-energy generation system, for which technical possibilities have evolved and seem set to expand.

In countries such as Australia, the construction sector and certain urban politicians argue for an ample supply of land to deliver more affordable housing. Even if cheaper to purchase than in urban centres, housing on the distant urban green fringes is typically bereft of infrastructure when house building starts and can remain so for years. Instead, cohousing developments can be prioritised in compact inner-urban infill or brownfield sites. Neighbourhood plans and evaluations might include a checklist including various forms of collaborative living. Moreover, eco-collaborative living offers a beneficial form of land use on boundaries of urban parklands, such as the Can Masdeu squat in Collserolla Natural Park (Barcelona) and the ELZ model (described above) enhancing state conservation goals.[56]

NETWORKS: KNOWLEDGE TRANSFER AND ENGAGEMENT

As governments come to acknowledge that various forms of collaborative housing are legitimate and advantageous practices, public financing of community-managed umbrella organisations is a relatively inexpensive form of support with numerous co-benefits for citizens and state agencies. Zsófia and Komlósi have identified awareness of collaborative housing, research and knowledge transfer of how to do collaborative housing as key steps to expanding cohousing options both in Hungary, where there doesn't seem to be any, and in Switzerland where 5 per cent of housing stock is in some form of collaborative housing. They identify 'the slow planning process, the complex maintenance structure and the unorthodox financial model', and dearth of skilled and confident initiators, as major barriers.[57]

While many projects have websites, giving them global visibility, face-to-face knowledge and skills-sharing and experiences are crucial for learning. National, regional and international networks can offer spaces for community, industry and government to learn and share information about collaborative housing at every level. They can be a key contact point at every stage of a project's development, offering options and contacts for inexperienced players. Habsburg has gone as far as to offer a government agency to provide such services.[58] Moreover, representative and open networks are visible and accessible points for engagement, consultation and negotiation by state authorities, especially for creating appropriate collaborative housing and neighbourhood planning policies, legislation and regulation.

German examples are the Forum for Collaborative Housing (Forum Gemeinschaftliches Wohnen), and the Institute for Creative Sustainability (id22) (2002–) directed by architect and cohousing resident, professor and activist, Michael LaFond, instrumental in co-founding the associated Co-Housing Berlin platform. id22 has 10-day 'Experiment Days' housing fairs that act like a dating pool of stakeholders in search of a collaborative team or groups wanting more residents. id22 has initiated 'experimentcity europe' with the same brief, but a larger canvas and possibilities for transferring effective policies, models and strategies for collaborative housing and urban life, including realising policies for inclusion and rights to the city and housing. Partners in the European platform include nationally representative organisations from Austria, Belgium, Finland, France, Italy, Poland, Romania, Sweden and the UK.[59]

Most other countries have national cohousing and intentional community organisations that promote collaborative housing initiatives through online directories and 'how to' guides, such as Kollectivhus NU, the Swedish National CoHousing Association NOW, established in 1981. As discussed in Chapter 6, the Global Ecovillage Network acts to advocate for and promote ecovillage developments to governments, and has engaged with United Nations agencies for some time.[60] (See Appendix 1: list of websites.) Communities acting as educative models for sustainable and socially progressive community-oriented living have very informative sites often detailing their constitutions, histories, and governance and financial structures.

During 2014–2015, a UK university ESRC-funded seminar series 'Collaborative Housing and Community Resilience', critically involving the UK Cohousing Network, brought together international and national advocates with personal experience, academics and other experts to share their understanding and analyses of collaborative housing along a series of key themes.[61] Such interactions are crucial if collaborative housing is to become a recognised area of intellectual discourse and policy relevance, to facilitate data-gathering and advance understandings of the rich but hidden culture of collaborative housing. As in an earlier cohousing conference in Stockholm (2010), the seminar series demonstrated a 'general consensus concerning the need to mobilise robust comparable data for particular projects, models and the sector as a whole'.[62]

As analysts of negative trends in carbon emissions urge policymakers to deal with affluence (overconsumption), creating policies, processes, legislation and regulation to facilitate eco-collaborative living is appropriate and, even, critical.[63] Daley's literature review of case studies of 30 ecovillage and cohousing ecological footprints concludes not only that 'there is evidence globally to suggest these communities are achieving significant reductions in environmental impact' but also that cohousing, as a 'community level innovative niche, or grassroots innovation', demands examination specifically because of its 'diversity of innovations and sustainable practices that may (or may not) be usefully transferred to mainstream systems'.[64] Lovell has pointed out that 'it is because eco-communities are composed of unfamiliar, radical innovations that demonstrating their work becomes so critical to any strategy aimed at encouraging further action towards sustainable development'.[65]

Similarly, Von Lüpke refers to ecovillagers as 'pioneers for cultural transformation', their practical and creative experimentation with potential futures proving that they 'walk their talk'. He emphasises that they have become a 'low-tech technology developer for the rest of society' and in the 'avant-garde in leading value-based ecological lifestyles, demonstrating to the rest of society that a reduced use of resources and energy can be combined with an actual growth in quality of life'.[66] In the same vein, Joubert has referred to ecovillages as 'precious playgrounds', inspirational demonstrations spaces for sustainable futures.[67] Thus, their learnings and demonstrations are significant in fields way beyond those citizens interested in establishing eco-collaborative housing and the professionals tasked with supporting them.

CONCLUSION

Clearly policies and legislation could, indeed should, be altered and developed to allow and enhance eco-collaborative housing. This would allow not only numerous erstwhile frustrated and demoralised groups to flourish, but also existing groups, such as housing cooperatives, might have the option to transform in collaborative directions, with alternative forms of governance to mainstream hierarchies and silo-specialisation, enabling greater powers of collective organisation.

This final part of *Small is Necessary* focuses on three distinct drivers and directions for eco-community housing and living: 'government', 'market' and 'community'. As most cases show, projects and communities are rarely the result of just one type of driver. Still, many can be categorised as dominantly of a particular type, or their histories characterised by a change in main driver or direction. For example, a government initiative might devolve all ownership and management to the housing community once the project is established. Table 7.1 shows how the interests of drivers are likely to influence models, characteristics and directions.

The typology in Table 7.1 is useful to frame futures for eco-collaborative housing. For instance, if governments fail to support such housing and, especially if land supply and prices remain under pressure and financing of projects is difficult for housing groups, then the generic direction of eco-collaborative housing might well end up relying more on market-based provision, as explored in Chapter 8.

The short history of government-facilitated, government-supported and even government-driven collaborative housing shows a change in agendas of governments after the devastation of the Second World War, when many European governments proactively supported public housing, a priority swept aside by neoliberal currents. Simultaneously driven to accommodate a grassroots demand, and acknowledging their complementarity with urban sustainability principles, contemporary city

Table 7.1 Typology of drivers of eco-collaborative housing models in the twenty-first century

DRIVER: Dominant or Sole Decision-Maker/Owner	Community of Members	Designer–Architects, Sustainability and Building Experts	State Agency and/or NGO	Commercial and/or Financial Interests
Driver's Approaches and Key Interests	Of, for and by the community Directly and collectively decide (plus represent future inhabitants) Deliberation and vision are key – even if the community employs professionals and receives support from government	Professional skills uppermost in applying participatory design and design for sustainability and community Approach community as clients directly or along with a state agency, NGO or commercial interest Developing and demonstrating saleable skill with projects as demonstration sites and construed as models	Generically plan for and regulate models and sites Community householders are clients or co-producers Employ supervisory professionals Regulatory, bureaucratic framework, even if somewhat flexible and creative Criteria: affordable, socially beneficial and environmentally sustainable	Market and private property-based, for profit Centre on selling – even continuously managing – a community-oriented eco-dwelling-precinct Follow pre-existing community- or state-driven models, cherry-picking profitable aspects for inclusion
Generic Examples, Often Illustrative	Eco-cohousing, plus eco-landscape plus eco-community Eco-communes Eco-intentional communities Ecovillages Ecosquats	Twentieth-century cohousing models Twenty-first century ecovillages Community-managed eco-social housing		Twenty-first century ecovillage and cohousing projects

governments such as Berlin have proactively included eco-collaborative housing and neighbourhoods as legitimate urban forms. Yet German collaborative housing activists and researchers have been quick to point out that progress would be facilitated by more government attention. As other governments follow suit and pressures from interested citizens remain strong, a summary statement here can do little more than acknowledge the current state of flux and potential of governments as drivers, not simply facilitators or regulators, of eco-collaborative housing in the future.

8

'To Market, to Market':
Eco-collaborative Housing for Sale

Architects, sustainability experts, developers and building industry entrepreneurs have stepped in to support, lead and even substitute for, resident-based initiatives to create more community-oriented and sustainability-based housing projects. Challenging definitions of collaborative housing as self-organised and community-led housing, market-based interventions present limits and benefits associated with financial arrangements, commercial interests, community values and grassroots control.

This chapter considers certain ways that professional-cum-commercial interests have supported, partnered and led ostensibly community-oriented and environmentally-efficient housing, by focusing on an ecovillage, several cohousing projects and self-build groups. Next, forms of 'marginal' housing are discussed within a wider critique of the market focus of sharing movement notions of a 'sharing city' and 'sharing economy'. Concluding observations introduce themes of genuinely community-led collaborative housing (Chapter 9).

EXPERT-LED 'COLLABORATIVE' HOUSING:
ECOVILLAGE AT CURRUMBIN

From the mid-1980s, Australian and United States (US) planners and developers formed a standard approach to growing suburbs, centring on the formation of master planned estates. Gwyther refers to their 'neo-communitarian' marketing strategy as centring on 'the promise of "community"', including through so-called 'community compacts' (covenants) committing neighbours to conform to certain standards in the presentation and upkeep of their homes. The Ecovillage in Currumbin (Queensland, Australia) replicates this conventional commercial model albeit with a niche green and smart sustainability content.[1]

Developer-led by Land Matters Currumbin Valley, Ecovillage at Currumbin has appeared in the online Fellowship of Intentional Communities directory as a sustainability-oriented housing settlement in the south-eastern section of the Gold Coast region. Half of the 110 hectares under 'community title' is forest regrowth and planted hoop pine reserve while 147 lots with freehold title (450–8000sq m) take up 20 per cent, and the remainder is used for horticulture and recreation. The first house was built in 2006; there were 450 residents a decade later. Plans for the village benefited from detailed advice from a sympathetic council and, in its first decade, the Ecovillage at Currumbin attracted more than 30 international, national and local government and industry awards for sustainability and design, including from the United Nations Association of Australia.[2]

The aim was to establish a sustainable estate by setting a series of conditions on purchasers of lots: air conditioners and pets were banned, heating appliances discouraged, permaculture techniques advised for food gardening, passive thermal building standards, roof water collection for household and onsite use, waste (including sewerage) management onsite, solar and gas energy, and smart metre monitoring for household management. Beyond attracting residents with sustainability values, household practices were modified by such infrastructure. Research conducted after the first few years showed that householders had deliberated over house design and become knowledgeable, skilled and efficient regarding use of water, energy and manual ventilation. Strengers concluded that 'co-management' of environmental resources and services showed resident adaptation to achieve levels of comfort with which they had become 'highly satisfied'.[3]

However, this settlement is 5km from major shopping and commercial centres; without public transport and concerted car-pooling or car-sharing, residents cannot claim strong sustainability achievements in terms of travel. Moreover, unlike genuine eco-cohousing projects, the settlement is spacious and dwellings are large, replete with bathrooms and cars. Houses are neither modest in size nor value.

In 2015, the average house had just 2.7 bedrooms for 2.7 occupants but was 194sq m in size and occupied a lot of 1000sq m. Moreover, in the September quarter 2016, when the mean price of an Australian residential dwelling was around A$610,000, the asking price for one four-bedroom, two-bathroom and two-car garage ecovillage house on a block of 1272sq m in the Ecovillage in Currumbin was A$985,000 (mid-December 2016). Similarly, the owner of another four-bedroom, three-bathroom home with parking for three cars on a 1196sq m ecovillage block was asking A$790,000. Seemingly more modest, was a two-bedroom, one-bathroom and two-car house available on a 475sq m lot for A$599,000. Furthermore, a block of 746sq m with two dwellings – a two-bedroom home and one-bedroom self-contained studio – had sold for A$696,000 in October. A study of the first 64 ecovillage households reported that most fell into the mid- to high-income range; the ecovillage is in an area where median house prices are significantly above the Australian average.[4]

Research data published in 2012 indicated that the average ecovillage household still used 50 per cent (10kWh) of the state average household energy daily consumption (20kWh), although half was sourced from onsite generation. Embodied house energy costs, ecological footprints and broader household consumption data were unavailable. However, householders clearly fell short of the One Planet Living target for limiting energy use followed, say in Westwyck (Melbourne, Australia), another developer-led urban 'ecovillage' (more accurately described as 'eco-cohousing') where a reported 75 per cent savings had been made and all energy used was renewable. Although collected and stored onsite, water use of the average resident of Ecovillage at Currumbin was similar to the state average, indicating few consumption efficiencies.[5]

More than A$30m worth of ecovillage lots had been sold by 2009 when it was being described as a 'model for commercial viability' for building in sustainability into housing developments. The level of developer control and market-orientation was indicated when the Planning Institute of Australia pointed out that, even if they received gratis in-kind support in terms of local planners' attention to the project, Land Matters Currumbin Valley 'deliberately did not seek the financial involvement of government of any level due to a belief that relying on a subsidy would have put the development at the mercy of government'.[6]

One of its developers referred to Ecovillage at Currumbin as 'the future' of the building industry – 'essentially just a very well designed land estate with [a] major emphasis on community living'.[7] Yet, its operation and governance appears closer to an ordinary body corporate structure than the typical cohousing model, residents complying with the developers' environmental directives and guidance. Co-developer O'Callaghan suggests a trivial level of community participation distinguishing it from:

a pure cohousing model which suggests residents should make all the decisions, typically using a consensus decision making approach. Our experience suggests such models can be taxing on volunteers who struggle to deal with critical items in a timely manner.[8]

Control held by the developer in establishment continued via ongoing specialist advice and management: 'We design, build and help manage each community – so unlike traditional developers – we're community partners for the long-term.' Perhaps it is not surprising that when this particular developer was a co-researcher evaluating the ecovillage, they used a Quality of Life approach to find that the sustainability features of the houses were a more likely source of sustainability practices than the characteristics of householders.[9]

In short, in contrast to community-driven and deeply environmentally concerned ecovillage models discussed in Chapter 6, management of this highly acclaimed commercial project seems both patronising and contradictory. Sustainability is positioned in the built and natural environments rather than the community which, in fact, is managed rather than self-organising. The intentionality is received and accepted rather than a living, beating, participatory cooperative model. Finally, the websites of this and similar developments seem closer to housing estate marketing models, with invitations to buy sustainability advisory services rather than engage in the relatively free sharing that is more common amongst genuinely collaborative, self-organising models.

ARCHITECT-LED COHOUSING

In the latter decades of the twentieth century, government-facilitated collaborative housing in northern European countries often arose with the support of semi-public housing associations or housing firms subject to government policies. In contrast, in North America, the delayed development of cohousing was promoted, if not spearheaded, by architectural and construction project management enterprises. In Europe, collaborative developments were influenced by architects and householders with a social and solidarity tradition of cooperatives, and a social housing (even if middle-class owner-occupier) welfare rationale. In North America, the slant was market-oriented, with entry and exit to cohousing on relatively conventional market terms and a bias towards private ownership and traditional housing styles. In both

European and North American cases eco-collaborative housing came later, with a practical community-orientation characterising most environmentally-concerned groups and projects.

Architects' interest in collaborative housing models has been inquisitive and natural in terms of their disciplinary concern with changing forms of the 'household' and residential design of space and form. Moreover, certain architects were attracted to living in collaborative housing. Many collaborative housing projects have been designed, if not project-managed, by architects. Both the sheer size of the developments and council requirements have necessitated architectural and associated professional advice. Dealing with a group, rather than an individual or couple as the client, has demanded the development of a specific set of skills, often learned and streamlined on the job and, thereon in, offered as a niche service. Architects can exercise two avenues of leadership, first, in terms of design and workshopping the design process; second, in extending oversight of construction to project management proper, including financing details and even directly contributing to financing. Architects' models range from a managerial style of assessing a group's requirements to a more genuinely action-research participatory collaborative approach.

The fact that many collaborative housing projects are architecturally designed almost certainly means better design than mainstream housing although a comparison is not straightforward due to other differences. A more straightforward claim, in terms of clear evidence, is the impact on collaborative housing literature of architects' involvement in cohousing, particularly in North America, which has seen a discourse dominated by elements of design, by the participatory design process and re-iterations of the significance of design for the success of collaborative housing. In contrast, literature on intentional communities more broadly has frequently focused on aspects of community, spirituality, governance and, only more recently, sustainability.[10]

Architects can take a market-based approach, using a competitive and managerial style: 'We are *the* choice for clientele seeking to build elite cohousing communities' states the introductory page of the United States (US) McCamant and Durrett Architects website. The site promotes Charles Durrett, and publications highlighting his approach and style. The sister 'Cohousing Solutions' website shows Kathryn McCamant as a leading cohousing architect-developer, offering a one-year course for 'sustainable development entrepreneurs', aiming to make cohousing 'the new normal'. A leading quote claims: '*If we are to "save the world," we must strive for more sustainable market-driven models that are attractive to the American middle class*' (italics in original). Engineer-developer Jim Leach, founder and president of Wonderland Hill Development Company, has been McCamant's business partner, first in Cohousing Partners and later in Cohousing Solutions, 'pioneering structures for developers to partner with cohousing groups'. This entrepreneurial approach clashes with the cooperative, self-organising and self-directed character of collaborative housing processes that emphasise listening and consensual decision-making. This commercial tendency, owner-occupier and market-orientation of US developments is less evident, or at least more subtle, in Europe.[11]

The rural-cum-greenfield development Ecovillage at Currumbin and a more recent coastal development with higher sustainability standards with respect to homes and infrastructure, The Cape at Cape Patterson, are sustainability-expert-cum-design-led housing projects. Located a 100-minute drive from Melbourne, the capital of Victoria (Australia), The Cape is a small estate. Its entrepreneur Brendan Condon iterates O'Callaghan's refrain that 'we've really set out to prove the whole industry can adopt what we're doing at Cape Paterson'.[12] While laudable compared with regular construction and developer practice, these models are best described as eco-housing developments rather than cohousing or ecovillages.

In contrast to sustainability-expert led eco-constructions, architects such as Zanderroth Architekten have created responsive contemporary models of collaborative housing since the 1990s in Berlin. Adjusting designs for affordability, floor plans for flexibility, enhancing energy efficiency and optimising spatial layout, they have overcome financial hurdles by forward deposit agreements with purchasers to buy cheap lots.[13] Long after these developments multiplied in Europe (see Chapter 7), alternatives are evolving in the Australian capitals of Melbourne and Sydney. They allow for self-organising amongst prospective householders, who become a group client made up of individuals responding to a call out by architect-developers interested in establishing community- and sustainability-oriented living.

As with *Baugruppen*, they hold certain characteristics in common, yet each project differs in its specific financial arrangement, design features, the group's social mix and level of affordability. For instance, one of the projects detailed below (Nightingale 3.0) is to be built on land that the vendor was prepared to release on the basis of his mortgage being paid off and the promise of a three-bedroom apartment and shop space in the proposed development.[14] Similar to certain *Baugruppen* operations, Northcote (Melbourne) co-investment firm Property Collectives is a property syndicate that includes users and offers support to free-wheeling communities of prospective household-developers, from land purchase through to joint design and development processes, with legal (including tax) and financial advice.[15]

Architect-led rhizome in inner-suburban Melbourne

Melbourne has seen one specific rhizome spread of architect-cum-developer-led urban community- and sustainability-oriented single apartment block developments. The 'rhizome' metaphor refers to the interconnected character of the network of architects in question. The impact-investment firm Small Giants is involved in both The Cape at Cape Paterson and Melbourne developments. The latter initiatives have similarities with Beddington Zero Energy Development (BedZED) in Hackbridge (London), focusing on a compact urban development with dozens of dwellings rather than a suburban estate or urban eco-district. An apartment block is a familiar scale for an architect and, therefore, an easy step to trial moving to extensive project management. Indeed, these cases show architects collaborating financially, as developers, and finding financial partners.[16]

Back in 2013 – when interviewed about developments such as the Murundaka Cohousing Community in the Melbourne suburb of Heidelberg Heights – managing director of placemaking consultancy Village Well, Gilbert Rochecouste argued: 'We need new models.' 'To be blunt,' he added, 'there's money to be made here.' His advice was: 'make it savvy and about lifestyle, make it funky and use all the best technology, and make it fun.'[17] That year, The Commons evolved in Brunswick (Melbourne) as a prototype with architect participants and umpteen architects, and other investors, in tow.

Originated by Jeremy McLeod, this community-oriented sustainability-styled block of apartments, with studios and a café, was completed by Small Giants. Subsequently, in 2014, The Commons gained 13 professional and industry, national and state awards. It attracted so much interest that, by December 2016, 'Nightingale 1.0' was in construction opposite The Commons in Brunswick, again driven by

McLeod's Breathe Architecture firm. Moreover, Nightingale 2.0, a bit further from the central business district (CBD) in Fairfield, was in late development managed by architectural firm Six Degrees. Furthermore, Nightingale 3.0, led by Austin Maynard Architects, was on the drawing board with a site in Brunswick, closer to the CBD than the other three developments. Finally, Nightingale 4.0 was in very early development by Clare Cousins Architecture and licences were out for tender for Nightingale versions in Sydney.[18]

Each Nightingale has 20–25 'angel investors', a significant proportion of them architects prepared to accept the 'minimum profit allowed by banks' (15 per cent), established on a *Baugruppen* architect-led self-build model, subsequently referred to by Sharam et al. as a designer-led 'deliberative development model' in a 'sharing economy' framing.[19] While prompted by McLeod, the Nightingale model has involved not only various other construction-related professionals but also, each iteration met local council planning and state appeal mechanism hurdles, such as resistance to no or few car parking spaces per development.[20]

The developers' aim for the Nightingale model to deliver 'quality' housing design to satisfy social health, connectivity and neighbourly needs and environmental sustainability criteria. Additionally, while bearing transparent cost prices, for the first 20 years, purchasers will be constrained by a caveat on the title to limit on-selling prices to the original purchase price plus the average price increase for the suburb. Still, Nightingale 1.0 prices for one- and two-bedroom apartments (50–75sq m plus and average balcony space of 8sq m) were A$400,000 and A$645,000 respectively in a suburb where, by December 2016, the average one- and two-bedroom apartment selling prices were A$355,000–475,000 and the average apartment was realising an annual growth of more than 5.5 per cent (2013–2016). In short, the model is neither inexpensive nor likely to avoid inner-urban and local gentrification price pressures because average price growth is inbuilt in the caveat cap. Still, the caveat prevents a particular form of gentrification or price hike attached to these specific developments.[21]

The Nightingale model covers the costs of sustainability features – high thermal standards using insulation and double-glazing, passive design, solar panels, hydronic heating, vertical gardens and natural ventilation techniques contributing to coolth from the summer sun – by avoiding conventional marketing. The developer has lengthy waiting lists of seriously interested owner-purchasers, ideally able to deposit 20–40 per cent of the expected cost. Further savings are made by surveying purchasers on their expectations and preparedness to compromise through, say, common laundry and drying spaces, and by avoiding car parking spaces, air conditioning and extra bathrooms. The Commons and Nightingale 1.0 make environmental economies on travel via proximity to public train, tram and bus services and a bike-friendly neighbourhood.[22]

The Commons two-bedroom apartments have 25 per cent of the energy footprint of a two-bedroom suburban detached house and their overall energy efficiency has potential to reduce heating and cooling to 10 per cent of a five-star rated dwelling. However, solar panels target common areas and Australia's energy sources are comparatively highly carbon polluting so, while three times better than the average Victorian apartment, in this respect The Commons is well below achievements of the United Kingdom (UK) One Brighton (Bioregional). Still, the Commons does very well in rankings on travel, almost as well as the model sustainable district Vauban (2000) in Freiburg in terms of short trips. The Commons has a perfect score for being totally car-free onsite and offering common bike storage. However, some residents do own cars and engage in offsite car-sharing arrangements. While domestic water use is only fractionally less than the Australian average, landscaping just uses water collected onsite.[23]

In short, these developments customise as much in the way of sustainability features as their niche market can bear but are not generally affordable. They are heavily designer-led and only post-occupancy audits could confirm what real achievements might be made in terms of creating housing communities that cooperate for communal and environmental efficiencies.

COMMERCIAL SELF-BUILD GROUP

'Self-build', aka 'owner-built', where the owner-occupier is the project manager and/or offers sweat-equity by working on the housing project, can be an individual or group enterprise. Many get together to group self-build with no intention of developing a permanent community with communal spaces and facilities. Some self-build groups comprise of owner-occupiers of separately located properties but others work on attached dwellings, say retrofitting a big building for sustainability, or an apartment block. Eco-self-build ventures have certain parallels with fully blown collaborative housing projects although often forgo ongoing environmental economies of intentional eco-collaborative living.

This self-build tradition is especially accepted in Germany although other governments have offered self-build programs periodically. Brought up in Germany, architect Walter Segal pioneered self-build council housing in the UK. His system of owner self-build as variously applied – including by Lewisham Council (London) and the Hedgehog Housing Coop (Hogs Edge, Brighton) – has gained attention for innovation in simplicity and self-help.[24] An interesting market-based case of self-build is 'On the Rise', which Froud describes as 'not an "intentional community" of shared values (of the non-pecuniary kind, anyway)'. Yet, for its architect, the project presented similar challenges to designing collaborative housing.

Here, seven neighbours in Hafer Road, Clapham Junction, Battersea (London) formed a limited company as shareholders and operated like a cooperative to successfully offer to purchase the freehold from Wandsworth Council, demolish the 'substandard, undersized' dwellings they lived in, rebuild around a courtyard to include more dwellings and, then, sold the extra dwellings to finance the whole operation (2011–2016). Gaining finance required them to engage a project manager, an expense generally forgone as a key saving for self-builders yet they benefitted from exemptions from including affordable housing and paying a Community Infrastructure Levy. Their new construction complemented the terrace-style neighbourhood; all apartments had distinct interiors, most just two bedrooms.[25] This initiative was bravely out of the norm but not particularly community-oriented, sustainability-focused or affordable.

In another case, the regular 20 per cent profit gained by a developer was saved in the 3xGrun self-build group's 13-household, five-level timber apartment block in Pankow, Berlin. Wood was chosen for its carbon-saving properties. The average cost was €307,000 per apartment of varying sizes, 100–200sq m. One of its designers (Philip Koch, Atelier PK Architekten) resides there. At the end of a shared development experience, they co-manage their garden and all enjoy green views. Koch attributes their success to financial and organisational structures that support these types of *Baugruppen* in Germany (see Chapter 7).[26] Indeed this German case offers greater sustainability, community and affordability outcomes than the previous example, which was a unique out-of-the-mainstream UK initiative.

Just as *Baugruppen* and, more recently UK collaborative housing models, are supported by several financial institutions, late in 2016 the CommBank (Commonwealth Bank Group, one of Australia's 'Big Four' banks) acknowledged that collaborative living and buying models, such as cohousing, group loans, communities in common, and 'crowd housing' might well alter housing lenders' practices to 'meet the needs of Australian home buyers in the future.'[27] However, market-based 'collaborative' models incorporate few of the more generally accepted common principles of collaborative housing and living outlined in Part II. Furthermore, self-interested, private-property-oriented developments tend to have relatively few environmental features. 'Crowd housing' refers to matches made between developers and prospective households through an Internet site, a tool the developer uses to seek the specific wants of householders, negotiating packages to fulfil stakeholders' economic constraints through appropriate environmental decision-making, and 'sharing' opportunities. This Internet-facilitated process posits such developments in a broader market-based paradigm of 'sharing economies' and 'sharing cities', a topic to which we now turn.

FROM SHARED HOUSING TO A SHARING MOVEMENT: SHARING CITIES

So-called 'sharing economies' refer to participants sharing products and services by means of digital technology in variously formal or informal, temporary and expanding, commercial or nonmonetary networks. High-profile sharing economy enterprises include the car service Uber and accommodation service Airbnb. Underground examples include pop-up swap meets promoted via email networks, and on dedicated Facebook pages, for nonmonetary gift exchange of, say, second-hand clothes and home grown or surplus food through to market and profit-centred businesses. As shown in Part II, collaborative housing offers a perfect social context and built environment for localised sharing. However, 'sharing cities' is a major focus of sharing economy advocates.

The sharing economy

In practice, holistic sharing economies do not exist; the notion of a 'sharing economy' evolves from ideas of scaling up and integrating networks of practices of sharing within consumption, (re)distributive networks and collaborative production. A sharing economy would connect initiatives centring on sharing the use of goods and services (aka collaborative consumption), and equipment and production processes (a pottery kiln or 3D printer). Associated notions of a 'peer-to-peer (P2P) economy' and 'on-demand economy' are both simply techniques for producing rather than structures for either relations or means of production. A sister paradigm is the 'social and solidarity economy' that focuses on a mutual aid tradition of cooperatives, a 'fair price', democratic workplaces, reasonable remuneration for work, and balancing the skewed relations of capitalist trade between economies of the Global South and North.

Sharing practices typically entail joint use and re-use of products, as well as cooperative or client-focused service provision in peer-based digital technology networks. As such these networks have been touted as offering new forms of environmental and social resource efficiency, waste reduction and, sometimes contradictorily, wider access to resources. These supposed characteristics parallel similar assumptions made for collaborative housing initiatives. Yet, well-known commercial sharing initiatives promoted as global and disruptive have been in the news for adverse impacts on workers' rights (Uber) and for disturbing neighbourhoods, including through commercialisation, unwanted tourism and gentrification (Airbnb). While car-share networks more broadly have been hailed for economising on car and petrol use, US research by Schor and others shows that, in fact, their very cheapness can encourage increased trips by riders and detract from environmentally better public transport options. In short, direct efficiencies, say not travelling so much by car, trumps sharing practices for absolute environmental savings.[28]

If practical results do not auger well for sharing economies, what about the allied notion of a 'sharing city'?

Sharing cities

Despite presenting and tempering their arguments with values of inclusivity, 'just sustainabilities' and social justice, McLaren and Agyeman express the triumphal urbanist and smart ecomodernist spirit of the early twenty-first century in *Sharing Cities: A Case for Truly Smart and Sustainable Cities*. Ignoring the vast ecological footprints that cities cast as dark shadows on the rest of the planet, they argue that 'well-planned and -governed cities are potentially the form of human organization that could keep us within environmental limits while simultaneously building the social foundations prescribed by human rights, dignity, and a decent quality of life'.[29]

Although McLaren and Agyeman distinguish between communal and commercial approaches, and criticise 'monetizing and monetized' collaborative consumption, their politico-cultural conceptualisation of the 'sharing paradigm' covers individual, collective and public sharing of goods, services and activities, and essentially blurs non-market and market interaction. Even while they recognise that certain forms of the sharing economy 'can deepen inequalities and deliver injustice', they epitomise social and solidarity economy currents that see the market as an institution that can be contained, better driven or redesigned to work for the interests of the majority, specifically through the proliferation of cooperative models. Within this paradigm, they laud cohousing, squatting, self-build and social housing as housing activities with characteristics that mirror a broader sharing mentality.[30]

Similarly, the San Francisco-based Shareable online hub for sharing initiatives and sharing cities, which is supported mainly by millennials and their successors, highlights collaborative housing. This hub promoted a Shareable & Sustainable Economies Law Centre report that encourages planners to remove or relax restrictions hampering or disallowing collaborative housing and to create appropriate zones and codes allowing for cooperative housing, accessory dwelling units (ADUs), tiny house clusters, short-term visitors, cohousing and ecovillages. Frequently prohibited due to density standards, parking requirements and even US local government ordinances that 'limit the number of unrelated people who may live in a housing unit', the report recommends 'that cities promote development of smaller homes including micro-apartments, tiny houses, yurts, container homes, and other humble abodes, which produce more affordable and sustainable housing options, and promote sharing'.[31] Micro-apartments, ADUs, cohousing and ecovillages are dealt with elsewhere. In this section, I briefly discuss examples of cooperative housing, tiny house clusters and alternative habitations that fail to fulfil standards set out in regular building and planning codes and, as such, are seen by authorities as 'marginal housing'.

Cooperative housing as collaborative housing

The cooperative housing sector is very heterogeneous, extending from radical, independent income-sharing collaborative living models through to the more typical, highly managed not-for-profit philan-thropic and state-owned subsidised rental models. As already discussed, only certain types with specific characteristics are of interest in this book; housing cooperatives deserve attention here in as much as they are an outcome of market-based activities and potentially influenced by more community- and sustainability-based models.

Many countries have seen the rise of a 'new cooperativism' in the housing cooperative sector in recent decades. This new wave shares with the old cooperativist sector primary characteristics of solidarity and catering for low-incomes, but is differentiated by greater emphasis on a decentralised bottom-up, rather than top-down, decision-making structure and more market-oriented operating principles. The new cooperative sector reflects wider concerns for the environmental sus-tainability of housing and household practices, and has a greater capacity to implement environmentally friendly developments than the old cooperative sector. As Kadriu and Wendorf argue with respect to German developments, a community- and household-based eco-centric approach is likely to be more effective than a simply techno-centric one.[32]

Despite shared responsibilities for ownership and/or management of cooperative dwellings, only an indeterminate fraction of the housing cooperative sector is collaborative housing as defined here. Some have few or no communal spaces and facilities; 'in most, life is still focused on individual dwellings'. Moreover, Clapham points out that most shares exchange on market-based value, as with UK commonhold and leasehold ownerships; only some owner-occupier cooperatives have par-value shares where, on exiting, member-residents only receive the amount paid on entering. Tenant management cooperatives characteristic of social housing in the US, UK and Scandinavia show various arrangements with respect to the delineation of management and administrative responsi-bilities between landlord and tenants.[33]

Even while attracting some government support, Clapham explains that the cooperative sector evolved with similar market-associated ideals to the current sharing economy, and social and solidarity economy, movements – prioritising self-governing, mutually supportive, small and simple market-integrated models for self-help and criticising big capital, big government and neoliberalism. Writing in 2012, Silver emphasised neoliberal pressures to privatise state-supported cooperative housing and to trade shares and dwellings at market rates.[34]

By the mid-2010s, German housing cooperatives numbered around 2000, with three million members and five million residents in around two million apartments equating to 10 per cent of German housing stock. More than two in five housing cooperatives in East Berlin, and one in five in West Berlin, originated relatively recently, in the 1990s. Rental cooperatives are characteristic of North Germany and owner-occupied housing cooperatives characterise the South. Regulated rents make cooperative tenancies secure. Housing cooperatives are foci of local government social welfare and sustainability policies, with a national target for all dwellings to be 'climate neutral' by 2050, and offering a distinctive model avoiding the classic 'landlord–tenant dilemma'. To maintain their attraction to residents, cooperatives offer environmental features and access government energy-efficiency programs. Some remarkable examples include the private citizen-initiated Möckernkiez Genossenschaft (Berlin). With 1400 members, this 'cooperative for self-governed, social and ecological living' began construction in mid-2016 on a well-located carpark-free neighbourhood site, with plans for 471 dwellings (27–150sq m) at a Passivhaus plus standard, and most with a balcony, in 14 apartment blocks.[35]

Murundaka cohousing community (2011) in Heidelberg Heights, an established outer suburb of Melbourne, offers an example of an affordable, community-managed and environmentally concerned rental cooperative – in a country where the cooperative housing sector is considerably less than 0.1 per cent of housing stock. A tenants-only cooperative, eligibility requires a low income of which rental is set at 25 per cent. There are 18 apartments in the complex with multiple common areas inside and outside, including productive gardens and bike storage. The buildings were designed with sustainability in mind, with solar hot water systems and tanks with a capacity for 80,000l of roof-collected water. Numbers of residents do not own a car but, instead, car-share. Residents elected to limit the number of bins collected by the council as a waste management strategy. Their community laundry, of just three washing machines, has an 'open closet exchange space' for re-using clothes.

Murundaka is owned, and the asset is managed, by a community not-for-profit housing association. The project benefited from a federal government stimulus package after the Global Financial Crisis. Combined private and shared dwelling space amounts to circa 165sq m per household which, when built, cost around A$410,000. All residents are low-income and asset-poor tenants paying affordable rents. Resident management is extensive, choosing new member-residents, collecting rent, administering finances, organising dwelling maintenance and maintaining records. These and other community-based activities, including more than a dozen working-groups, demand from each member around two to three hours per week.[36]

Another type of eco-cooperative rental housing is represented by Sunwise Coop (Davis, California), owned by the Solar Community Housing Association, a case of mini-coliving in a large shared household of eight low-income members in one house.[37] Somewhat similar are the eco-houses purchased and environmentally renovated by the UK Co-operative Living Freehold Society, Cordata Housing Co-operative Ltd (Withington, South Manchester), a fully mutual housing cooperative. A dual structure allows for sharing skills, knowledge and effort between households; members benefit from moving into an already established eco-retrofitted house on the expectation that, once sufficiently established, they will put time into renovating a future cooperative house. Beyond belonging to a household and living in a house over which they have almost total control, members have a mutually beneficial arrangement within a cooperative of cooperatives, inculcating outward-looking solidarity. The main point of including this atypical cooperative is to demonstrate fleet-of-foot market cooperative agents taking ecological concerns seriously and approaching them affordably. However, this specific model does not seem to have rapidly expanded in the UK.[38]

In contrast, the Mietshäuser Syndikat (Germany) has attracted a good deal of interest and is growing. An umbrella housing organisation that aims to 'neutralise' property or remove it from speculation, this limited liability company – with much lower maintenance and governance costs than a cooperative – operates alongside a decentralised structure of autonomous housing projects where mature, independent housing communities assist in financing new entrants. The independent legal status of the organisations gives the housing community relative autonomy yet sale of the community house (re-privatisation) is highly unlikely because both relevant bodies would need to agree to it. Unlike a foundation, the Syndikat, can lend money to housing projects directly, at little or no interest.

A similar network of housing (and worker) cooperatives is the UK Radical Routes (1992–), which restricts membership to fully mutual cooperative groups substantially working for 'positive social change', who can demonstrate that they are 'committed to a low impact lifestyle'. Pre-empting themes in Chapter 9, Radical Routes has a strong position:

> We want to see a world based on equality and co-operation, where people give according to their ability and receive according to their needs, where work is fulfilling and useful and creativity is encouraged, where decision making is open to everyone with no hierarchies, where the environment is valued and respected in its own right rather than exploited.

> We want to take control over all aspects of our lives. However, as we are not all in a position of control we are forced to compromise in order to exist.[39]

In short, a cooperative structure is being used across the spectrum of collaborative housing organisations; a legal cooperative, in and of itself, is no guarantee of values and processes that are socially just or environmentally sustainable. Indeed, generally, market-based cooperatives advance capitalism. The minority of dissident cooperatives are painfully aware of the inherent deficiencies of market dynamics and pressures.

Clusters of tiny houses and other unusual habitations

Shareable promotes an assortment of alternative shelters that exist marginally in the property market and legally, illegally or in tension with mainstream dwelling regulations. They include barges and other boats used as homes, such as some Boaters in London and along Britain's extensive canal network. Intentionally connected and using sustainable practices, a critical number could comprise a low impact quasi-community but, in reality, life on a boat can be as individualistic, eco-unfriendly and luxurious as a wealthy person's city-pad.[40] Similarly, transportable tiny houses – burgeoning as a movement, especially of millennials seeking home ownership of a minimal kind – often appear alone, only occasionally as 'ecovillages'.[41] Other examples, such as ex-shipping container housing-cum-working studios and caravans, cabins and manufactured homes in residential villages are generally oriented around simply providing affordable accommodation rather than eco-collaborative living spaces.[42]

In most countries the definition of a 'mobile home' is straightforward and similar – a dwelling either on wheels, say a caravan, or capable of being moved, such as a transportable manufactured home, with regulations, including maximum sizes. In the UK the definition covers railway carriages not on tracks but rather re-purposed and adapted to a dwelling, 'dormobiles', and touring 'caravanettes', but not tents. Tipi Valley (Llandeilo, Wales) rightly belongs to the themes in Chapter 9 – with its anarchic governance and 'we belong to the Earth' eco-naturalism of the valley's congregation of 'light, portable, relatively cheap and gentle' tipis.[43] Coates has called clusters of mobile homes in park sites 'co-housing in all but name' and pointed to the evolution of the Findhorn Park (Scotland) intentional community as a prototype. He suggests that 'eco-snobbery' is probably the main barrier to them populating the countryside.[44]

A high-profile example of marginal housing is self-built, or marketed, tiny houses (Figure 8.1). Developed in a longer history of bottom-up innovations in creating cheap housing, tiny house clusters are rare although government and not-for-profits are trialling tiny house settlements for the homeless. An experimental and educational Wurruk'an cluster in rural Victoria (Australia) imitates the communal and environmental history of collaborative eco-living on a micro-scale and accommodates a tenuous land arrangement. Wurruk'an community advocates simple living for degrowth futures.[45] Although very few such tiny house villages have emerged, demand is demonstrated in media reports of group plans that list council planning, other government agency regulations and costs as key barriers.[46] Meanwhile, entrepreneurs have taken up the challenge.

The Las Vegas Airstream park evolved unintentionally from a failed hotel plan. The brainchild of – and supervised by – an almost-billionaire Tony Hseih, Llamapolis is an 'experimental' one-acre park of micro-habitations including 30 sleek Airstreams. In early 2016, a 240sq ft Airstream trailer cost a not-so-cheap US$1200 per month to rent, including Wi-Fi and other utilities.[47] Along with more modest commercially produced Tumbleweeds (tiny houses), the park has a common kitchen (shipping container), pantry and laundry, outdoor living space with fire pits and buses to cowork in.[48] Luxury Airstreams hardly qualify as eco because their signature appearance is polished aluminium, the end product of a highly energy-intensive process of refining bauxite, a far cry from the off-grid eco-DIO models of tiny

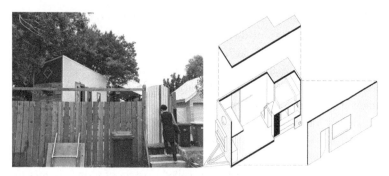

Figure 8.1   Photo and sketch of tiny house, West Australia
Source: Post- (architectural practice, Perth), West Australia

houses.[49] The average Tumbleweed model tiny house, by comparison, has been promoted as 'made with only 4,800 pounds of building materials' generating a construction waste of 'less than 100 pounds' and operating environmental cost of 'less than 4 tons' of greenhouse gas in 'a typical Minnesota winter'.[50] Regarding overall environmental impacts, Tumbleweed founder Jay Schaefer highlights the freedom and extra spending power tiny house living creates, giving pause for serious concerns on extra consumption.[51]

A study of Australian 'marginal rental housing' – primarily boarding houses and permanent tenants in residential parks with caravans, cabins and/or manufactured houses – noted the tendency to gentrification of parks in well-serviced and attractive locations such as the eastern coast of New South Wales. Tenants complained of increasing rents that threatened to force them to move from their home. Furthermore, in 2012, certain highly priced homes of owner-renters on rented parkland lots were realising more than A$700,000 in the open market.[52] The sources of gentrification included village sites having been bought as long-term investments and only temporarily, strategically, being used as income-earning parks while waiting for the right time to sell as well as growth in demand from retirees. This study suggested that residents might:

> increase control of their living arrangements through new co-operative ownership and governance arrangements ... achieved by removing the barriers that restrict the development of public-private partnerships and direct investment and guarantor mechanisms that hold the potential to establish rights that are closer to those enjoyed

by home owners while retaining the collective or community-based characteristics that attract residents to buy into residential parks.[53]

This policy advice could be transferred, or adapted, to other types of alternative dwelling clusters allowing for, but not limited to, collaborative housing that was affordable, low impact and self-managed.

Semi-permanent stay-on-inns: coliving

Coworking is occupying a shared space to work in, with Wi-Fi for freelancing. Coworking embodies the sharing economy and grew 10 times by 2016 from just over 1000 spaces in 2011.[54] Coworking entrepreneurs, such as WeWork (worth around US$15bn in 2016), have spread into supplying space for accommodation marketed to millennials who work and travel.[55] WeLive is sold as coliving but, in reality, it is a monetary host–guest or landlord–boarder relationship.[56] Despite the protestation that 'coliving is, from the outset, built around an intention to create a tight, productive community to accelerate personal and community development', this sharing economy is clearly framed by the market.[57]

Leo Hollis has analysed the negatives of 'startup urbanism' and sharing cities using the example of Downtown Las Vegas where Tony Hsieh (owner of the aforementioned Llamapolis) aimed to make his 20-block 'collisionability' development the international 'coworking capital'. Referring to the famous community-based urbanist Jane Jacobs, Hollis contends that developers such as Hsieh speak with a forked-tongue, talking 'the language of community to disguise their plans to make a killing' and end up with old-fashioned gentrification in a city which heightens inequality. 'It has become increasingly prevalent to "Jane-wash" a project with the promise of bike lanes, placemaking, and walkability.' Hollis refers to *Los Angeles Times* reports of local opposition and impacts: local stores and residents unable to pay increasing rents and rising fees for education and day-care. Similarly driven by '24/7 capitalism', Hollis sees London's Tech City showing how the sharing city is one big marketplace, 'a community defined, and dominated, by work'.[58] It seems as if coworking and coliving might become the apogee of the sharing economy and sharing city, quite a different story from the narratives of advocates of the so-called sharing economy and sharing city.

Fernández summarises critiques of the sharing cities paradigm, and its pretensions to prompt commoning, by distinguishing commons from either private or public property: 'The "commons," that which is communal, is goods that belong to a community, a group of real people, a demos, that manages it jointly and directly.' Instead, private property is preserved in most sharing economy relations: 'In most municipal "biking" or "car-sharing" services, the bikes belong to a company or city hall itself.' Genuine bike-sharing would mean sharing bikes in a network committed to managing the bike's use.[59]

Eco-collaborative housing and the sharing economy paradigm

Generalisations can be made about eco-collaborative housing in the sharing paradigm. First, the emphasis is on housing, rather than living or working. Moreover, where living is involved, it is commodified as far as possible, traded and managed, and 'working' looks like what we are used to in capitalism. Furthermore, those kinds of housing suggested by Shareable as affordable, and with environmental sustainability benefits, share dubious generic characteristics of 'marginal housing'. Thus, it is incumbent for cases such as Radical Routes to explicitly identify with an anti-market, anti-state tradition rather than the sharing paradigm.

Second, the sharing economy movement aims to mould market structures, if necessary with government support. Residents of Shareable's preferred housing options might participate in wider sharing networks that include food, transport, clothing and coworking but, more often than not, trade stitches together these apparent aspects of a sharing economy in the making. The assumption is that, given the right drivers, the market could deliver community, substantive democracy and environmental sustainability – despite firms making decisions about what and how to produce, and the fact that prices do not (and cannot) reflect environmental values, and money arising in production for trade creates divisions between people into 'haves', 'have nots' and those who 'have a bit'.[60] The Shareable vision is of class harmonisation and aspiration, not deep change: 'Where the poor are lifted up, the middle class is strengthened, and the rich are respected because they all work together for the common good.'[61]

Third, there is a contradiction in the extent to which various sharing economy initiatives seek government support yet flout or undermine regulation. As with entrepreneurial movements in general, the sharing movement argues for government to regulate for their free play, implying that the market is an appropriate structure for organising our everyday affairs. At the same time, there is a muted struggle in the sharing movement, and vocal criticism outside of it, on the level of monetisation that it involves, with conclusions that commercialisation is the defining dynamic of the sharing economy. In a brief discussion of this and related arguments, the final section serves as a bridge to the next chapter on eco-collaborative living models that have been substantially grassroots affairs eschewing, or neglected by, the state and market.

CONCLUSION: MONETISING COMMUNITY AND SUSTAINABILITY

Sharing economy initiatives often present their aims in terms of ethical, social, environmental, local and community-oriented values yet, as Schor points out, there has been little robust research assessing the extent to which sharing networks fulfil their professed social and environmental aims in practice. Relying on markets for their operation implicitly limits sharing, demanding compliance with market dynamics and pressures, and generating social tensions and contradictions that, historically, played out most visibly in cooperatives producing for trade and, today, as shown by critics such as Slee, Hollis and Richardson. A less cynical view of market limitations inspires sharing economy proponents who tend to explain such anomalies via a critical divide in (un)ethical practices between small and large capital, as in Lovell's view of eco-communities as 'organised in either a "top-down" (housing developer or government-led) or "bottom-up" (entrepreneurial or community-led) way'.[62]

In the types of housing considered in this chapter, market forces of supply and demand, competition and profit produce unaffordability and gentrification, which impacts on owner-occupiers and tenants alike. The market remains the framework within which subsidies, or partially income- or asset-sharing arrangements take place in many models of collaborative housing. Sharing costs as in certain cooperatives, say with par equity shares, and community land trust and mutual home ownership models, relies on higher-income residents absorbing costs for lower-income residents. Where schemes, such as Nightingale, attempt to avoid speculation, an oblique transference of wealth occurs between original and later owners that Morris, reasonably, considers unfair.[63] In these cases there are member benefits and disadvantages but no impact on broader market dwelling prices or affordability, even in countries where they are most extensive, such as The Netherlands and Germany.

To the extent that professionals and commercial developers are attracted to eco-collaborative living models, they generally receive salaries and even profits, just as architects and other construction professionals, project managers and property owners earn in market-based activities. For instance, being prepared to make a limit of 15 per cent profit in comparison to a purported 20 per cent average – as in the Nightingale case – is hardly a great sacrifice. Efficiencies are gained through cutting out a process or professional altogether, such as the developer in the 3xGrun case. Economies of scale are realised along with savings because of special treatment from government, including with access to land and in planning matters (say fast-tracking or giving special consideration to a project), as well as in financial arrangements (such as a government-guaranteed loan). This is why such models are often criticised as tinkering at the sidelines, and as middle-class welfare or gentrifying trends.

With the decrease of public housing and transfer to social housing models delivered by not-for-profit housing associations, market-based calculations and arrangements typify collaborative rental, say cooperative, housing even if affordability is taken into account. Often, a chief objective in making habitations more environmentally sustainable has been to improve affordability of operating costs. Furthermore, the goals of both private and public social welfare agencies can be fulfilled in collaborative housing models that are physically safe, economically secure and community-supported living arrangements as is visible with seniors' aging in place within intergenerational housing.[64]

These points are significant because many adherents to the sharing paradigm perceive the market as malleable by market players, even expecting progressive changes in market values, rules and dynamics. Proponents argue that peer-to-peer 'disruptive technologies' will inevitably introduce a multiplicity of social and environmental values, apparently dominating monetary values (prices, monetary calculations and profit) even as they simultaneously reproduce markets. Yet, critical analysts of market-based eco-collaborative developments of all kinds question whether they are really as community-oriented, affordable and sustainable as nonmonetary sharing initiatives that avoid or minimise interactions with market actors and marketplace activities. Indeed, this chapter has tried to show that the market has not delivered collaborative housing or living with beneficial qualities but, rather, has most often failed. Sharing economy advocates generally fail to appreciate that the market is a structure and key institution of capitalism, and that the market and capitalism structure inequity, competition and private property continuously preventing or eroding sharing and commons.

Although often overlooked in sharing-paradigm analyses, sharing networks include freely shared knowledge, seeds, second-hand clothing, food and other goods and services. For instance, a multi-university research team in Lancaster and Birmingham (UK) found that, whereas market and government discourse around sharing cities centred on commercial sharing schemes, 'the kinds of sharing that we found when speaking with people, groups and communities as well as our research team often took smaller, more local forms'. The latter included free sharing networks, and contexts such as collaborative living where there are agreements, expectations, responsibilities and benefits to sharing freely without money or markets. Arguably, 'community' is most convincingly expressed, at least partially, as a gift economy of free exchange.[65]

In contrast to market-oriented actors – who tend to monetise relationships, to trade and produce for trade goods and services such as knowledge (education, patents and copyright), skills (learning), materials and equipment in the growing niche market for sustainability goods and services – the grassroots DIO movement has an economy of genuine efficiency, tending to avoid, re-use and hand on materials, energy, equipment, knowledge and skills via nonmonetary sharing and exchange. Yet, the significant line between market-based and non-market or 'alter-market' production and exchange (exchange occurring without money either changing hands or entering calculations related to decision-making) is not well-acknowledged.[66]

Drivers of cases highlighted in this chapter have associated their sense of independence and confidence in the market as a means to establish sustainability and community-oriented projects. Instead, the next chapter presents developments where the market was primarily seen as a necessary evil by communities that arose without critical state or market support in a conscious movement of radical, anti-systemic, community-based activity.

9
Grassroots Sustainability, Sociality and Governance

The grassroots, community-based drivers of collaborative living cases discussed in this chapter are representative of communities who chose independent strategies – defined by relative autonomy from the market and the state – to implement environmental sustainability and communally oriented practices. They include income-sharing communities that many would refer to as 'communes' and precarious squats of activists, intent both on challenging capitalism at a basic level of private property and instituting social and environmental justice. Each of the highly experimental models discussed demonstrate significant levels of creativity, will and preparedness to break with fundamental economic and political structures within capitalism. Certain observers dismiss these types of collaborative housing as inconsequential and marginal. Others speculate that such 'hybrids' might be prescient forms demonstrating distinctive directions beyond capitalism whilst compromising in certain ways with prevailing governance and economic systems simply in order to survive.[1]

Scaling up these models certainly implies broadening the practices of commoning and the potential for the full flowering of nonmonetary sharing in terms of both production and exchange, specifically governing for collective sufficiency and ecological regeneration. Is it possible that models of horizontal governance, environmentally friendly practices and collective sustainability might evolve as nodes and drivers of inter-networked locally sufficient neighbourhood settlements and communities spread over a relatively peaceful planet? Does such a vision promise the establishment of a balance between humans and the rest of nature, maintained by holistic practices of dedicated stewardship?

One vision of scaling up might well have various institutions for self-governance substituting for the state while compacts based on human need, planetary capacity and justly shared effort replace competitive and environmentally wasteful production for the market supported by the limited and formal democracies characteristic of market-based states. The kinds of arrangements, values and relationships that typify the collaborative housing and living discussed in this chapter are more-or-less compatible with such a vision. The inter-personal and governance skills developed and demonstrated in these cases and their eco-sustainability practices – stretching from micro-techniques of growing and preparing food through to off-grid neighbourhood renewable energy and water systems – could constitute the fibres for the fabric of a new society beyond capitalism.[2]

This chapter begins with a discussion of revolutionary political currents and tensions reflected, and embodied, in collaborative housing movements and policies in France. I follow with themes of scaling up and precarious, antagonistic relationships with state and market that characterise radical environmentally sustainable communities, starting at the micro-scale with the dozen or so resident-members of Tinkers Bubble in the United Kingdom (UK) through to the average-sized substantial communities of Twin Oaks in the United States (US) and ufaFabrik (Germany), on to the macro-scale of around 900 residents of Christiania (Freetown), a veritable quarter of the global city of Copenhagen (Denmark), concluding with a discussion of Calafou (Catalonia), a node in the multi-various networks of the Catalan Integral Cooperative in Barcelona and its surrounds, which involves thousands of participants.

'LONG LIVE THE COMMUNE!'

For more than half a century, farmers and locals threatened with expropriation – and their national and international supporters – resisted the construction of an airport for Nantes that would endanger 4000 acres of ecologically rich forests, wetlands and farming land. This Zone À Défendre (ZAD) had been occupied, since 1974, by protesters rallying around a concept of political autonomy that only strengthened by the mid-2010s. The ZAD has been a highly contested space where the global and local connection is as strong as an umbilical cord and the echo of history a leitmotif. By way of an illustration, referring to the location (Le Bourget) of the international climate negotiations known as the Conference of Parties 21 (COP21) and their own advance in a cavalcade to Paris on 28 November 2015, ZAD defenders rallied: 'Keep the Bourget, we're taking Versailles. Long live the Commune!'[3]

In *Communal Luxury: The Political Imaginary of the Paris Commune*, Kristen Ross explores the basis of this living legacy of those momentous ten weeks, mid-March to the end of May 1871, when 'a worker-led insurrection transformed the city of Paris into an autonomous Commune and set about improvising the free organization of its social life according to the principles of association and cooperation'. Ross elaborates:

> The Communal imagination operated on the preferred scale of the local autonomous unit within an internationalist horizon. It had little room for the nation, or, for that matter, for the market or the state.[4]

Indeed, both in the radical imagination and for practical political purposes, the ZAD has been more than the defence of a space – extending to a genuinely democratic practice of politics, a holistic fight against management of people and land. Pointing to migrants obscurely evicted on a daily basis, a ZAD Communique from early 2016 stated: 'we want to continue to make this place a crossroad for struggles, so we can support, create solidarity, and share with each other'.[5] Contra mainstream views that such spaces as the ZAD are unique and marginal; during the 2010s the term '*habitat participatif*' (collaborative housing) spread to cover a multiplicity of French housing arrangements that pursued 'a response to the housing issue based on mobilizing civil society rather than on State intervention or market forces'.[6]

Habitat participatif

Bresson and Denèfle trace the cultural background to the contemporary *habitat participatif* in state-supported low-income-oriented housing cooperatives of the late nineteenth century and the self-management-oriented post-Second World War housing cooperative movement that promoted solidarity and sharing. They identify three, more recent, precursors of 2010s *habitat participatif* in projects begun in the 1970s, namely the Béalières, Hélix and Les Naïfs projects highlighting eco-design, self-management by co-owners and tenants, and common activities, spaces and facilities. Subsequently, the twenty-first century has seen new push and pull factors among young middle-class French citizens facing precarious employment, rising house prices and environmentally unsustainable lifestyles. Distinct from former housing movements, they are intent on managing 'aspects previously left to the market' and demonstrate a 'broad rejection of institutions' along with a 'wish to resolve their own problems here and now'.[7]

Grenoble has been a site of significant activity for both radical experiments and mainstream council-supported private-ownership models. Practising participatory urban planning, Grenoble council has proactively supported collaborative housing projects and demonstrated agency in national council bodies promoting them. However, such support came with expectations and conditions, precipitating differences, indeed factions, in and between *habitat participatif* groups and associated organisations. Bresson and Denèfle have identified several positions with softer- and harder-line engagements with councils after occupying buildings fated for demolition, both lines being 'criticized by some squat activists who reject any compromise with the authorities, while others accept the idea of contractual arrangements'. Moreover:

> Self-build and restoration housing operations can also be found in the Grenoble region, carried out by extreme left-wing activists who use social networks to raise funds to gain access to property that they then aim to dissociate from private ownership and all capitalist-based economic forms.[8]

I have observed the same types of groups and conflicts between them in Australia, as have analysts of the squatting movement in Europe more generally. Political fractures became widespread as neoliberal currents made squatting illegal, and increased the monitoring and punishing of squatters, especially during the 1980s in Europe. Ultimately, in October 2010, the Netherlands made squatting illegal after it had been effectively permitted by laws established early in the twentieth century. Delgado has lauded squats for their capacity to reinvigorate deprived and neglected urban neighbourhoods by offering spaces for locals: to work; to hold and attend convivial educational and entertainment events; to practise, perform and exhibit art; and, to enjoy inexpensive cafés and participate in collaborative dining.[9]

A range of types of squatters with distinctive political leanings and positions have been identified by Hans Pruijt: 'deprivation-based squatting' is easily co-opted and prone to external leadership of a hierarchical nature whereas squatting as an 'alternative housing strategy' finds resident-members more likely to be self-managing, autonomous and politically independent. The latter tend to generate networked cultural, social and political centres and organisations, as demonstrated by Christiania and ufaFabrik, discussed below. Similarly, 'entrepreneurial squatting', 'conservational squatters' and 'political squatting' manifest distinctive characteristics with differing political positions and influences.[10] As Delgado and Pruijt argue, squatters have the capacity to effectively embody or perform a critique of the failures of state and market on several levels, such as provisioning, services and governance.

In contrast, referring to a range of collaborative housing, Bresson and Denèfle describe French middle-class 'cohousing' as replete with humanistic and environmental values but reluctant to take a radical stand because, ultimately, they simply want more power in the established order.[11] In short, cases of alternative collaborative housing arise in a multitude of contexts and tend to be internally ridden with highly political conflicts over strategic directions. The argument that collaborative living is marginal is hard to maintain once it is acknowledged that the internal dynamics of associated movements are deeply linked to contemporary politics and that their socio-cultural and political activities are replete with inclusionary and environmentally concerned principles.

This chapter describes some key examples of the autonomous type to demonstrate how – in the face of heightened political, environmental and economic tensions – alternative communities and neighbourhoods have developed and refined more equitable, income-sharing, financial arrangements and horizontal decision-making techniques to support their existence to persist, and even blossom, in undoubtedly troubled times.

TINKERS BUBBLE: TRAVELLERS SETTLE NEAR A SPRING

'The fire pit is the heart of the community, where we often have breakfast or lunch together,' writes resident-member Pedro Brace: 'We eat together every night, taking turns to cook.' Most of the food that they eat is grown on site or sourced from an ethical wholesaler, just as the alcohol and juice they drink has been made on site from apples grown there. Practically all their energy comes from renewable sources, mainly wood from the 40 acres of fir plantation, woodland and orchards that they inhabit and some 12V solar power for lights, computers and stereos.[12] Water, accessed from a natural spring feeding a stream on the property, is only on tap at the community building, readily accessible for use in the shared kitchen and bathhouse but carried elsewhere, say to their small dwellings which only need sleeping and living spaces, along with waterless compost toilets.[13] They take wood for fuel, buildings and furniture, and leave the rest to fulfil services for other animals and plants. As resident Rosie Lancaster says 'you 'come so attached to nature, you can't separate yourself out'.[14]

Low impact community: planning

The original Tinkers Bubble residents were brought together protesting against automobile infrastructure, such as the M3 extension at a Twyford Down camp. The 1994 land purchase in Somerset (UK) was mainly financed by one founder, along with potential residents and 'interest-free loans from outside supporters'. Remarkably, no loan contracts were entered into: 'it was all based on trust'. However, they formed a cooperative that continues to include non-resident and ex-resident shareholders alongside communally held shares and individual resident shareholders. The first dwellings were temporary 'benders', tarpaulin-covered hazel wood frames (a kind of Celtic yurt) and tents. Locals complained to the council about this planning breach.[15]

A five-year planning struggle ensued. It was driven, on the Tinkers Bubble side, by Simon Fairlie who, as mentioned previously, coined the term 'low impact development'. The original application was knocked back, only to be granted on appeal. Then, the Secretary of the Department of Environment overturned that outcome. A further application by the intransigent Tinkers Bubble was lost in the High Court. Subsequently, when a new application was submitted – this time to a Labour, rather than Conservative, government – it succeeded. Even then, in 1999, 'success' only meant permission for five years, extended or renewed for temporary periods up to a decade at a time.[16]

In 2016, Tinkers Bubble succeeded in their application for a further 10-year temporary planning permission provided they fulfil conditions similar to the Welsh One Planet Development policy (see Chapter 6), which seems limited to 'hard-core would-be peasants', in Fairlie's words. He argues that, in reality, 'there is a huge demand for low impact housing which is not tied to agricultural or forestry livelihoods but', rather, 'provides people with access to a modest area of land for food and energy production, and for home-based businesses'. Speaking of the 'allergic reaction' of planners to genuine applications, especially 'for the sort of people who do not aspire to keep goats and burn charcoal on a Welsh mountainside', Fairlie has cogently argued that allowing for appropriate developments simply demands codification by planners. When, in the mid-2010s, the slight National Planning Policy Framework succeeded the previous massive guidelines, Fairlie duly advised groups wanting to start a communal sustainability venture to keep challenging planners, who now had more discretionary power to approve them, or resort to starting without permission and applying retrospectively.[17]

Drilling down into the drivers of their autonomy, we find that the will and visions of the 11 adult residents of Tinkers Bubble (2016) might vary yet unite on achieving sustainable futures. Mike, who had been a lead programmer in the video-games industry, wanted to prove fossil-fuel-free living was feasible. John Gollie expresses a deep, abiding and passionate commitment to low impact living when he says: 'that I hardly leave any trace, that's really important.'[18]

Economy

Tinkers Bubble residents are foresters, organic orchardists and gardeners. They eat road kill, pigeons and squirrels. Lancaster emphasises their 'strong work ethic'. Twenty-eight acres of Douglas fir, larch and mixed broadleaf woodland is managed by planting and thinning using horses, two-person saws and a sawmill with a wood-fired steam-engine. They often use no-dig methods. They keep chickens, pigs and bees, and one resident specialises in medicinal herbs. They wash clothes by hand and schedule turns to use the bath house.

Beyond collective sufficiency, they produce for local farmers' markets. They press Bramley, and other apple varieties by hand and process them through a wood-fired pasteurising station to make juice for sale. Their preserves include pickles, chutney and jams, wine and elderflower champagne. They sell raw cider vinegar locally, using traditional oak barrels for maturation. Yet, most industry is around collective sufficiency; in 2012, Brace estimated that each adult might only need £100 per month. In other words, compared with mainstream UK households, this off-grid community only marginally relies on the market.[19]

A critical chapter in Jenny Pickerill's *Eco-Homes* explores 'a disturbing persistence' of gendered cultures in eco-communities through notions, expectations and practices of 'embodiment'. Yet, she celebrates that a Tinkers' Bubble woman without much prior experience or training and 'no money' built here 'a beautiful, cosy small building out of natural materials'. Pickerill argues that this kind of determination and realisation of women's abilities across the board is necessary to establish a socio-cultural environment of free activity beyond external and internalised limitations associated with gender, not only in the mainstream workforce and social culture but also even in communities where there is a conscious effort to enact social change.[20]

In Tinkers Bubble we see several characteristics common to communities examined in this chapter. Residents often have an activist background. They do not wait for government or industry to lead a transition to a sustainable future. The state has been a strong barrier to their development. They substitute activities in capitalist markets as consumers and workers with self-provisioning, nonmonetary work and exchanges, and trade locally, ethically and informally only as necessary. They are instituting environmental sustainability through an, often antagonistic, autonomy from both state and market. Without ignoring deficiencies – certain building methods fail to fulfil a high thermal performance (a weakness minimised due to the small size of dwellings)[21] – Tinkers Bubble residents are achieving environmental goals without smart technology or clever design but through the practice of bricolage. They are *bricoleurs* and *bricoleuses* dancing their way to the revolution (Figure 9.1).

Figure 9.1   A Ceilidh at Tinkers Bubble

Source: Katja Testroet (photographer)

COLLECTIVE SUFFICIENCY: TWIN OAKS

Many sizable ecovillages tend to settle around a resident population of 90–150 – perhaps evidence of Dunbar's Number, which limits close relationships for any one person to 150? Illustrations of this tendency are the rural Twin Oaks (1967) in Virginia (US) and Sieben Linden (1997, Germany), with populations in early 2017 of 105 and 140, respectively. Both intentional communities demonstrate strong commitments to, and achievements in, environmentally oriented collective sufficiency.[22]

For reasons of space, the emphasis here is on Twin Oaks. It suffices to point out that, unlike Twin Oaks, Sieben Linden is not an income-sharing community, but its sub-community Club 99 has income-shared and achieved impressive environmental efficiencies. Along with maximum house space per capita and strict regulations over building, Sieben Linden members had already cut their carbon footprint back to 28 per cent of the German average by 2004. Provisional calculations in progress as this manuscript was submitted (mid-2017) suggest further savings, in terms of consumption, over the decade ending 2014 – one-quarter with respect to water, one-third regarding firewood and more than half with respect to electricity. In 2014, Litfin recorded members' per capita annual income as less than US$12,000.[23]

Although it had a rocky start, and was inspired by B.F. Skinner's behaviourist ideas, Twin Oaks endogenously developed a practical and feasible set of principles and practices around governance, work, and sharing their joint product. Their relationships and values, processes and protocol – based on 'cooperation, sharing, nonviolence, equality, and ecology' – contrast markedly with the dynamics of the market economy, which they only operate in marginally and as much on their own terms as possible. Similarly, the community's relationship to the state has been carefully crafted. The direct participatory democracy exercised in Twin Oaks starkly contrasts with the formal representative democracy of US governments at all levels. Valerie Renwick, who has lived at Twin Oaks for decades, explains that another world is not only possible: 'For us, another world is happening and we are living it.' This section sketches political and economic aspects of the community and its current operation rather than dwelling on its rich 50-year history and culture.[24]

Today Twin Oaks has 142 contiguous hectares of land, much of it woodland, and another 61 hectares of detached forest. There is flat and sloping agricultural land, pasture, dairy cattle, acres of vegetable plantings, fruit trees, massive greenhouse and ecological niches, including a lake. Solar energy and wood from their land heats most buildings. There are many outbuildings and seven large group dwellings, a children's building, Unicorn School, a big community centre with a large hospitality-style kitchen, dining spaces inside and out, and industrial buildings. No-one owns the property; they enter and remain its stewards. Twin Oaks is an incorporated association without capital stock; it has a similar tax status to a monastery though there is no common religion. While you live at Twin Oaks you cannot earn income from assets you own outside. Personal property is confined to what you can fit into your small to average-sized bedroom. Equality, incorporating diversity, is a lived reality.[25] Member Sabrina's testimonial in Box 9.1 featured on a placard for a 2012 Occupy demo.

Box 9.1   An Occupy placard created by Sabrina from Twin Oaks, 2012

I live communally with 100 people in Virginia. We run a miniature society, with government and businesses we collectively own, and produce lots of our own food. We aren't tuned into TV/iPhones. We each earn $5000 a year (on average) and all of the money goes to the community. By sharing what we have – seven big houses, fifteen cars, a variety of talents and skills – we get by on very little. We have no leader and there is always plenty of food, comfortable shelter and no trouble getting bills paid. We are all lucky to be secure and happy with our lives. I choose to live this way because corporatism is destroying American government and society, and because I am the 99%.

Thank you Occupy Wall St!!

Source: Derived from photo of Sabrina with placard, *Leaves of Twin Oaks* (Winter 2011/2012 #111)

Twin Oaks Community assumes and demonstrates that sharing incomes and resources has a range of benefits beyond expressing equal access and justice. There are economies of collectivisation which include use rights to more resources. There is greater security and insurance in mutual support. Nonmonetary, say domestic, tasks are viewed similarly to monetary, business-oriented work; everyone is recognised and appreciated for doing Twin-Oaks-defined work. Tighter relationships form due to their deep level of sharing. Twin Oaks has been able to construct a far more flexible, robust and successful economy with greater inbuilt resilience and relative autonomy from the mainstream market than any individual or family might attain. Drawing on research by Alexis Ziegler (of Living Energy Farm), Paxus reported (late in 2014) that, compared with US average consumption of energy and generation of solid wastes, Twin Oaks was already achieving the 80 per cent reduction in carbon emissions that the UN Intergovernmental Panel on Climate Change set as a target for 2050.[26]

Work

When I spent three weeks on the Twin Oaks visitor program (2012), I worked a bit less than the set quota of around 42 hours per week because the quota reduces after turning 55 years' old. The quota includes most domestic and non-domestic work chores to compare favourably with combined statistics of paid and unpaid work by mainstream workers (the average US adult spends around 20 hours per week on unpaid, mainly domestic, work).[27] Visitors attended numbers of talks and demonstrations on various aspects of living and working at Twin Oaks, many counting as hours for our quota. Sometimes we got a ride into town in a shared vehicle or simply put in a request for something to be bought or collected for us by the person on duty doing such errands that day. On site we followed local practice, walking or picking up and using any bike lying around and parking it once we'd arrived at our destination for any other person wanting it to take. No-one has a personal vehicle.

Each week managers put in their requirements, and every one indicates jobs they want and can do, signalling ideal and impossible times of the day and days to work. From this input, managers work out a draft schedule, so everyone gets a personal draft timetable for the week. This schedule goes out for comment and necessary changes and, then, is re-issued as a final draft. Subsequently, changes need to be negotiated, say by swapping with someone else or by talking with the area manager concerned. Time off for sickness and vacations are catered for in rules that apply equally to everyone. You learn on the job guided by a manager or crew member. I think that waiving aside the mainstream obsession with qualifications and experience is a great advantage (although Pickerill shows its downsides in a discussion specifically related to building).[28]

I spent time preparing food, cooking and washing dishes with the kitchen crew. At lunch and dinner times a big smorgasbord was available, catering for diverse tastes and diets with dishes labelled accordingly. I prepared for work in the tofu hut, cutting and packaging tofu, then cleaning down the room. I worked in the vegetable fields where Twin Oaks has a major crew weeding, planting, hoeing and harvesting. We took what we harvested straight to the kitchen or adjacent pantries. On hot days anyone wanting to took off their tops but we didn't if it was a day public visitors were around. (The nudity policy has been one of the most controversial Twin Oaks policies.) I worked on making hammocks, constructing boxes and filling them.

We went over to Twin Oak's community offspring Acorn and put seeds in packets. We spent time gardening around fruit trees and plants at a fellow-traveller's farm space. I worked on ornamental plants and with a member whose book project had been allocated a quota of work. I might have worked on laundry duties or child-care, repairing bikes, in the dairy or cheese-making, on political activities deemed work – such as one of the annual conferences that Twin Oaks hosts – or any number of other chores which you can read about at their site.

Most of the tofu and hammocks are sold offsite but most work done is not production for trade. There is a strong level of collective sufficiency and Twin Oaks swaps and shares human and other resources and products with other like-communities. The three-week-visitor brief includes the following questions: 'Consider if all your basic needs are met, can you live on $2 a day? Will you be comfortable with lots of public and common space and relatively small private space? Can you cooperate with people and share goods and responsibilities? What are your needs and desires around community?'[29]

Governance

Weekly general assemblies are places to make a public statement. There are constant personal and group conversations, the circulation of proposals, and the posting of opinions on a notice board in the main dining space wall. The governance structure certainly reflects, and clearly adapts from, Skinner's *Walden Two* (1948). There are discrete areas of activity coordinated horizontally by managers, including co-managers. They include all work areas, businesses, domestic and outdoor tasks, events, projects, land care, building and vehicle maintenance, energy and water systems. At the broadest scale, three planners work alongside one another in 18-month staggered terms to execute community decisions, deal with external relations and monitor that Twin Oaks is on course. Unless a candidate gains considerable support they do not become a planner and any of the decisions they make can be challenged and overturned.

Twin Oaks' democracy and complementary economy offers a set of processes and outcomes that are quite distinctive from mainstream standardisation, professional standards and state regulation. As Valerie reports:

> The key difference, for me, between how we do it and the mainstream does it is that, here, we're the ones making decisions about how of all those different aspects are going to look ... At Twin Oaks nobody's creating these values and these structures but us. So we have a really high degree of choice and we can consciously manifest our own values in the world throughout all stages of life.[30]

CULTURAL ECO-CONVIVIALITY: UFAFABRIK, BERLIN

Anarchist and women's liberationist Emma Goldman (1869–1940) was disgusted by a young boy counselling her not to dance so exuberantly because: 'My frivolity would only hurt the Cause.' Goldman saw dancing as the essence of revolution: 'I want freedom, the right to self-expression, everybody's right to beautiful, radiant things.'[31] This emphasis on holistic creative being is the essence of ufaFabrik, an outstanding urban sustainability demonstration centre and performance space in Berlin. There, collective solidarity, tolerant diversity in unity, exists as an exuberant and creative celebration driving the deep art of collaborative governance, of living with, and by, one another. After visiting in the late 2000s, Karen Litfin would write, 'I got the sense that ufaFabrik's motto was, "If it's not fun, don't do it."'[32]

Occupy

In 1979, more than 100 activists peacefully occupied a deserted film factory in Berlin, which had operated 1923–1964 as a subsidiary of the famous Universum Film AG (UFA) and was now a contested space waiting to be demolished. Some of the occupiers already knew one another through the first food cooperative established in Berlin and by performing for six weeks in an alternative cultural festival that had included demonstrating environmental techniques and technologies. With an independent direction, neither capitalist nor socialist but rather based on 'friendship first', their vision was to live modestly and communally and to 'create an interdisciplinary, multicultural meeting place, and a vibrant people-friendly oasis for creativity, art, and social and environmental creative processes'. Consequently, they placed a 'Welcome' banner at the entry of the property they envisaged as ideal for collaborative activities.[33]

Within a few weeks, the Berlin Senate agreed that they could remain on the site they had occupied. After a few months, 45 members of the now income-sharing commune were paying rent with an enhanced vision of co-creating a sustainable village in the world-famous capital. They started by making a combined heat and power (CHP) plant from a truck engine they called 'Mao Diesel'. In the 1980s, they began vegetating roofs and facades. Despite violent clashes with police later in 1980, further negotiations gave them security as tenants for at least three years; they have continued to develop the property for more than 35 years, now with a permanent lease through to the 2040s. Moreover, they have received regular subsidies from the City of Berlin for fulfilling cultural and social functions. The community worked step-by-step, starting in an emblematic way with a circus and a bakery, the trading success of which meant they could renovate their first theatre. Within a decade, however, they had a financial-cum-institutional crisis only resolved by introducing more formality and relative autonomy to distinct activities all operating under the umbrella ufaFabrik Berlin e.V.[34]

International Centre for Culture and Ecology

An International Centre for Culture and Ecology spread over 1.85 hectares in south Berlin (Templehof), UN Habitat acknowledged ufaFabrik in its 2004 shortlist of projects demonstrating 'Best Practice in Improving the Living Environment'.[35] Indeed, by the mid-1990s, they had: installed an expanded CHP; taken central control of ventilation and heating; turned over to energy-saving lights and devices; started biologically treating integrated rainwater collection to feed lawns and for flushing toilets; improved techniques for composting, re-use, recycling and separating wastes; insulated their Eco-Exhibition building with recycled paper; covered their walls with natural home-made mineral, and casein, paints; and, installed a 3m rotor wind turbine and 1000W generator, developing a high-efficiency slotted rotor to boot. These were integrated sustainability developments: for instance, Werner Wiartalla, an experienced physicist when joining ufaFabrik decades ago, has explained that condensation from the green roofs enables the solar panels to produce more energy.[36]

Further developments had ufaFabrik spreading their activities in participatory social change, community development and sustainability learning. By 1997, again using innovative techniques, ufaFabrik sustainably retrofitted many buildings, installing the largest existing array of solar panels in Berlin and creating an organic noise barrier. By the turn of the century, the ufaFabrik solar research centre boasted 12 different solar-related systems, they had initiated the id22 for thematic praxis on sustainable development, prepared for the id22 Festival for Ecology, Culture and Community, and embarked on a large and lengthy urban participatory planning project for their neighbourhood Templehof Harbour.[37]

In the 2010s, ufaFabrik continues to support original, international through to local, proposals for activities centring on cultural, social and environmental change and integrating ecology and creative arts. Much thought has gone into staging performances in eco-friendly ways, such as using energy from their in-house solar panels and two basement CHPs. Lighting systems use energy-saving lightbulbs, and vegetative insulation techniques enhance air quality. Using the Internet for local-cum-global transmission, ufaFabrik offers an instructional YouTube video on creating bike infrastructure for visiting peddlers to power a cinema.[38]

Today, a live-in community of 30 residents incorporate five or six times their number of workers in onsite multimedia, international and local community activities that attract hundreds of thousands of visitors every year: Café Olé, the ufaCircus and its children's circus school, a renowned samba band, production services for performative artists and activities, a large covered outdoor stage for more than 500 seats and multi-functional stages with 90, 180, and 260 seats, production, dance, sport and music studios, a bakery, a guesthouse (that I can recommend), an animal farmlet, markets and a neighbourhood self-help centre offering health and care services and support for all ages and abilities. The latter gave birth to an independent not-for-profit organisation with its headquarters in ufaFabrik but spreading over Berlin, with more than 30 facilities and projects and almost 300 employees working alongside volunteers. Members live on site, pay rent, work in ufaFabrik businesses and self-organise using consensus. ufaFabrik supports youth cultural talent and activities, live-in artist residencies and offers spaces for workshops, talks, tours and seminars on creative, social and environmental topics. Cultural diversity and participation is the veritable 'basis for our peaceful coexistence'.[39]

In short, decades ago, ufaFabrik established itself as a European demonstration space for community, culture and ecology. As municipal councils and industry players plan for integrated and off-grid neighbourhood-based urban power, water and waste systems as the way of the future, ufaFabrik pioneered such systems. Simultaneously, they are an innovative and vibrant international, national and local cultural centre where you can enjoy 'not too experimental' cabaret, vaudeville, musicals, puppetry, choirs, musicians with instruments from drums and didgeridoos to guitars, film festivals, 'medi-tainment', world music, poetry slams, singalongs, documentaries, theatre sports, and dancers of samba, flamenco and tango. ufaFabrik takes Shakespeare's 'all the world's a stage' to a revolutionary space of assembly, collaborative self-expression, creativity, consensual decision-making, diversity, conflict, dramatic resolution and celebration. Emma Goldman would be in her element.

FREETOWN CHRISTIANIA (COPENHAGEN, DENMARK)

Even with around 900 residents Freetown Christiania is not the most populous example of collaborative living in the world. Yet, this 'autonomous town', born in 1971 as a squat of the disused 34-hectare Bådsmandsstræde Barracks, has been attracting around one million tourists every year, certainly making it the most open and well-known model. Indeed, through its spontaneous mix of 'political resistance' and 'playful, resourceful atmosphere', Wendler has referred to it as 'one of the most influential attempts to create an alternative and self-determined life in the middle of, but independent from, mainstream society'.[40] Christiania's culture is radical and it has become 'a central node in international networks of activism and counterculture', especially significant within the European squatting movement.[41]

Freetown not only attracts tourists but also contributes to the culture of Copenhagen, for instance with 'Christiania bikes' (cargo tricycles) and by offering the only mixed-user bathhouse in the capital, low-cost meals, entertainment and cultural opportunities for local residents – see Figure 9.2. A complex urban organism that turns 50 years old in 2021, Christiania could be analysed from numerous angles. Here, I make a simple analysis of housing.

Until mid-2012, when a controversial agreement was signed with the Danish government to 'normalise' the settlement, allocation of housing

Figure 9.2   Christiania 2011

Source: Kim Wyon, photographer (VisitDenmark)

had followed particularly progressive protocol and principles based on need and capacity to pay, a simple tenure of use right, and build but leave, if you go. Then, to ensure its permanency, Christiania agreed to come under certain state regulations that limit making decisions on resource allocation and use based solely on social and environmental values. A brief summary of this rapprochement in terms of housing succinctly shows the binding connections between state and market forces, and the separation between, on the one hand, private property and monetary relations and, on the other hand, the simple and straight-forward satisfaction of needs through sharing.

When journalist Tom Freston revisited Christiania in 2013 – 40 years after an initial foray left him thinking it was too much like a festival to have a permanent future – he would reflect:

Christiania has grown up to be a cool, verdant little village in a corner of Copenhagen. I had underestimated the work ethic and the diligence of the Danes. They have built an entire settlement of spare, humble, Hobbit-like homes that surrounds a lake and runs along gravel paths and cobblestone roads that wind through woods to the seaside. Older buildings have been restored and are often covered in murals. There are bars, cafés, grocery shops, a huge building-supply store, a museum, art galleries, a concert hall, a skateboard park, a recycling center, even a recording studio (inside a shipping container). I noticed electric hand dryers in a café bathroom. Buildings had satellite dishes. Children rode around on multicolored bikes and groups of young tourists wandered the streets in short pants, sandals, and black hoodies.[42]

Residents of this car-free settlement had endogenously formed protocol for self-regulation, collective sustainability and horizontally negotiated agency that flew in the face of accepted market and state principles of private property. Rather than the direct and immediate sufficiency of a rural commune, their claims to sustainability relied not only on hospitality, cultural entrepreneurship and trade (including in drugs and with tourists), but also frugal convivial living and living off the waste of a profligate Global North city. Cattaneo argues that such tenuous and limited sustainability is an inevitable straightjacket of urban twenty-first century squats.[43]

Christiania has had a series of agreements with Danish state institutions, including parliament, starting in 1972 when the Defence Ministry approved use provided that they pay electricity and water fees. In the 1970s, the Social Democrat government referred to Christiania legally as 'a social experiment'. Residents upgraded the 150 buildings onsite, adapting and refurbishing them in eco-conservative ways, and built further modest structures using salvaged at-hand materials in a process that Jarvis remarks amounted to 'reclaiming from "experts" and "commerce" the intimate significance of habitation'.[44] By the mid-1970s, the settlement had already reached almost the number of residents it has today.

The Christiania Law of 1989 concretised their use rights by defining their space into building-free rural and building-full urban zones. The law was renegotiated, but a firm intent by the state clarified 'normalisation' of Christiania (2004), ultimately meaning engagement with private property, building and urban regulations. By 2011, Christiania seemed to face a grim choice: compromise or disappear. Of course, what made negotiating controversial was the option of standing firm with the ultimate ideal of autonomy in a highly dangerous fight to either live the dream or die. They certainly had external support, including from Danish urbanists and architects who made their opinions public.[45]

The 2012 agreement – only made after the community lost a Supreme Court case – sealed the sale of a portion of the land and buildings they occupied into collective ownership of the Christiania Foundation (which had been formed for the purpose), with remaining land and buildings reserved for rent. The payment was well under market rates for Copenhagen: almost €14 million, the first half of which was paid mid-2012 partly through a loan, the other half due by 2018. Coppola and Vanolo argue that city planners had a vested interest in ensuring that the space remained a tourist attraction under City of Copenhagen and Danish state regulation.[46]

Christiania had established fair, resident-managed allocation of housing 'based on values of communality, informality, trust and local sovereignty'. This meant familiarity with the housing applicant and decisions made by meetings of the appropriate local area – of which there were 14 of various sizes. Rooms in houses were allocated in house meetings on similar principles of subsidiarity and familiarity. In contrast, 'normalisation' would introduce a right of appeal to a 'higher authority', a 'third party'.[47] A stay was put on independent house-building, and a bureaucratic process enforced whereby proposals needed to be passed by four levels of Christiania and city council bureaucracy. Simultaneously, bans were put on procuring recycled goods from government recycling sites, shrinking ready sources of building materials to the 24-hour site at Christiania.[48]

The effect of these changes to the contexts within which houses were built and democratic decision-making exercised over Christiania's residents' everyday lives, cannot be underestimated. Wendler, for instance, has described Christiania's self-built 'incremental, recycled' alternative homes as 'immediately recognisable':

> ... their colourfulness, striking materials and unique architecture is an intrinsic expression of Christiania's spirit and many of them feature on postcards and photographs. They are also one of the main Christiania 'inventions' ... They reflect the diversity of the autonomous town: they are personal, lived alternatives with their own unique trajectories, yet they express related ideas about making alternative urban life possible. It is in this interplay of tendencies that Christiania's experimentality is rooted.[49]

Normalisation has risked gentrification and 'Disneyfication' as residents unable to afford rents feel like they are selling themselves and their locale to keep up with the qualitative and quantitative increase in monetising their lives – along with 'concerns regarding the loss of Christiania's distinctive qualities of social inclusiveness and cultural originality'.[50] Under Christiania's established system, if someone had been late in paying their rent, they would be reminded, there might be discussion on addressing the cause or some remedy suggested. As resident Ole Lykke told Freston, by 2013, failure to pay rent suddenly meant a threatening notice that, after three months, 'the state can throw everybody out':

> We now pay double for half the freedom, considering the interest cost and increased rent. We have moved into a capitalist structure. Money talks now. It's possible for the state to keep turning the wheel on the rent and the banks to keep making the interest higher. It will be harder and harder for older people, disabled people, to keep a home here.[51]

In short, the encroachment of state and market threaten to starve and stifle essential aspects of residents' responsibilities and rights to create their own living space. Freetown is at risk of becoming an unfree-town.

CALAFOU: FROM STATE AND MARKET TO 'OUR-RULE'

Just as France has a revolutionary history of struggling for grassroots autonomy, so does Catalonia. This has been clear in its century-long struggle to gain independence from Spain, heightened by efforts to regain autonomy within the Spanish state since it was abolished by Franco in 1938. The Catalan language and autonomy are dearly held ideals in Catalans' hearts and their everyday culture and practices. Thus, the Spanish anti-austerity pro-democracy 15-M (Indignados) movement was particularly vibrant in Barcelona, as thousands of protesters extended their 15 May 2011 street demonstration into an occupation of the central Plaça de Catalunya that ensued for several weeks, despite police assaults. The distinctive 'real democracy' politics of Catalan protesters reappeared in May 2015, when Ada Colau, a radical housing activist prominent in the Platform for Mortgage Victims, became Barcelona's mayor.[52]

It is in this context that Calafou, located close to the town of Vallbona d'Anoia, around 60km from Barcelona, was reborn. Today it is a self-proclaimed 'eco-industrial post-capitalist colony', with housing and work spaces for a collective of around 50 residents plus others with whom they collaborate. Originally, Calafou had been an industrial textile colony innovatively developed more than seven centuries ago. Later a paper-manufacturing enterprise, prior to its current function it had become a hydroelectric plant. Calafou started in a practical sense in July 2011 when around 30 people, mainly ex-squatters from Barcelona, pooled their resources and, as a housing cooperative, raised a mortgage to buy the abandoned ruins and surrounding land, including a river, for circa €500,000.[53]

Catalan Integral Cooperative

The establishment of Calafou was associated with a growing network, the Catalan Integral Cooperative (*Cooperativa Integral Catalana*, CIC). Calafou has become a key node in CIC, which is an alternative economic network with its own set of relatively autonomous assemblies and interlinked currencies ('ecos') that had several thousands of Catalan participants by early 2017. CIC started in 2010 after eco-networks (*ecoxarxes*) in Montseny and Tarragona had developed an alternative currency (2009) within a community exchange system where accounts of members were tracked via an online platform. Later, an endogenous IntegralCES platform united many of the Catalan eco-networks into horizontally connected politico-economic infrastructures in order to co-ordinate, and holistically structure, them. This structure includes bioregional assemblies uniting eco-networks within either a north or south bioregion.[54]

As just one (if notable) node, Calafou illustrates the distributed and relatively autonomous productive bases of CIC, focusing on producing and value-adding food and other basic products and services including health, learning and housing. These units are dotted around the region emanating from participants' homes, and self-governing spaces such as the well-used Aurea Social space located in the centre of Barcelona, which has been a venue for general assemblies. The CIC includes transport, warehouse and distribution networks connecting the eco-networks with one another. Didac Costa estimates that there could be up to 200 food cooperatives, and Carolina Zerpa has referred to CIC food activities and relationships as the largest network of farmers, consumers and processors across Catalonia. Each eco-network develops its own sets of projects, relationships with other environmental and social movements, and activities, including free-sharing and mutual support.[55]

Calafou[56]

Calafou offers 2.8 hectares of space for productive, residential, political and cultural activities. It has a strong technological, postmodern, focus that contrasts with its centuries' old buildings. Almost 30 apartments have been in a process of refurbishment. When I visited, in mid-2012, the most organised sections seemed to be the hacklab working on hardware and software, and the mechanic's workshop dealing with all kinds of vehicles from motorbikes to trucks. The site had a rather surreal feel in places, such as when in sight of a highway pass buttressed by great columns jutting out from the surrounding rural green landscape.

By the end of 2016 expanding activities at Calafou included a wood workshop repairing and creating furniture, a metal foundry and workshop, cloth printing and clothes making, recycling oils into detergent, and a biolab. As with CIC, the aim is for individuals and groups within, and working alongside, Calafou to generate activities with relative autonomy but, nevertheless, effectively interconnected. Other productive activities include food production, food preparation and food sharing. Although located in a rural area, Calafou suffers from soil and water pollution from previous onsite industrial activities, and pollution from activities upstream. Thus, food production is constrained and challenged but benefits from ecological and permaculture approaches and practices (Figure 9.3).

The general assembles and other political processes and principles followed at Calafou have great similarities with other collaborative housing, living and working cases presented in this chapter. As such, there are 'collective projects' that Calafou self-manages and gains (actually profits) from, an 'autonomous project' is the name for an enterprise controlled by an individual or collective organised for that particular purpose, and there are 'collective spaces' for initiating projects and conducting members' everyday affairs, embracing inclusive values of outreach. The horizontal politics, production and exchange protocol of Calafou and CIC project a post-capitalist mesh of ways of relating and values that are works-in-progress and represent experiments in the here and now towards up-scaled and future-oriented structures.

Figure 9.3   Calafou (2012)

I have raised questions in other work about the superficial radicalism of the 'alternative currencies' (including digital currencies) that CIC employs.[57] In this – as in its horizontal politics, collaborative work units and approaches to financing – the techniques used are representative of a range of practices used in experimental housing, living and working models in many other places. Such models share similar environmental and social values and respectful relationships between members. However, CIC incorporates a remarkably high level of committed participants and, as such, presents an unusual level of sustained effort towards unifying their systems as a direct and holistic alternative to the capitalist order.

The last word is reserved for the caution Calafou makes to visitors, that it is 'not a vacation destination, but a political project for social transformation, as well as the home of a community.'

'FROM LITTLE THINGS BIG THINGS GROW'

The context of the early years of CIC is detailed in a general study of alternative activities of everyday life in Barcelona since the Global Financial Crisis, with a special emphasis on nonmonetary production and exchange. The authors of *Otra Vida es Posible* ('another life is possible') set up a discourse connecting local projects and individuals' experiences to themes of wholesale social change.[58] Indeed, the most remarkable cases of eco-communal living are so politically aware and connected, so far removed from self-absorbed cults, that they could be seen to cast mainstream urban life into a quirky, out-of-date and marginal light.

This chapter has shown how certain collaborative living projects have grown from activism and remain deeply connected to broader socio-economic and cultural transformation. They operate on political principles and processes that highlight autonomy and collective sufficiency, horizontal relationships, and approach resources as commons and via commoning. Intended and real impacts on local through to national environments proceed like ripples from a stone thrown into water, ever-growing, ever-moving; upscaling seems organic.

In the early 1990s, Australian singer-songwriter-musicians Kev Carmody and Paul Kelly collaborated on a now globally known song 'From little things big things grow'. This song celebrated the implicit association between the Gurindji strike on a Northern Territory cattle station in 1966 and both the Indigenous peoples' movement to gain Native Title of traditional lands and black and white reconciliation across Australia. Similarly, cases in this chapter, and this book more generally, show that collaborative housing can blossom into alternative living, nonmarket economies and grassroots governance, rehearsing post-capitalist futures. In short, from little things, big things do grow.

Conclusion

10

Small Is Necessary and, with Sharing, Feasible

Small is necessary because the ecological footprint of the average human occupant of our earth breaches the planet's regenerative capacity. The most severe challenge associated with our future is our environmentally unsustainable practices, a challenge linked to the ways we live collectively as a species. The greatest threat comes from generic ways of living in countries from the Global North, the central focus of this book.

Despite all the conventional emphasis on the environmental features of residences – the materials out of which a house is made, its operating costs in terms of energy and how renewable its energy sources are – the relative size and per capita floor space of our dwellings – is a broad, if not always reliable, indicator of the ecological footprint of its inhabitants. As elaborated in Part I, this point would not be so significant if, during the twentieth century, the average sizes of dwellings in many regions and cities of the world had not grown exponentially while the average sizes of households shrank. Furthermore, whereas many houses and households a few hundred years ago were still units of production, since the nineteenth century houses and households have become primary units of consumption.

Beyond the physical efficiencies of sharing spaces, infrastructure, and resources such as water and energy in various forms of eco-collaborative housing, as described in parts II and III, the socio-cultural impacts of encouraging, monitoring and regulating for low impact co-living is crucial for residents' everyday practices. Certainly the built environments of eco-collaborative housing reflect qualities of durability and light ecological footedness, but it is critical that they proactively adopt, adapt and develop sharing models that emphasise efficient use of food, clothing and vehicular resources along with re-using, recycling and minimising waste. Thus, sharing is a critical component of genuinely small footprint, or low impact, living.

Eco-collaborative housing models that incorporate initiatives and infrastructure towards collective sufficiency at least in food, water and energy not only represent the cutting edge of more sustainable lifestyles but also seem to prefigure post-capitalist values and relations of production and exchange. Holistic change has co-evolved forms of governance that turn the vertical layering of powers within the capitalist milieu on their head. Within such communities, horizontal power means participatory, delegated and shared responsibilities supported by consensual decision-making. Extensive and complex collaborative housing offers new forms of both material sustenance and political governance.

Perhaps it is this essential radicalism of alternative housing-cum-living that accounts for its grindingly slow progress primarily against state and market forces, as explored in Part III. The lack of appropriate planning codes and financial support remain key barriers for numbers of people keen to participate in collaborative models of all kinds.

FURTHER RESEARCH

The transdisciplinary 'smaller is better' and 'sharing is best' framing of this exploration of collaborative housing and living is distinct within literatures of this field, which are often discipline-associated if not disciplinary-based or case-by-case interdisciplinary analyses. While the cases, literatures and discourses drawn on here mainly fall in the realms of planning, housing, urban architecture, interior design, and environmental and sustainability studies, I have freely referred to and engaged with topics related to the implicitly interdisciplinary fields of sociology, community development, ecological economics, political activism and utopian or futures studies. It is highly likely that most fruitful future research will emerge from holistic and transdisciplinary perspectives.

Iterated throughout this work are comments on the paucity of statistics on all types of collaborative housing that have been so frequently marginalised in mainstream housing policy, residential planning codes and building regulations, and by conventional home loans, except in key northern European countries and, more recently, further afield. Even when accepted within regulation for mainstream housing, the devil emerges in the detail as authorities seem more concerned to conform to obsolete ideals such as a standard 'family' home and household with ample parking spaces for cars, than to promote significant sustainability features that, for instance, collaborative housing and their community of households offer. It is not surprising, then, that further difficulties with quantitative primary research arise because many developments are barely visible and conveniently remain off government agencies' radars. While it is probably more feasible, effective and efficient to open planning codes and building regulations to eco-collaborative housing at a national level, local governments are likely to be the appropriate authority to monitor and keep reliable records of existing and prospective eco-collaborative housing developments in their territory.

Qualitative studies of co-owners, ecovillagers, cohousers and squatters generally take the form of community histories, community-oriented sociological studies or autobiographical testimonies. Moreover, there are many 'how-to' works by residents or professionals involved in supporting the built, legal, social and financial development of alternative communities. Many of these primary sources are rich in experiential detail. Other qualitative research uses ethnographic methods, such as analyses of records of participant-observers or of interviews, many applying the lenses of social constructionism, grounded or critical theories. However, there are large gaps in comparative studies because the case-based studies have customised approaches and cannot be easily drawn on to create a reliable database for generic reviews. It is incumbent on funding bodies to support extensive comparative studies to inform various residential, professional, industry and government stakeholders.

Collaborative housing and living has become so attractive to potential members that many communities keen to share their experience and encourage interest have very informative websites. Recently, certain researchers interested in transformation and social change and acknowledging the critical need for more environmentally sustainable living and local economies have focused on such communities and their settlements. This is an area of cutting-edge research, which seems to drill down to the essence of what eco-collaborative housing can offer with respect to developing more sustainable, socially just and democratic futures.

This potentially rich field of studies on alternative communities and collaborative housing demands much more attention than it currently receives. Beyond progress in data gathering, especially in terms of detailed statistics, there are many questionable assumptions, untested hypotheses and methodological queries to challenge researchers. For instance, although I have relied on ecological footprints as a method of comparison, this measure is neither perfect nor comprehensive (see

Chapter 6). In fact, an ecological footprint is not a pure standard at all but varies across regions specifically (though ironically) to make it both a more accurate and comparable unit of measure. Arguably, it is a more accurate measure in the same place across time, rather than comparatively at a moment in time. I justify using it here due to its generality and relevance to speculating for futures characterised by social justice and environmental sustainability.

Comparative levels of collective sufficiency and ecological regeneration, the diversity of community management techniques of a whole range of ecological resources, buildings, infrastructure and services, as well as internal governance of activities and relationships are amongst a range of topics that might tempt rigorous researchers.

ACTIVISM

Beyond citizens curious to know more about collaborative housing, this book was written with two audiences in mind: a scholarly, academic and student audience mainly interested in thinking about, researching and supporting such developments in a range of professional ways; and activists keen to know more, and eager for material to assist them in advocacy and their personal-is-the-political journeys. Collaborative housing reveals models and practices that embody and connect with a plethora of social and environmental movements and causes: climate justice, degrowth, commoning and sharing, food sovereignty, anti-consumerism, permaculture, solidarity economies, and inclusive and diverse neighbourhoods, to name a few.

Collaborative housing and living attracts many more people this century than the last for reasons related to affordability, sustainability and community. Housing has become increasingly unaffordable, especially in the bastions of capitalism, our global cities. Residents are seeking cheaper ways to accommodate themselves on a permanent basis. They are more aware of the costs of residential services, such as water and energy, and of a plethora of unnecessary goods in societies that seemingly only grow more consumptive and inequitable. Thus, there is an economic imperative to be concerned about environmental sustainability. At the same time, housing ourselves more sustainably and changing household practices with one or two related others often presents as a lonely, challenging and de-spiriting struggle. The power of community, of doing it ourselves, has strong potential not only for economic and environmental efficiencies, but also offers various and numerous benefits related to a diversity of people experimenting with and showcasing improved forms of living.

BEYOND A CONCLUSION

I have tried to show that many dedicated cases of collaborative housing are replete with positive and negative, clear and subtle lessons for our uncertain future. Given the environmental and socio-political challenges that capitalism presents, that future sometimes seems like a cliff that we, like lemmings, are all bent on chasing one another over to end up in freefall into an abyss. At the same time, don't we pride ourselves in the human capacities of consciousness, will, cooperation and freedom of action?

I have structured this book to show current, dynamic and interrelated forces at play: the state, the market and citizens as a collective. I have intervened in a discordant set of discourses in provocative ways, but set my course with a singular intention in mind. Certainly I wanted to reveal the various potentials of too-readily hidden and dismissed realities. But, more than that, my intention has been to contribute to debates and action that might cut loose imaginations straightjacketed by mainstream forms of living, working and governing. At a point of seeming collapse, not only of the systems that dominate how we cooperate but also of our response, I wanted to show that the personal is the political, and that infectious change can start by adopting sustainable practices as members of collective households and genuine communities in heartfelt neighbourhoods. What the world needs now is a spectacular reawakening of human creativity, collectivity, solidarity and localism in practice.

Appendix
Key Sources and Links

This set of key and representative English sources and links for topics raised in this book was current for mid-2017 and selective along the themes and topics considered significant here. It is a simple guide to searching for more information. One of my selection criteria was that the source included links and other leads to even more data and relevant topics. As iterated throughout the book, you will find that practically all communities discussed in it – and many more such communities – have elaborate and living websites replete with information on associated topics. I have left them out; you only need your search engine to identify them. Of course, the endnotes include many of them and offer a lot more in the way of sources.

GENERIC COLLABORATIVE HOUSING ORGANISATIONS

Since 2002, the Institute for Creative Sustainability (id22) has been a not-for-profit organisation based in Berlin promoting sustainable cohousing cultures ('cohousing' used here in the widest sense of the term, similar to how 'collaborative housing' is defined in this book). id22 coordinates an 'experimentcity' initiative, offers events such as guided tours and manages an interactive website for housing groups to promote their projects, to network and to share data – http://id22.net/en/themen/#cohousing

Michael LaFond and Thomas Honeck (eds), *CoHousing Cultures: Handbuch für Selbstorganisiertes, Gemeinschaftliches Und Nachhaltiges Wohnen/Handbook for Self-Organized, Community Oriented and Sustainable Housing*, Berlin: jovis, 2012. The CoHousing Cultures book website includes links to all national contact points – http://cohousing-cultures.net/cohousing-platform/

The most recent publication in English and German is Michael LaFond and Larisa Tsvetkova (eds) *CoHousing Inclusive: Self-organized, Community-led Housing for All*, Berlin: jovis, 2017 – www.jovis.de/en/books/details/product/cohousing_inclusive.html

The Fellowship for Intentional Communities (FIC) is a not-for-profit body promoting a wide range of intentional communities and a sharing, cooperative culture. Based in the US, the body has an international online directory, a journal and other resources – www.ic.org/

The not-for-profit collective Diggers and Dreamers ('The Guide to Communal Living in Britain'), which started in 1989, offers numerous printed, audio-visual and online resources to a range of alternative living events, options and topics, including a directory to alternative housing across Britain. Look out for their publications on cohousing, low impact living, communes and more – www.diggersanddreamers.org.uk/

The UK National Custom and Self Build Association (NaCSBA) has a site 'endorsed by the Government', which includes a page on 'Independent community collaboration' – www.selfbuildportal.org.uk/independent-community-collaboration

COHOUSING ASSOCIATIONS

The Cohousing Association of the United States website has a directory of cohousing projects and offers resources on governance and seniors' cohousing – www.cohousing.org/

Similarly, the Canadian Cohousing Network, established in 1992, offers a directory of communities on its website, along with a range of other resources – http://cohousing.ca/

The UK counterpart is UK Cohousing – https://cohousing.org.uk/

COMMUNITY GOVERNANCE

Glen Ochre, *Getting Our Act Together: How to Harness the Power of Groups*, Melbourne: Groupwork Press, 2013.

Seeds for Change Lancaster Cooperative has published (2013) *A Consensus Handbook: Cooperative Decision-Making for Activists, Co-Ops and Communities* – www.seedsforchange.org.uk/handbook

Sociocracy is a popular approach offering useful techniques – http://thesociocracygroup.com/

COOPERATIVE HOUSING

The Co-operative Housing International (CHI), under the umbrella International Co-operative Alliance organisation, aims to represent and promote the international cooperative housing movement. Its website offers an interactive guide to search for registered national organisations: www.housinginternational.coop/housing-co-operatives-worldwide/

Nic Bliss (compiler), *1,001 Co-operative and Community-led Homes: The Housing Revolution Starts Here*, Liverpool: Confederation of Co-operative Housing, undated.

ECOVILLAGES

The Global Ecovillage Network (GEN) supports communities that focus on regenerative activities right across the world, promoting their aims to government, entrepreneurs, researchers, activists and other interested parties and citizens – https://ecovillage.org/

Karen T. Litfin, *Ecovillages: Lessons for Sustainable Community*, Cambridge (UK)/Malden (Massachusetts): Polity, 2014.

FINANCIAL AND LEGAL STRUCTURES

Many of the generic sites on collaborative housing include pages and other resources on financial and legal models. The implications and pros and cons of the various models can take a long time to absorb. Advice from local and national professionals who specialise in collaborative housing is usually very useful because specific legal systems constrain and permit building and planning and financial aspects of models in various ways.

Check out the housing section at Sustainable Economies Law Centre (California) – www.theselc.org/rethinking-home

Janelle Orsi's associated collaborative housing work can be found here – http://janelleorsi.com/

Significant grassroots models include the German Mietshäuser Syndikat – www.syndikat.org/en/ and UK Radical Routes, 'a network of housing and worker co-operatives working for radical social change' – http://radicalroutes.org.uk/

LOW IMPACT LIVING

Sarah Bunker, Chris Coates, James Dennis and Jonathan How, *Low Impact Living Communities in Britain: A Diggers and Dreamers Review*, London: Diggers and Dreamers Publications, 2014.

Paul Chatterton, *Low Impact Living: A Field Guide to Ecological, Affordable Community Building*, London: Routledge, 2015.

Members of Redfield Community (Buckingham, UK) started Lowimpact.org, a not-for-profit educational organisation the activities of which include distributing online information – www.lowimpact.org/

PERMACULTURE

David Holmgren, *Permaculture: Principles and Pathways Beyond Sustainability*, Hepburn: Holmgren Design Services, 2002. This classic is just one of many works by co-founder of permaculture whose website has many free resources – www.holmgren.com.au/

Rosemary Morrow, *The Earth User's Guide to Permaculture*, 2nd edn, Pymble (Sydney): Kangaroo Press, 2006. There is more information at the website of the Blue Mountains Permaculture Institute that she cofounded – www.bluemountainspermacultureinstitute.com.au/

The Permaculture Association (UK) website features many events and resources – www.permaculture.org.uk/ – as does the UK Permaculture Magazine website – www.permaculture.co.uk/

Jan Martin Bang, *Permaculture: A Student's Guide to the Theory and Practice of Ecovillage Design*, Edinburgh: Floris Books, 2015.

COLLABORATIVE HOUSING RESEARCH HIGHLIGHTS

Karin Krokfors (ed.) *Built Environment – Special Issue: Cohousing in the Making*, 38(3), 2012.

Lidewij Tummers, 'The re-emergence of self-managed co-housing in Europe: A critical review of co-housing research', *Urban Studies* 53(10), 2016, pp. 2023–2040.

Lidewij Tummers (ed.) *Journal of Urban Research and Practice – Special Issue: Taking Apart Co-Housing: Towards a Long-Term Perspective of Self-Managed Collaborative Housing Initiatives* 7(1), 2015.

Dick Urban Vestbro (ed.) *Living Together: Cohousing Ideas and Realities Around the World* is a selection of articles generated by the first International Conference on Collaborative Housing (Stockholm, Sweden), May 2010.

A useful list of references, *Cohousing Academic Research Bibliography with Abstracts*, can be found at the Cohousing Research Network,

a working group of the Cohousing Association of the US – www.
cohousingresearchnetwork.org/wp-content/uploads/2017/05/CRN-
Academic-Bibliography.pdf

Another source of publications and research activities is the European
Co-Housing Research network – http://cohousingresearch.wbb-nrw.de/

SQUATTING

Claudio Cattaneo and Miguel A. Martínez (eds) for the Squatting Europe
Collective, *The Squatters' Movement in Europe: Commons and Autonomy
as Alternatives to Capitalism*, London: Pluto Press, 2010.

Bart van der Steen, Ask Katzeff and Leendert van Hoogenhuijze (eds)
The City is Ours: Squatting and Autonomous Movements in Europe,
Oakland (California): PM Press, 2014.

Squatting Europe Kollective (ed.) *Squatting in Europe: Radical
Spaces, Urban Struggles*, Wivenhoe/New York/Port Watson: Minor
Compositions, 2013.

Alexander Vasudevan, *The Autonomous City: A History of Urban
Squatting*, London: Verso, 2017.

For up-to-date news and links on squatting internationally, see the
Squat!net website, established in 1997 – http://planet.squat.net/

The Squatting Europe Collective has a map of squat locations here –
https://maps.squat.net/en/cities

For more on squatting in England and Wales see the SQUASH
(Squatters Action for Secure Homes) website – www.squashcampaign.
org/

TINY HOUSES

Lloyd Kahn, *Tiny Homes: Simple Shelters – Scaling Back in the 21st
Century*, Bolinas (California): Shelter Publications, 2012.

Shay Salomon, *Little House on a Small Planet*, Guilford (Connecticut):
Lyons Press, 2nd edn 2010.

Two tiny houses YouTube videos are especially worth checking out:
Ana White, Open Concept Modern Tiny House with Elevator Bed,
30 January 2017 – www.youtube.com/watch?v=lHjJd4tkvSU – and
University of Oregon, April Anson's Tiny House, 21 March 2013 – www.
youtube.com/watch?v=waunFoKkJEs

April Anson offers a critique of tiny house living in 'Framing degrowth: The radical potential of tiny house mobility' in Anitra Nelson and François Schneider (eds) *Housing for Degrowth: Principles, Models, Challenges and Opportunities*, London: Routledge-Earthscan Environmental Humanities Series, 2018.

Notes

Chapter 1

All URLs current at 20 April 2017.

1. Dan Hancox, 'Only the rich and old will own homes in 2025, says study', *The Guardian Weekly*, 10 February 2016, p. 15.
2. Demographia *12th Annual Demographia International Housing Affordability Survey* (2015, 3rd quarter), Christchurch (NZ): Performance Urban Planning, 2016, p. 7.
3. Ric Battellino, 'Housing and the economy – remarks by Mr Ric Battellino, Deputy Governor of the Reserve Bank of Australia' (to the 6th National Housing Conference, Melbourne, 25 November 2009) in *BIS Review*, 154/2009.
4. NHF, *Home Truths 2015/2016: The Housing Market in London*, London: National Housing Federation, 2016.
5. OECD, 'Figure 1.13 House prices have risen fast amid large household debt', in *Economic Policy Reforms 2016*, Paris: Organisation for Economic Co-operation and Development Publishing, 2016.
6. UN, 'Preparing for growing numbers of urban residents', in *Integrating Population Issues into Sustainable Development, Including in the Post-2015 Development Agenda – A Concise Report*, NYC: United Nations, 2015, pp. 27–29.
7. R. McLellan, L. Iyengar, B. Jeffries and N. Oerlemans (eds), *Living Planet Report 2014: Species and Spaces, People and Places*, Gland (Switzerland): WWF, 2014, p. 4.
8. Ibid, pp. 9, 32–33.
9. WWF, *Living Planet Report 2016: Risk and Resilience in a New Era*, Gland (Switzerland): WWF International, 2016, p. 83.
10. IPCC, *Climate Change 2014: Mitigation of Climate Change. Contribution of Working Group III to the Fifth Assessment Report of the Intergovernmental Panel on Climate Change* – O. Edenhofer, R. Pichs-Madruga, Y. Sokona, E. Farahani, S. Kadner, K. Seyboth, A. Adler, I. Baum, S. Brunner, P. Eickemeier, B. Kriemann, J. Savolainen, S. Schlömer, C. von Stechow, T. Zwickel and J. C. Minx, Cambridge/NYC: Cambridge University Press, 2014, pp. 675–77.
11. Brian Edwards and Paul Hyett, *Rough Guide to Sustainability*, London: Royal Institute of British Architects, 2001, p. 97.
12. Simon Guy and Steven A. Moore, *Sustainable Architectures: Cultures and Natures in Europe and North America*, Oxford: Spon Press, 2005, pp. 4–5.
13. Kevin McCloud, UK Channel 4, *Grand Designs Revisited*, Series 4 Episode 4, 'The Woodsmans cottage: revisited', 26 October 2005 – http://www.channel4.com; Ben Law – http://www.ben-law.co.uk
14. Kevin McCloud, UK Channel 4, *Grand Designs* Series 3 Episode 3, 'The larch-clad house', 31 October 2012 – http://www.channel4.com/programmes/

grand-designs/; Rural Design Architects site, 'Kendrum turf house' – http://www.ruraldesign.co.uk/Kendram-Turf-House

15. Kevin McCloud's company HAB and Green Square partnered to produce Haboakus, three community-oriented developments (2007–2014) – http://www.haboakus.co.uk; Roger Hunt, 'We Hab a dream', *Eco House*, pp. 71–76 – http://huntwriter.com

16. Michael Short, 'Melbourne's housing crisis: would you live in a floating apartment?', *The Age*, 24 March 2015 – http://www.theage.com.au/

17. Sarah Booth 'Backyard bungalows: Emilio and Anna', *Assemble Papers*, 7 November 2014 – http://assemblepapers.com.au/

18. Shannon Bouton, David Cis, Lenny Mendonca, Herbert Pohl, Jaana Remes, Henry Ritchie and Jonathan Woetzel, *How to Make a City Great*, NYC: McKinsey and Company, 2013, p. 16 – http://www.mckinsey.com/

19. Lloyd Kahn, *Tiny Homes: Simple Shelter*, Bolinas (Calinfornia): Shelter Publications, 2012.

20. Matthieu Lietaert, 'The growth of cohousing in Europe', The Cohousing Association of the United States, 16 December 2007 – http://www.cohousing.org/print/313

Chapter 2

URLs current at 25 April 2017 unless otherwise indicated.

1. K. J. Mee and N. Vaughan 'Experiencing home', in Susan J. Smith (ed.), *International Encyclopedia of Housing and Home*, Amsterdam: Elsevier, 2012, pp. 146–51.

2. Judith Flanders, *The Making of Home*, London: Atlantic Books, 2014, p. 49.

3. Ibid, pp. 192–95.

4. Nora Bohnert, Anne Milan and Heather Lathe, 'Living arrangements of children in Canada: A century of change', in Statistics Canada (Cat. No. 75-006-X), *Insights on Canadian Society*, 2014, pp. 1–2.

5. Flanders, *The Making of Home*, pp. 28–31, 91.

6. John Burnett, *A Social History of Housing: 1815–1985*, 2nd edn, London/New York: Methuen, 1986, pp. 98–99.

7. Ibid, pp. 102–5.

8. On 'gender' in the home, see J. Hollows 'Domesticity', in Smith (ed.), *International Encyclopedia of Housing and Home*, pp. 405–14.

9. Flanders, *The Making of Home*, pp. 66–67, 92, 127–28, 140–41.

10. History.com Staff, 'Tenements', 2010 – http://www.history.com/topics/tenements

11. Gwendolyn Wright, *Building the Dream*, Cambridge, MA: MIT Press, 1988, p. 27.

12. Burnett, *A Social History of Housing*, p. 336.

13. Peter W. Ward, *A History of Domestic Space*, Vancouver: UBC Press, 1999, p. 81.

14. Burnett, *A Social History of Housing*, pp. 144–45.

15. OECD, 'Housing', in *OECD Better Life Index*, Paris: Organisation for Economic Co-operation and Development, 2015 – http://www.oecdbetterlifeindex.org/topics/housing

16. Burnett, *A Social History of Housing*, pp. 331–32.

17. Ibid, pp. 283, 300–02, 318–19, 321, 332–34, 337, 340.

18. Ibid, pp. 309, 315.
19. Gwendolyn Wright, 'Design and affordable American housing', *Cityscape: A Journal of Policy Development and Research*, 16(2), 2014, pp. 69–86, esp. p. 75.
20. Burnett, *A Social History of Housing*, pp. 344–45.
21. Malcolm Morgan and Heather Cruickshank, 'Quantifying the extent of space shortages: English dwellings', *Building Research & Information*, 42(6), 2014, pp. 710–24.
22. Mayor of London, *Housing Space Standards: A Report by HATC Ltd for the Greater London Authority*, London: HATC Ltd, 2006, pp. 33–35.
23. Burnett, *A Social History of Housing*, p. 336.
24. Flanders, *The Making of Home*, p. 242.
25. Burnett, *A Social History of Housing*, pp. 333–34.
26. Ibid, pp. 339–40.
27. Ibid, pp. 257–58; Elaine L. Chao and Kathleen P. Utgoff, *100 Years of U.S. Consumer Spending: Data for the Nation, New York City, and Boston*, 2006, NYC: US Department of Labor and Bureau of Labor Statistics, p. 16 – http://www.bls.gov/opub/uscs/
28. Flanders, *The Making of Home*, p. 264; Ebenezer Howard, *Garden Cities of To-Morrow*, London: Routledge, 2013 [1889].
29. Flanders, *The Making of Home*, pp. 273–77; Patrick Geddes, *City in Evolution*, London: Williams and Norgate, 1915.
30. Lorna Fox O'Mahony, 'Meanings of home', in Smith (ed.), *International Encyclopedia of Housing and Home*, pp. 231–39, esp. pp. 232–33.
31. Flanders, *The Making of Home*, pp. 174–76.
32. Cuffley, *Australian Houses of the Forties and Fifties*, pp. 74, 77.
33. Burnett, *A Social History of Housing*, p. 234.
34. Ibid, p. 250.
35. K. D. Vandell 'Housing supply', in Smith (ed.), *International Encyclopedia of Housing and Home*, pp. 644–58, esp. p. 648.
36. Marshall Colin, 'Levittown, the prototypical American suburb – a history of cities in 50 buildings, day 25', *The Guardian*, 28 April 2015 – http://www.theguardian.com
37. Flanders, *The Making of Home*, p. 269.
38. Patrick Sisson, 'Wright-inspired tiny home Resurfaces in Indiana town', *Curbed*, 3 March 2016 – http://www.curbed.com
39. Emma Wiffen, 'Winter Park: suburban nature' *Assemble Papers*, 4 July 2015 – http://assemblepapers.com.au
40. Mumford, *The City in History: Its Origins, Its Transformations and Its Prospects*, p. 496.
41. Boyd, *Australia's Home: Its Origins, Builders and Occupiers*, pp. 29, 129–30.
42. Alan Ehrenhalt, *The Great Inversion and the Future of the American City*, NYC: Vintage, 2013.
43. OECD, 'Housing', in *OECD Better Life Index*, Paris: Organisation for Economic Co-operation and Development, 2015 – http://www.oecdbetterlifeindex.org/topics/housing/
44. ABS, 1301.0 'Households and families', extract from Population Chapter in *Year Book Australia, 2002*, Canberra: Australian Bureau of Statistics, 2002 – http://www.abs.gov.au

45. DIRD, *State of Australian Cities 2010*, Canberra: Department of Infrastructure and Regional Development, 2010, pp. 38–39.

46. ABS 1301.0, *Year Book Australia, 2005*, Canberra: Australian Bureau of Statistics, 2005 – http://www.abs.gov.au

47. R. Simpson, 'Households and families', in Smith (ed.), *International Encyclopedia of Housing and Home*, pp. 227–33, esp. pp. 229–32.

48. Wright, 'Design and affordable American housing', p. 72.

49. Vandell, 'Housing supply', p. 648.

50. Ibid, p. 656.

51. J. Hoekstra, M. Haffner, H. van der Heijden and M. Oxley, 'Private Rental Landlords: Europe', in Smith (ed.), *International Encyclopedia of Housing and Home*, pp. 387–92.

52. Angelica Salvi del Pero, Willem Adema, Valeria Ferraro and Valérie Frey, 'Policies to promote access to good-quality affordable housing in OECD countries', *OECD Social, Employment and Migration Working Papers*, No. 176, Paris: OECD Publishing, 2016, pp. 4–5 – http://dx.doi.org/10.1787/5jm3p5 gl4djd-en

53. Walker Rosie and Jeraj Samir, 'Infographic: The Rent Trap: How We Fell into It and How We Get Out of It', London: Pluto Press with Left Book Club, 2016 – http://therenttrap.co.uk

54. DCLG, *English Housing Survey: Headline Report 2014-2015*, London: Department of Communities and Local Government, 2016 pp. 3, 7–10 – http://www.gov.uk/dclg

55. Salvi del Pero et al., 'Policies to promote access to good-quality affordable housing in OECD countries', pp. 14–15.

56. Robin Goodman, Anitra Nelson, Tony Dalton, Melek Cigdem, Michelle Gabriel and Keith Jacobs, *The Experience of Marginal Rental Housing in Australia*, AHURI Final Report 210, Melbourne: Australian Housing and Urban Research Institute, 2013, p. 2.

57. Benoît Bréville, 'Mobile Homes Can't Move on', *Le Monde Diplomatique*, English Edition #1603, March 2016, pp. 12–13.

58. Goodman et al., *The Experience of Marginal Rental Housing in Australia*.

59. Alexandra Lange, '2016 Pritzker Prize goes to Alenjandro Aravena, Chilean architect behind innovative affordable housing', *Cubed*, 13 January 2016 – http://www.curbed.com; Jenna McKnight, 'Alejandro Aravena makes housing designs available to the public for free', *Dezeen*, 6 April 2016 – https://www.dezeen.com

60. Olivier Namias, 'Half a good home isn't enough', *Le Monde Diplomatique* English edn, #1604, April 2016, p. 16; check out the numerous projects at Elemental – http://www.elementalchile.cl/en/proyectos/

61. Justin McGuirk, *Radical Cities: Across Latin America in Search of a New Architecture*, London/Brooklyn: Verso, 2014, pp. 82, 88–9.

62. A. Stephan and R. H. Crawford, 'House size and future building energy efficiency regulations in Australia,' in R. H. Crawford and A. Stephan (eds), *Living and Learning: Research for a Better Built Environment: 49th International Conference of the Architectural Science Association 2015*, 2015, pp. 342–51, esp. p. 349.

63. ABS, 8752.0 *Feature article: Average floor area of new residential buildings*, Australian Bureau of Statistics, Canberra, 2013 – http://www.abs.gov.au

64. Stephen Clune, John Morrissey and Trivess Moore, 'Size matters: house size and thermal efficiency as policy strategies to reduce net emissions of new developments', *Energy Policy*, 48, 2012, pp. 657–67, esp. pp. 662–64; B. Güneralp and K. C. Seto, 'Can gains in efficiency offset the resource demands and CO_2 emissions from constructing and operating the built environment?', *Applied Geography*, 32, 2012, pp. 40–50.

65. Trivess Moore, Stephen Clune and John Morrissey, 'The importance of house size in the pursuit of low carbon housing', in Kristian Ruming, Bill Randolph and Nicole Gurran (eds), *State of Australian Cities Conference 2013: Refereed Proceedings*, State of Australian Cities Research Network, 2013 – http://www.soacconference.com.au

66. ABS 'Household Projections' in Cat. No. 3236.0 – *Household and Family Projections, Australia, 2011 to 2036*, Canberra: Australian Bureau of Statistics, 2015.

67. Statistics Bureau Japan, *Statistical Handbook of Japan 2011*. Tokyo: Statistics Bureau, 2011, pp. 21–22.

68. G. Powells, 'Housing dynamics: environmental aspects', in Smith (ed.), *International Encyclopedia of Housing and Home*, pp. 429–35, esp. p. 431.

69. A.M. Yezer, F. Lui and W. Larson, 'Energy consumption, housing, and urban development policy', in Smith (ed.), *International Encyclopedia of Housing and Home*, pp. 80–86, esp. p. 81.

70. Xinkuo Xu, Liyan Han and Xiaofeng Lv, 'Household carbon inequality in urban China, its sources and determinants', *Ecological Economics*, 128, 2016, pp. 77–86.

Chapter 3

All html links successfully accessed 15 April 2016.

1. Burnett, *A Social History of Housing: 1815–1985*, pp. 54–96.

2. Stanley I. Kutler, *Dictionary of American History*, 3rd edn, NYC: Charles Scribner's Sons (Macmillan Reference USA), 2003.

3. Burnett, *A Social History of Housing*, pp. 153–54.

4. Ibid, pp. 209–10.

5. Ibid, pp. 233–34, 236–37, 243–47; the Mass Observation archives are housed at University of Sussex – http://www.massobs.org.uk

6. Burnett, *A Social History of Housing*, pp. 236, 300, 304 and 308.

7. DCLG, *English Housing Survey: Headline Report 2014–2015*, London: Department for Communities and Local Government, 2016, p. 31.

8. Boyd, *Australia's Home: Its Origins, Builders and Occupiers*, pp. 110–12.

9. Commonwealth Bureau of Census and Statistics, *Census of the Commonwealth of Australia, 30th June, 1933: Part XXXVI Dwellings*, 1938, Canberra: Commonwealth Government Printer, p. 7 – http://www.abs.gov.au/

10. Alderman McFadyen quote in *Hornsby Advocate* (7 June 1929) cited in Caroline Butler-Bowdon and Charles Pickett, *Homes in the Sky: Apartment Living in Australia*, Carlton: Miegunyah Press, 2007, p. 10.

11. Boyd, *Australia's Home*, pp. 192–3, 292.

12. Ibid, pp. 260, 291; Ray Edgar, 'Don't fence me in', Spectrum (insert), *The Age*, 14 May 2016, pp. 12–13.

13. Butler-Bowdon and Pickett, *Homes in the Sky*, pp. 12–14, 98–9, 108–9, 112, 158.

14. Simone Alexander, *Predicting the Growth Suburbs of the Future*, 2013, Melbourne: .id, p. 12 – http://home.id.com.au/

15. Peter Atkins, Richard Marson and Brendon Brann, *State of Australian Cities 2014–2015: Progress in Australian Regions*, 2015, Canberra: Commonwealth of Australia (Department of Infrastructure and Regional Development), p. 42 – http://www.infrastructure.gov.au

16. Nenad (Team Forecast), 'Population densities of Australian capital cities – Melbourne and Sydney', *.id Blog*, 15 June 2015 – http://blog.id.com.au

17. Save Our Suburbs Inc. (Victoria) – http://www.saveoursuburbs.org.au

18. Elihu Rubin, 'Viewpoint: new in town – the Californian garden apartment in the 1960s', *Building and Landscapes*, 21(1), Spring 2014, pp. 1–26, esp. p. 14.

19. Jin-Ann Lin and Liang-Chuan Chen, 'The modern vernacular reassessed: the socio-architectural origin of the Taipei walk-up apartments', *Journal of Urban History*, 41(5), September 2015, pp. 908–26.

20. Richard Dennis, 'Apartment housing in Canadian cities, 1900–1940', *Urban History Review*, 26(2), March 1998, pp. 17ff.

21. CMHC, *Canadian Housing Observer 2013*, 2013, Ottawa (Ontario) Canada Mortgage and Housing Corporation, pp. 1–2, 1–8, 1–9, 2–3, 2–19, 2–21, 5–22 – http://www.cmhc.ca

22. Linda Mitrojorgji, 'Urban regeneration in Berlin, Germany: new approaches at the neighbourhood level', 2003 (Concentration paper), Urbana-Champaign: University of Illinois Department of Urban and Regional Planning.

23. INURA, 'Berlin, Germany', Berlin: International Network for Urban Research and Action, 2014 – http://www.inura.org/v2/wp-content/uploads/2014/01/INURA11_Berlin.pdf

24. J. Doling 'Housing policy trends', in Smith (ed.), *International Encyclopedia of Housing and Home*, pp. 596–605; J. Hoekstra, M. Haffner, H. van der Heijden and M. Oxley, 'Private rental landlords Europe', ibid, pp. 387–92.

25. Feargus O'Sullivan, 'Berlin just showed the world how to keep housing affordable', (*The Atlantic*) *CityLab*, 12 November 2015 – http://www.citylab.com

26. Angelica Salvi del Pero, Willem Adema, Valeria Ferraro and Valérie Frey, 'Policies to promote access to good-quality affordable housing in OECD countries', OECD (Organisation for Economic Co-operation and Development) Social, Employment and Migration Working Papers No. 176, Paris: OECD Publishing, 2016.

27. Nicole Vrenegor, 'Next stop: sell-out city – urban activism in Hamburg', *Eurozine*, 10 September 2012 – http:// www.eurozine.com

28. Flanders, *The Making of Home*, p. 91.

29. Edwin Heathcote, 'The historic mixed-use courtyard buildings of central Europe', *Financial Times*, 6 October 2014 – https://www.ft.com

30. Edward Glaeser, *Triumph of the City*, London: Pan Books, 2011, pp. 138–9.

31. Ibid, pp. 98–101, 477.

32. David Harvey, *Paris: Capital of Modernity*, NYC: Routledge, 2003.

33. Eliza Ferguson, 'The cosmos of the Paris apartment: working class family life in the nineteenth century', *Journal of Urban History*, 37(1), 2011, pp. 59–67.

34. Kenneth Baar, 'The national movement to halt the spread of multifamily housing, 1890–1926', *Journal of the American Planning Association*, 58(1), Winter 1992, pp. 39–48.

35. Dennis, 'Apartment housing in Canadian cities, 1900–1940', pp. 17ff.

36. Mumford, *The City in History*, p. 433.
37. Tim Redway, Housing Density and Design PowerPoint, Planning Institute of Australia Seminar, June 2008 – https://www.planning.org.au/documents/item/1752
38. CommSec 'Australian homes are biggest in the world', *Business News*, 23 August 2011 – http://www.switzer.com.au/business-news
39. Dolores Hayden, *The Grand Domestic Revolution* (1982[1995]) Cambridge (MA)/London: MIT Press, p. 67.
40. Ibid, pp. 72–73.
41. Ibid, pp. 230–41.
42. Ibid, pp. 138–39.
43. M. Levine, D. Ürge-Vorsatz, K. Blok, L. Geng, D. Harvey, S. Lang, G. Levermore, A. Mongameli Mehlwana, S. Mirasgedis, A. Novikova, J. Rilling, H. Yoshino, 'Residential and commercial buildings', in B. Metz, O. R. Davidson, P. R. Bosch, R. Dave and L. A. Meyer (eds), *Climate Change 2007: Mitigation. Contribution of Working Group III to the Fourth Assessment Report of the Intergovernmental Panel on Climate Change*, Cambridge (UK)/NYC: Cambridge University Press, 2007.
44. G. Xie, W. Chen, S. Cao, C. Lu, Y. Xiao, C. Zhang, N. Li and S. Wang, 'The outward extension of an ecological footprint in city expansion: the case of Beijing', *Sustainability*, 6, 2014, pp. 9371–86.
45. E. Stôa, 'Adaptable housing', in Smith (ed.), *International Encyclopedia of Housing and Home*, pp. 51–57.
46. Glaeser, *Triumph of the City*, pp. 74ff. David Owen *Green Metropolis: Why Living Smaller, Living Closer, and Driving Less are the Keys to Sustainability*, NYC: Riverhead Books, 2009.
47. ACF, *Consuming Australia: Main Findings*, Australian Conservation Foundation, 2007, p. 7 – http://www.acfonline.org.au
48. Ibid, pp. 5, 6 and 10.
49. CSE, *Fact Sheet: ACT State of the Environment Report*, Canberra: Commissioner for Sustainability and the Environment, 2015 – http://www.envcomm.act.gov.au
50. Arunima Malik, Jun Lan and Manfred Lenzen, 'Trends in global greenhouse gas emissions from 1990 to 2010', *Environmental Science and Technology*, 50(9), pp. 4722–30.
51. Herbert Girardet, *Cities, People, Planet: Liveable Cities for a Sustainable World*, Chichester: Wiley-Academy, 2004, pp. 112–15.
52. Anon. 'Moshe Safdie used "All the Lego in Montreal" to design Habitat '67', *Dezeen Magazine*, 19 December 2014 – http://www.dezeen.com
53. Alex Bozikovic, 'A renovated flat in Moshe Safdie's Habitat '67', *Dwell*, 30 December 2012 – http://www.dwell.com
54. Anon. 'Brutalist buildings: Habitat '67, Montreal by Moshe Safdie', *Dezeen Magazine*, 11 September 2014 – http://www.dezeen.com
55. Anon. 'Moshe Safdie completes Singapore Sky Habitat featuring aerial "streets" and gardens', *Dezeen Magazine*, 9 February 2016 – http://www.dezeen.com
56. Yasmin Beevi, 'Sky Habitat review', *Property Guru*, 25 January 2016 – http://www.propertyguru.com.sg
57. Anon. 'The oasis of Aboukir green wall by Patrick Blanc', *Dezeen Magazine*, 8 September 2013 – http://www.dezeen.com/
58. Joan Roca i Albert, Mireia Freixa and Mar Leniz, 'Park Güell: over a hundred years of history', Historical Museum of Barcelona – http://www.parkguell.cat; Dr

Dickson Despommier, *The Vertical Farm: Feeding the World in the 21st Century*, New York: St Martin's Press, 2010.

59. Amy Frearson, 'Stefano Boeri's "Vertical Forest" nears completion', *Dezeen Magazine*, 15 May 2014 – http://www.dezeen.com

60. *Daily Mail* reporter, 29 October 2011, 'Towers of trees: vertical forests in the sky are the height of green living', *Daily Mail*, – http://www.dailymail.co.uk.

61. 'Two bedroom apartments for sale', *Right Move Overseas* – http://www.rightmove.co.uk; Patrick Collinson, 'Average UK house price reaches £288,000', *The Guardian*, 17 February 2016 – http://www.theguardian.com

62. Edwin Heathcote, 'Legacy of the pod-fathers', *Financial Times*, 10 May 2013 – http://www.ft.com

63. Lloyd Kahn, *Tiny Homes: Simple Shelters*, 2012, Bolinas (CA): Shelter Publications, pp. 78–79; Daniel Miller, 'Living in a box: the desperate workers forced to live in tiny "coffin" apartments of Tokyo – which cost up to £400 a month to rent', *Daily Mail*, 1 March 2013 – http://www.dailymail.co.uk/

64. Anon., 'Boxhome – Rintala Eggertsson Architects', *Arch Daily*, 6 May 2014 – http://www.archdaily.com

65. Multifamily Research Committee, *The Macro View on Micro Units*, Washington DC, Urban Land Institute, 2014, pp. 4, 13, 17, 19–20.

66. Ibid, pp. 5, 22, 25.

67. Amelia Barnes, 'Stylish studio apartments to make you rethink micro living', *Domain*, 22 August 2015 – http://www.domain.com.au; James Stephens, 'The Cairo: romance and the minimum flat', 18 June 2012 – http://assemblepapers.com.au

68. Hana R. Alberts, 'Tour a totally liveable 242-square-foot west village apartment', *Curbed*, 3 September 2014 – http://ny.curbed.com

69. Jessica Daley, '5 super-efficient tiny New York apartments', *Inhabitat: New York City*, 7 November 2012 – http://inhabitat.com

70. Multifamily Research Committee, *The Macro View on Micro Units*, pp. 5, 16, 26–27, 28.

71. Ibid, pp. 7, 9, 15.

72. Bruce Haden, 'Living small in the big city', *The Canadian Architect*, 59(1), 2014, pp. 14–17; Gary Chang, 'Tiny Hong Kong apartment turns in 24 rooms', 2 June 2010 – https://youtu.be/DQM7a5Yjp9g; Kirsten Dirksen, 'Lego-style apartment transform into infinite spaces', faircompanies.com and https://www.youtube.com

73. Glaeser, *Triumph of the City*, pp. 74ff; Owen, *Green Metropolis*.

74. Mumford, *The City in History*, p. 525.

75. Glaeser, *Triumph of the City*, p. 191.

76. James Hansen, M. Sato, P. Hearty, R. Ruedy, M. Kelley, V. Masson-Delmotte, G. Russell, G. Tselioudis, J. Cao, E. Rignot, I. Velicogna, B. Tormey, B. Donovan, E. Kandiano, K. von Schuckmann, P. Kharecha, A. N. Legrande, M. Bauer and K.-W. Lo, 'Ice melt, sea level rise and superstorms: evidence from paleoclimate data, climate modelling, and modern observations that 2°C global warming could be dangerous', *Atmospheric Chemistry and Physics*, 16, 2016, pp. 3761–812.

77. Felipe Fernández-Armesto, *Millenium: A History of our Last Thousand Years*, London: Bantam Press (Transworld Publishers), 1995, pp. 707–8.

78. Ralph Horne, John Fien, Beau B. Beza and Anitra Nelson (eds), *Sustainability Citizenship in Cities: Theory and Practice*, London: Earthscan-Routledge, 2016.

Chapter 4

URLs accessed 10 May 2016.

1. Flanders, *The Making of Home*, p. 56.
2. Ibid, pp. 118–19.
3. Andrew Drury, 'Space in the home: what is being built and is the customer happy?', paper presented at the RIBA Research Symposium 2008: Space at Home, 23 September, London.
4. Flanders, *The Making of Home*, p. 112.
5. Ibid, p. 115.
6. Lesley Head, Kate Mayhew, Chris Gibson, Gordon Waitt, Nick Gill, Carol Farbotko, Natascha Klocker and Elyse Stanes, *The Connected Household: Understanding the Role of Australian Households in Sustainability and Climate Change*, Wollongong: Australian Centre for Cultural Environmental Research (University of Wollongong), 2013, pp. 8–11, 34–35.
7. Ibid, pp. 6–7, 20.
8. Zeenat Kotval-K and Igor Vojnovic, 'A socio-ecological exploration into urban form: the environmental costs of travel', *Ecological Economics*, 128, 2016, pp. 87–98.
9. Head et al., *The Connected Household*, p. 17.
10. City of Melbourne, *Understanding the Quality of Housing Design*, Issue 2 Final Report, Melbourne: City of Melbourne, February 2013, pp. 24, 37–38.
11. City of Melbourne, *Understanding the Quality of Housing Design*.
12. Trivess Moore, Ralph Horne, Andrew Martel, Geoffrey London and Tom Alves 'Valuing form and function: perspectives from practitioners about the costs and benefits of good apartment design', in *Conference Proceedings of the 7th International Urban Design Conference: Designing Productive Cities*, 2014, pp. 68–75; Ralph Horne, Geoffrey London, Trivess Moore, Andrew Martel and Tom Alves, 'Placing a value on good design for cities: evidence and prospects', paper for the 7th Making Cities Liveable Conference, Kingscliff (NSW), 10–11 July 2014; Melinda Dodson, 'Living small? An architectural exploration of occupant behaviours and community preferences to medium density compact housing precincts in Canberra', in *Conference Proceedings of the 7th International Urban Design Conference: Designing Productive Cities*, 2014, pp. 33–44.
13. DELWP, *Better Apartments for Victorians: Improving the Liveability and Sustainability of Apartments in Victoria*, Melbourne: State of Victoria Department of Environment, Land, Water and Planning, 2016, p. 2.
14. City of Melbourne, *Understanding the Quality of Housing Design*, pp. 5–6.
15. Andrew Drury and Eleanor Somers, *Room to Swing a Cat? The Amount and Use of Space in New Dwellings in London and the South East*, Ilkley: HATC Ltd, 2010, pp. 7, 17–18, 32, 41.
16. Flanders, *The Making of Home*, pp. 68–73 and 86.
17. Ibid, pp. 251–52.
18. Elizabeth Shove site – http://wp.lancs.ac.uk/elizabeth-shove; Elizabeth Shove 'Size is everything at Christmas and your oven is no exception', *The Conversation*, 23 December 2014; Sustainable Practices Research Group site – http://www.sprg.ac.uk/
19. Flanders, *The Making of Home*, pp. 237–38.

20. Ibid, pp. 238–40.

21. Steven Parissien, *Interiors: The Home Since 1700*, 2009, London: Laurence King Publishing, p. 255.

22. Flanders, *The Making of Home*, pp. 18 and 82.

23. Parissien, *Interiors*, p. 258.

24. David Higgins and Trivess Moore, 'What gives to keep that price point? High-density residential developments', *Pacific Rim Property Research Journal*, 21(1), 2015, pp. 37–49; Andrew Drury, Gary Welsh and Nick Allen, *Resident Satisfaction with Space in the Home: A Report for CABE*, 2009, HATC Ltd and Ipsos MORI.

25. Drury et al., *Resident Satisfaction with Space in the Home*; Andrew Drury, 'Space in the home'.

26. Terence Conran, *Small Spaces: Inspiring Ideas and Creative Solutions*, NYC: Clarkson Potter/Publishers, 2001, pp. 24–51, quote p. 24.

27. Ibid, pp. 64–69.

28. Ibid, pp. 90–95.

29. Ibid, pp. 140–45.

30. Mayor of London, *Housing Space Standards: A Report by HATC Ltd for the Greater London Authority*, London: HATC Ltd, 2006, p. 56.

31. Sarah Susanka and Marc Vassallo, *Inside the Not So Big House*, Newtown (Connecticut): The Taunton Press, 2005, esp. pp. 6–7, 143–9, 159–65; see too, Terence Conran, *How to Live in Small Spaces: Design, Furnishing, Decoration, Detail for the Small Home*, 2nd edn, Buffalo (NY): Firefly Books.

32. Max Jacobson, Murray Silverstein and Barbara Winslow, *Patterns of Home: The Ten Essentials of Enduring Design*, Newtown (Connecticut): The Taunton Press 2002, pp. 10–17.

33. Chris Reardon, 'Housing of the future: affordability', in *Your Home: Australia's Guide to Environmentally Sustainable Homes*, 5th edn, Sydney: Department of Industry, 2013, pp. 461–69.

34. Diana Ürge-Vorsatz, Sergio Tirado Herrero, Navroz K. Dubash and Franck Lecocq, 'Measuring the co-benefits of climate change mitigation', *The Annual Review of Environment and Resources*, 39, 2014: pp. 549–82.

35. Megan Lee, Stephen Smith and Andrew T. Carswell, 'Green housing', in Nevin Cohen and Paul Robbins (eds), *Green Cities: An A–Z Guide*, Thousand Oaks: SAGE Publications, 2015, pp. 218–23.

36. Nicola Szibbo, 'Lessons for LEED® for neighborhood development, social equity, and affordable housing', *Journal of the American Planning Association*, 82(1), 2016, pp. 37–49, esp. pp. 40, 44.

37. Christine Long, 'Taking a punt on tiny living', *The Age*, 27 April 2016.

38. Gabrielle Gwyther, 'Paradise planned: community formation and the master planned estate', *Urban Policy and Research*, 23(1), 2006: pp. 57–72.

39. Kevin McCloud 'How I let loose my constructive rage: people deserve better designs than the tired old models churned out by dinosaur developers [Eire Region]', *The Times*, October, 2009, pp. 21, 24; Glenn Howells Architects – https://glennhowells.co.uk/project/triangle-swindon/; Roger Hunt, 'We Hab a dream', EcoHouse, pp. 71–76; Footprint, 'FIRST LOOK: Glenn Howells' Triangle for Kevin McCloud', *Footprint* (Eco-Projects) 2011.

40. BioRegional, *BedZED Seven Years On: The Impact of the UK's Best-Known Eco-Village and its Residents*, 2009, Wallington: BioRegional Development Group: pp. 2, 5–6, 8–9, 32, 37–40.

41. Marcella Whitfield, *Performance in Sustainable Community Developments: Closing the Gap Between Perception and Reality*, Master of Design Studies thesis, Boston Architectural College, submitted 31 May 2014: pp. 53–60, 72–3.

42. Ibid, p. 29.

43. Onder Ozmetin, '403/9 Florence Street Brunswick – Environmentally Sustainable Living: Friendly Community Lifestyle', 13 June 2014 – http://www.realestate.com.au

44. Clay Lucas, 'No parking, no air con, no real estate agents, no worries', *The Age*, 5 April 2016 – http://www.theage.com.au

45. Tina Perinotto, 'Radical apartments: after the Commons, the Nightingale keeps ruffling feathers', *Fifth Estate*, 13 March 2015 – http://www.thefifthestate.com.au/; Breathe Architecture, 'Nightingale', 3 January 2016 version – http://www.maynardarchitects.com

46. International Living Future Institute, 'zHome: Issaquah, Washington', Living Building Challenge, 2015 – http://living-future.org/case-study/zhome

47. Eugenie Stockmann, 'Ecotown houses in the CBD' *The Owner Builder* 170, April–May 2012, pp. 23–27; The Green Swing: Towards a Sustainable Community (site), 'Genesis: planning approval'- http://thegreenswing.net; DELWP, *Better Apartments: Public Engagement Report*, Melbourne: State of Victoria Department of Environment, Land, Water and Planning, 2015, p. 6.

48. Leanne Hodyl, *Churchill Fellowship Report: To Investigate Planning Policies that Deliver Positive Social Outcomes in Hyper-Dense, High-Rise Residential Environments*, 2015, pp. 36–37.

49. Ibid, pp. 28–29, 36.

50. Marta Bausells, 'Superblocks to the rescue: Barcelona's plan to give streets back to residents' *The Guardian*, 17 May 2016 – http://www.theguardian.com

51. Adele Peters, 'Madrid is covering itself in plants to help fight rising temperatures', *Fast Company*, 2 March 2016 – http://www.fastcompany.com

52. Liam S. Whittaker, 'France declares all new buildings must be topped with plants or solar panels', CSglobe, 8 April 2015 – http://www.csglobe.com

53. Evelyn Schultz, 'Beyond modernism', in Claudia Hildner, *Future Living: Collective Living in Japan*, 2014, Basel: Birkhäuser Verlag, pp. 11–26, esp. pp. 15–20.

54. Ibid, pp. 21–22.

55. Claudia Hildner, *Future Living*, p. 7.

56. Anti-Eviction Mapping (project site) – http://www.antievictionmap.com

Chapter 5

URLs current at 10 May 2017, unless otherwise specified.

1. Bill Metcalf 'Sustainable communal living around the globe', in Sarah Bunker, Chris Coates, David Johnson and Jonathan How (eds), *The Guide to Communal Living: The New Millennium Edition 2000–2001*, London: Diggers and Dreamers Publications, 1999, pp. 5–19.

2. Karen Bush, Louise Machinist and Jean McQuillin, *My House Our House: Living Far Better for Far Less in a Cooperative Household*, Pittsburgh: St Lynne's Press,

2013, esp. pp. 87, 121 and 'General Partnership Agreement', pp. 177–82; see too E. Doskow and Jannelle Orsi, *The Sharing Solution: How to Save Money, Simplify Your Life and Build Community*, Berkeley (California): Nolo, 2009.

3. Data on Summerland Mansions draws from: Carmel Shute, 'Farewell to Summerland Mansions', 13 December 2008 (speech, emailed to author); Richard Peterson, 'Summerland Mansions: 17–27 Fitzroy St, St Kilda', Chapter 15 in *A Place of Sensuous Resort: Buildings of St Kilda and Their People*, 2005, St Kilda: St Kilda Historical Society Inc.; Peter Mares (and Carmel Shute interviewed) *St Kilda: From Riches to Rags and Back Again* (final audio tour script) 12 November 2009, Heritage Council website – http://heritagecouncil.vic.gov.au

4. Mary Logan and Darcy Dugan 'Cooperative living', *A Prosperous Way Down* (blog), 5 May 2012 – http://prosperouswaydown.com/cooperative-living

5. Caitlin McGee and L. Wynne, 'Regenerating the suburbs: a model for compact resilient cities', in Paul Burton and Heather Shearer (eds), *State of Australian Cities Conference 2015: Refereed Proceedings*, Gold Coast: Urban Research Program at Griffith University on behalf of the Australian Cities Research Network, esp. p. 1 – http://soacconference.com.au

6. McGee and Wynne, 'Regenerating the suburbs', p. 8; Caitlin McGee and Suzanne Benn 'How co-housing could make homes cheaper and greener', *The Conversation*, 20 April 2015 – https://theconversation.com

7. Mount Alexander Sustainability Group, 'Zero net emissions by 2025: Sustainable House Education Day (SHeD) 28 February 2016', accessed 24 February 2016 – http://masg.org.au; Joanna Middleton and Bronwen Machin email to author 20 June 2017.

8. Hibi Farm (Pottery Studio) – https://hibifarm.com; Naomi Waller, 'Living sustainably in Banyule: Hibi Farm', *Sustainable Homes and Communities*, December 2012 – http://www.sustainablecommunities.vic.gov.au/Files/2012_case_study_Hibi_Farm.pdf

9. Rebecca Reid, 'Leaps of Faith 21', Fellowship for Intentional Community, April 2016 – http://www.ic.org/leaps-of-faith

10. Aprovecho: Living, Learning, Organizing and Educating to Inspire a Sustainable Culture – http://www.aprovecho.net

11. Abbey Quillan 'How to create a successful collective', Shareable, 12 April 2010 – http://www.shareable.net/blog/how-to-create-a-successful-collective

12. Kristen Ross. *Communal Luxury: The Political Imaginary of the Paris Commune*, London: Verso, 2015, pp. 91–116; Architektur E.V. and Common Room (NY) 'Communal Spaces/Community Places/Common Rooms' (interview with Joseph Vogl, 3 October 2003 and 31 posters, supplement to Exhibition at Common Room 2, NY, 12 June–20 July 2007 – shortened and revised reprint of *10: Gemeinschaftsräume* translated by Common Room – http://www.arkitektur.se

13. This timeline is rough due to controversy in reviewed literature on influences country to country.

14. Dick Urban Vestbro and Lisa Horelli, 'Design for gender equality: the history of co-housing design and gender equality' *Built Environment*, 38(3), July 2012, pp. 315–35, esp. p. 332.

15. UK Cohousing Network – http://cohousing.org.uk

16. See, for instance, Dick Urban Vestbro, 'Cohousing in Sweden: history and present situation', March 2014 – http://www.kollektivhus.nu/pdf/Swedish Cohousing14.pdf

17. Lidewij Tummers, 'Introduction to the special issue: towards a long term perspective of self-managed collaborative housing initiatives', *Urban Research and Practice*, 8(1), 2015, pp. 1–4, esp. p. 2.

18. Lidewij Tummers (2015), 'Understanding co-housing from a planning perspective: why and how?', *Urban Research & Practice*, 8(1), 2015, pp. 64–78, esp. pp. 64–65.

19. Christiane Droste, 'German co-housing: an opportunity for municipalities to foster socially inclusive urban development?', *Urban Research & Practice*, 8(1), 2015, pp. 79–92, esp. p. 86.

20. Peter Ache and Micha Fedrowitz, 'The development of co-housing initiative in Germany', *Built Environment*, 38(3), July 2012, pp. 395–412, esp. p. 398.

21. Droste 'German co-housing', p. 89.

22. Monica William-Olsson, 'Färdknäppen (One for the road)', in Michael LaFond and Thomas Honeck (eds), *CoHousing Cultures: Handbuch für Selbstorganisiertes, Gemeinschaftliches Und Nachhaltiges Wohnen/Handbook for Self-Organized, Community Oriented and Sustainable Housing*, Berlin: Jovis, 2012, pp. 68–83, esp. p. 71.

23. Albrecht Göschel, 'Collaborative housing in Germany', in Dick Urban Vestbro (ed.), *Living Together – Cohousing Ideas and Realities around the World: Proceedings from the International Collaborative Housing Conference in Stockholm 5–9 May 2010*. Stockholm: Division of Urban and Rural Studies, Royal Institute of Technology in collaboration with Kollectivhus NU, 2010, pp. 71–78, esp. p. 76; for another angle, see Lydia Coudroy de Lille 'Housing cooperatives in Poland: the origins of a deadlock', *Urban Research & Practice*, 8(1), 2015, pp. 17–31.

24. Alex Steep, 'How co-housing designs community into developments', *Spacing Toronto*, 16 June 2016 – http://spacing.ca

25. Lucy Sargisson 'Cohousing evolution in Scandinavia and the USA', pp. 23–42, esp. p. 25; Lucy Sargisson 'Second-wave cohousing: a modern Utopia', *Utopian Studies*, 23(1), 2012, pp. 28–56 with Kim Stanley Robinson (*Pacific Edge*, 1988, New York: Tom Doherty) quote cited on p. 51; Sabrina Bresson and Sylvette Denèfle, 'Diversity of self-managed co-housing initiatives in France', *Urban Research & Practice*, 8(1), 2015, pp. 5–16, esp. p. 14.

26. Jason L. Shedd, 'Sustainable Construction Practices of Intentional Communities: A Pilot Investigation in Loudoun County, Virginia and Frederick County, Maryland', Masters thesis submitted to Mississippi State University, Mississippi, August 2012, pp. 50, 63, 65, 75–76.

27. Graham Meltzer, *Sustainable Community: Learning from the Cohousing Model*, Victoria BC: Trafford, pp. 153–62.

28. Both of the following cited in Enkeleda Kadriu, 'The end of social housing, the beginning of co-housing?', 23rd European Network for Housing Research Conference, Toulouse (France), July 2011, esp. p. 5 – http://www.enhr2011.com/sites/default/files/Paper-Kadriu-WS10.pdf; T. Knorr-Siedow 'Innovations from below? A new concept for social housing in Germany', in C. Whitehead and K. Scanlon (eds), *Social Housing in Europe II, A Review of Policies and Outcomes*, London: LSE, 2008, pp: 131–44, esp. p. 136; H. Harms, 'Historical perspectives on the practice and purpose of self-help housing', in H. Ward (ed.), *Self-Help Housing: A Critique*, London: Mansell Publishing Ltd, Alexandrine Press and Contributors, 1982, pp. 17–55, esp. p. 18.

29. Tummers, 'Understanding cohousing from a planning perspective', pp. 64–78; Kathryn McCamant and Charles Durrett, *Creating Cohousing: Building Sustainable Communities*, Gabriola Island BC: New Society Publishers, 2011, pp. 275–81; Ralph Horne, John Fien, Beau B. Beza and Anitra Nelson, *Sustainability Citizenship and Cities: Theory and Practice*, London: Routledge, 2016.

30. McCamant and Durrett, *Creating Cohousing*, pp. 25, 275.

31. Helen Jarvis, 'Towards a deeper understanding of the social architecture of co-housing: evidence from the UK, USA and Australia', *Urban Research & Practice*, 8(1), 2015, pp. 93–105, esp. p. 94.

32. Kathryn McCamant and Charles Durrett, *Creating Cohousing: Building Sustainable Communities*, Gabriola island (BC): New Society Publishers, 2011, esp. p. 9. Furthermore, McCamant and Durrett are criticised for 'significantly contestable claims' in Sargisson, 'Second-wave co-housing', pp. 29, 34–37.

33. Cohousing Association of the United States, 'What Is Cohousing?', 4 October 2015 – http://www.cohousing.org/what_is_cohousing

34. Dick Urban Vestbro, 'Concepts and terminology', in Vestbro (ed.) *Living Together*, pp. 21–29.

35. Meltzer, *Sustainable Community*, pp. 8–9.

36. Chris Coates, 'From co-housekeeping to cohousing', in Sarah Bunker, Chris Coates, Martin Field and Jonathan How (2011), *Cohousing in Britain: A Diggers and Dreamers Review*, London: Diggers and Dreamers Publications, pp. 11–20.

37. Vestbro and Horelli, 'Design for gender equality', pp. 315–35.

38. K. Gram-Hanssen, R. H. Scherg and R. S. Christensen, 'One-person households – a growing challenge for sustainability and housing policy', paper presented at the European Housing Research Network Changing Housing Markets: Integration and Segmentation conference, Prague, 28 June–1 July 2009; J. Williams 'Innovative solutions for averting a potential resource crisis – the case of one-person households in England and Wales', *Environment, Development and Sustainability*, 9, 2007, pp. 325–54.

39. K. Gram-Hanssen, 'Households' energy use – which is the more important: efficient technologies or user practices? Paper presented at the World Renewable Energy Conference, Linköping University, Sweden, 7–13 May 2011.

40. Alan Heeks and Charles Couzens, 'Models from mud: Threshold Centre', in Bunker et al. (eds), *Cohousing in Britain*, pp. 79–92.

41. Graham Meltzer, 'Close relationships: learning from the cohousing model', in Bunker et al. (eds), *Cohousing in Britain*, pp. 43–57, esp. pp. 55–56.

42. Matthias Gütschow, 'Mühlenviertel', in LaFond and Honeck (eds), *CoHousing*, pp. 68–83, esp. p. 71.

43. Vestbro, 'Concepts and terminology'; LaFond and Honeck (eds), *CoHousing Cultures*.

44. Martin Field, 'Introduction: How far has cohousing in the UK come?' and 'Appendix A: A resumé characteristics of cohousing neighbourhoods', in Bunker et al. (eds), *Cohousing in Britain*, pp. 5–10 and pp. 150–52, respectively.

45. Michael LaFond, 'Learning from each other's housing: an inspiring diversity', in LaFond and Honeck (eds), *CoHousing Cultures*, pp. 182–95.

46. Ibid, pp. 183–85, 189.

47. Ibid, pp. 191–93; Urs Aeschbach, Leo Arnold, Ruedi Bachmann, Ulrich Kriese and Katherina Sommer, 'Bärenfelserstrasse 34', in LaFond and Honeck (eds), *CoHousing Cultures*, pp. 52–67.

48. Meltzer, 'Close relationships', esp. p. 46 (quote).

49. Anitra Nelson, 'Creating a Sharing Context: A Study of Sharing in the Ganas Community, NYC', confidential report solicited by Ganas, Staten Island, 2012; Earthsong Eco-Neighbourhood, 'Community', Earthsong – http://earthsong.org.nz/about/community.html

50. Meltzer, *Sustainable Community*, 135–36.

51. Ibid, pp. 119, 121–23.

52. Tummers (2015) 'Understanding co-housing from a planning perspective', p. 72.

53. Bella Marckmann, Kirsten Gram-Hanssen and Toke Haunstrup Christensen, 'Sustainable living and co-housing: evidence from a case study of eco-villages', *Built Environment*, 38(3), July 2012, pp. 413–29; another Danish study reached different conclusions: Vilma Ardzijauskaite, 'Ecovillages: Is it a Way to Reach Environmental Sustainability? Case Studies in Denmark', thesis submitted 1 October 2009, Maastricht University and Aalborg University.

54. Liz Laine 'Escape to the future', in Sarah Bunker, Chris Coates, James Dennis and Jonathan How, *Low Impact Living Communities in Britain: A Diggers and Dreamers Review*, London: Diggers and Dreamers Publications, 2014, pp. 41–52, esp. pp. 43–4, 46, 48–50; Hockerton Housing Project – http://www.hockertonhousingproject.org.uk; Robert Vale 'Housing project – Hockerton', in *Home: Design for Lifestyle and the Future* (Case 7.7b) – http://cavrep.com.au/H/housingdesigncasestudy.pdf; IEA–SCH Task 28 ECBCS Annex 38 'Hockerton Housing Project, UK', in International Energy Agency, *Sustainable Solar Housing* – https://www.iea-shc.org/data/sites/1/publications/task28-demonstration-uk_hockerton.pdf; Databuild, *The Hockerton Housing Project: Design Lessons for Developers and Clients* (factsheet), London/Belfast/Edinburgh/Cardiff: Energy Savings Trust, Energy Efficiency Best Practice in Housing – www.est.org.uk/bestpractice

55. Paul Chatterton, 'Towards an agenda for post-carbon cities: lessons from Lilac, the UK's first ecological, affordable cohousing community', *International Journal of Urban and Regional Research*, 37(5), pp. 1654–74, esp. p. 1667 (quote); LILAC Co-operative, 'Affordable ownership in a low impact setting: LILAC', in Bunker et al. (eds), *Cohousing in Britain*, pp. 93–100; Lilac – http://www.lilac.coop/learning-from-lilac.html

56. Mary Kraus, 'How working together can bring us together: participatory design as a key to sustainable society', *Northeast Sun*, Spring 2006, pp. 19–21; Kraus Fitch Architects – http://www.krausfitch.com/; Mary Kraus, 'Living green in cohousing: choices for a sustainable planet', *CoHousing Journal*, Fall 2002, pp. 14–17; Mary Kraus, 'Ecologically sustainable design for cohousing', *CoHousing Journal*, Spring 2002, pp. 8–13; Laura Fitch, 'Common-sense approaches to common house design decisions', *Cohousing eMagazine*, Spring 2004.

57. Quote from 'Christie Walk: a piece of ecocity', Urban Ecology Australia – http://www.urbanecology.org.au/eco-cities/christie-walk/; Sustainability Victoria, 'Christie Walk, Adelaide: Cooperative approach delivers community-focused eco-village', in *Building Models for Sustainable Precincts*, Melbourne: Sustainability Victoria – http://www.sustainability.vic.gov.au; Christie Walk: A piece of ecocity (video), Change Media, 2011, at YouTube – https://www.youtube.com/watch?v=T4NoXeMadjc

58. LaFond and Honeck, *CoHousing Cultures*, pp. 84–99, 187, 191.

59. Graham Meltzer, *Sustainable Community*, pp. 158–9; Margrethe Kähler, 'Collective housing and well-being', in Vestbro (ed.), *Living Together*, pp. 93–104, esp. pp. 97, 100–02; Matthieu Lietaert, 'The growth of cohousing in Europe', The Cohousing Association of the United States, 16 December 2007 – http://www.cohousing.org/node/1537; Jeff Loux, 'Cohousing and sustainability: Munksøgård', 27 July 2011 – http://ucdesustainability.blogspot.hu/2011/09/cohousing-and-sustainability-munksgaard.html

60. Bresson and Denèfle, 'Diversity of self-managed co-housing initiatives in France', pp. 5–16, esp. p. 5.

61. The 'pocket neighbourhood' approach applied Ross Chapin's architectural practice is detailed in Ross Chapin, *Pocket Neighbourhoods: Creating Small-scale Community in a Large-scale World*, Newtown (Connecticut): Taunton Press, 2011.

62. Vestbro, 'Concepts and terminology', p. 29.

Chapter 6

Unless otherwise stated, URLs accessed 15 May 2017.

1. Tao (formerly Paul) Wimbush, 'Interview, 4 March 2016', in Leon Greenwood, 'Could Low Impact Development be the Answer to the Current Housing Crisis Whilst Making Positive Social, Economic and Environmental Differences in the UK', thesis submitted for a BSc Construction, University Centre, Blackburn College, May 2016, pp. 44–66, esp. pp. 56, 60.

2. GEN, 'About GEN', Global Ecovillage Network – https://ecovillage.org

3. Westwyck – http://westwyck.com; 'BedZED', Bioregional – http://www.bioregional.com/bedzed

4. See projects by country at 'Ecovillage projects', GEN – https://ecovillage.org/projects

5. Karen T. Litfin, *Ecovillages: Lessons for a Sustainable Community*, Cambridge: Polity Press, 2014, pp. 12 (Box 1.1), 38.

6. For figures, see Marti Mueller and Lucilla Borio, *Global Ecovillage Network: Living and Learning Centres* (undated, 2010s), Belzig (Germany)/Forres (Scotland): GEN-Europe – http://gen.ecovillage.org/sites/default/files/files/ll_single.pdf; Jan Martin Bang, *Permaculture: A Student's Guide to the Theory and Practice of Ecovillage Design*, Glasgow: Floris Books, 2015; Michael Dresser, 'COP22 – Pan-African Ecovillage Development Programme', 14 February 2017, GEN – https://ecovillage.org/

7. Iris Kunze, 'Ecovillages: isolated islands or multipliers of social innovations?' Transformative Social Innovation Theory (blog), 9 October 2015 – http://www.transitsocialinnovation.eu/blog; Marcus Andreas and Felix Wagner, 'Introduction', in Marcus Andreas and Felix Wagner (eds), *Realizing Utopia: Ecovillage Endeavors and Academic Approaches*, Munich: Rachel Carson Centre Perspectives (#2012/8), pp. 5–16, esp. p. 5.

8. Bill Metcalf, 'Utopian struggle: preconceptions and realities of intentional communities', in Andreas and Wagner (eds), *Realizing Utopia*, pp. 11–16, esp. p. 13; Michael Würfel, 'The ecovillage: a model for a more sustainable, future-oriented lifestyle?', in Andreas and Wagner (eds), *Realizing Utopia*, pp. 21–29, esp. p. 28.

9. Sarah Bunker, Chris Coates, James Dennis and Jonathan How, *Low Impact Living Communities in Britain: A Diggers and Dreamers Review*, London: Diggers and Dreamers Publications, 2014, especially Chris Coates, 'Introduction: something has to be done', pp. 7–14; Paul Wimbush 'Lammas: key development stages', pp. 87–100, and Simon Fairlie 'What is stopping LID going mainstream?', pp. 133–42; also see Matthew Buxton, 'How Radical Politics Are Changing the Construction of the Rural: The Lammas Project Working Within the Planning System', thesis submitted to School of Applied Sciences, BA (Hons) Geography, University of South Wales, 2016, pp. 37–38.

10. Lammas, *Annual Monitoring Report for Tir y Gafel Ecovillage, 1 January–31 December 2015*, 2016, esp. pp. 5–7; downloaded from Lammas – http://lammas.org.uk

11. Paul Wimbush, 'The process: Lammas experience with the planning system, December 2006 to August 2009', and 'Lammas Low Impact Initiatives Ltd, 2009' – http://lammas.org.uk; Tony Wrench 'Having a £3k eco-home is more about attitude than building codes or regulations: interview with Tony Wrench', Lowimpact.org, 2 October 2016 – http://www.lowimpact.org/; Tao (formerly Paul) Wimbush, 'Interview 15 April 2016' in Buxton, 'How Radical Politics Are Changing the Construction of the Rural', pp. 34–38; Katherine Jones, 'Mainstreaming the Alternative: The Lammas Eco-Village and the Governance of Sustainable Development in Wales', PhD thesis submitted to Department of Geography and Earth Sciences, Aberystwyth University, 2015, pp. 115, 119–22, 181–85.

12. Sarah Bunker et al., *Low Impact Living Communities in Britain*, especially Coates, 'Introduction', Wimbush 'Lammas', and Fairlie 'What is Stopping LID Going Mainstream?'; Buxton, 'How Radical Politics Are Changing the Construction of the Rural', pp. 37–38.

13. Wimbush, 'Interview', in Greenwood, 'Could Low Impact Development be the Answer', pp. 49–50, 52.

14. One planet guidelines vary, depending on when and where established, and to which standards they refer. For Welsh One Planet Development policy, see documents at 'One Planet Development Practice Guide', Welsh government, 2012 – http://gov.wales/topics/planning/policy/guidanceandleaflets/oneplanet/?lang=en; On defining a global hectare, see Global Footprint Network, 'Glossary', 26 August 2015 – http://www.footprintnetwork.org; The London-based Bioregional 'one planet living' approach is based on a 'global fair share' and aspirational targets, typically to 2020 or 2050, see Bioregional – http://www.bioregional.com; For application by Bioregional Australia to 'achieve Ecological Footprints of 1.7 global-hectare/person as soon as possible and 1.25 global-hectare/person by 2050', see LandCorp, *White Gum Valley: One Planet Living Summary Report*, Perth: LandCorp (Government of Western Australia), June 2015, p. 4 – https://www.landcorp.com.au

15. Paul Wimbush with Nick Swallow, *Initial Carbon Investigation for The Lammas Project*, 2009 (November), p. 13 – http://lammas.org.uk; Anon., 'Carbon footprint', Global Footprint Network, 11 August 2016 – http://www.footprintnetwork.org

16. Lammas, *Annual Monitoring Report 2015*, pp. 5–6.

17. Oneplanet, 'Welsh government confirms commitment to ecological footprinting', One Planet Council, 7 December 2016 – http://www.oneplanetcouncil.org.uk

18. Wimbush, 'Interview', in Greenwood, 'Could Low Impact Development be the Answer', pp. 47–48.

19. Ibid. p. 46.

20. Lammas, 'A pioneering ecovillage in West Wales', 2016 – http://lammas.org.uk/ecovillage/; Wimbush, 'Lammas', in Bunker et al., *Low Impact Living Communities in Britain*, p. 98.

21. The first three paragraphs of this section draw on Villaneuva, 'L.A. Eco Village: 20 years as a model of sustainable living', an interview with Lois Arkin, KCET, 20 December 2013 – https://www.kcet.org/

22. LAEV, 'CRSP', Los Angeles Eco-Village, 2016 – http://laecovillage.org/crsp

23. 'About' and 'Beverly-Vermont Community Land Trust', Los Angeles Eco-Village – http://laecovillage.org/

24. LAEV, 'About', 2015 – http://laecovillage.org; Villaneuva, 'L.A. Eco Village'.

25. Stephen Tinsley and Heather George, *Ecological Footprint of the Findhorn Community and Foundation*, 2006, Foress (Scotland): Sustainable Development Research Centre, esp. pp. 17, 34; Jessica Hodge and Julia Haltrecht, *BedZED Seven Years On: The Impact of the UK's Best Known Eco-village and Its Residents*, London: Bioregional and Peabody, 2009.

26. 'Time bank', Los Angeles Eco-Village – https://laecovillage.wordpress.com; LAEV Food Coop (wiki) – https://urbansoil.net

27. Leiler Loezer, 'Enhancing Sustainability at the Community Level: Lessons from American Ecovillages', thesis submitted for a Master of Science in Architecture, University of Cincinnati, June 2011, pp. 80–87, 102–3.

28. Litfin, *Ecovillages*, pp. 30–32.

29. Ibid, p. 162. (A structuralist finds Litfin's definition of consciousness [p. 31] idealistic.)

30. Robert H. W. Boyer, 'Achieving one-planet living through transitions in social practice: A case study of Dancing Rabbit Ecovillage', *Sustainability: Science Practice, & Policy*, 12(1), Spring 2016, pp. 1–13.

31. Adonia Lugo, 'Los Angeles Eco-Village', *Critical Sustainabilities*, 1 June 2015 – http://critical-sustainabilities.ucsc.edu/la-eco-village

32. CE, 'About us', Cloughjordan Ecovillage – http://www.thevillage.ie/about-us

33. See caution in note 14 above re one planet guidelines: GFN, 'Cloughjordan Ecovillage leads the way toward sustainable living in Ireland', Global Footprint Network, 5 February 2015 – http://www.footprintnetwork.org

34. Peader Kirby, *Cloughjordan Ecovillage: Modelling the Transition to a Low-Carbon Society* (18-page draft of forthcoming book chapter) – http://www.thevillage.ie/wp-content/uploads/2014/11/Cloughjordan-Ecovillage-Modelling-low-carbon-society.pdf

35. Ibid, p. 9.

36. GFN, 'Cloughjordan Ecovillage leads the way toward sustainable living in Ireland', Global Footprint Network, 5 February 2015 – http://www.footprintnetwork.org

37. 'Community Farm', Cloughjordan Ecovillage, 12 October 2016 – http://www.thevillage.ie; Cloughjordan Community Farm – http://cloughjordancommunityfarm.ie; Oliver Moore, Olive McCarthy, Noreen Byrne and Michael Ward, 'Reflexive resilience and Community Supported Agriculture: the case that emerged from a place', *Journal of Agriculture, Food Systems, and Community Development*, 4(3), pp. 137–53.

38. On Cloughjordan's system, see Kirby, 'Cloughjordan Ecovillage', pp. 13–15.
39. Nessa Winston, 'Sustainable housing: a case study of the Cloughjordan Eco-Village, Ireland', in Anna Davies (ed.), *Enterprising Communities: Grassroots Sustainability Innovations*, Bradford: Emerald Group Publishing Limited, 2012, pp. 85–103, pp. 95–97; 'What's for Sale' and 'Building in the Ecovillage', Cloughjordan Ecovillage, 12 October 2016 – http://www.thevillage.ie
40. Tony Gallagher, '2 An Cusan Cuil, Ecovillage, Cloughjordan, Co. Tipperary', DAFT, 27 July 2016 (renewed 30 September 2016) – http://www.daft.ie/tipperary/houses-for-sale/cloughjordan/2-an-cusan-cuil-ecovillage-cloughjordan-tipperary-1276471
41. Robert H. W. Boyer, 'Grassroots innovation for urban sustainability: comparing the diffusion pathways of three ecovillage projects', *Environment and Planning A*, 45, 2015, pp. 320–37.
42. DRE, 'Dancing Rabbit Land Trust', Dancing Rabbit Ecovillage – http://www.dancingrabbit.org
43. DRE, 'Webinars', Dancing Rabbit Ecovillage – http://www.dancingrabbit.org/webinars
44. Rachel Beck and Alison Ormsby, 'A case study analysis of Dancing Rabbit Ecovillage, Missouri', *Communal Societies*, 35(1), 2016, pp. 1–24, esp. pp. 15–16, 20–21; DRE, 'Feminism, empowerment, and justice', Dancing Rabbit Ecovillage – http://www.dancingrabbit.org
45. Lucas Berard, 'Good soil to grow in: a Dancing Rabbit update', *The March Hare: The Dancing Rabbit Weekly Blog*, 24 January 2017 – https://www.dancingrabbit.org
46. Boyer, 'Achieving one-planet living through transitions in social practice', p. 5.
47. DRE, 'Dancing Rabbit Sustainability Guidelines' and 'Ecological Covenants', Dancing Rabbit Ecovillage, 2016 – http://www.dancingrabbit.org
48. Ted, 'Big burn, new kids, big game: a Dancing Rabbit update', *The March Hare: The Dancing Rabbit Weekly Blog*, 6 February 2017 – http://www.dancingrabbit.org; DRE, 'Our land', Dancing Rabbit Ecovillage – http://www.dancingrabbit.org
49. 'Cutting our carbon footprint', Dancing Rabbit Ecovillage, 2016 – http://www.dancingrabbit.org
50. DRE members, in drecovillage 'Who is Dancing Rabbit?', skillly.net, 8 January 2015 – https://youtu.be/GvxhX1r4Vzg
51. Anon., 'Top 10 eco homes: Lammas', *The Guardian*, 14 April 2014 – https://www.theguardian.com; 'Self-reliant residents live the good life in eco-village', *Wales Online*, 9 July 2011 and updated 22 March 2013 – http://www.walesonline.co.uk; Peader Kirby, 'Cloughjordan Village: Modelling the Transition to a Low-Carbon Society', *Communities*, 171, Summer 2016, pp. 49–53, esp. p. 53; Litfin, *Ecovillages*, pp. 29–30; DRE, '30 Days' (including linked pages), Dancing Rabbit Ecovillage – http://www.dancingrabbit.org
52. DRE, 'History', Dancing Rabbit Ecovillage – http://www.dancingrabbit.org
53. Wimbush, 'Lammas'; Jenny Pickerill, *Eco-Homes: People Places and Politics*, London: Zed Books, 2016, pp. 114–19.
54. Litfin, *Ecovillages*, pp. 29–30, 137.
55. Kirby, 'Cloughjordan Village', pp. 13–15.
56. Data on population derived from websites of the communities in question, or associated ecovillage directories, as follows: Crystal Waters – http://crystalwaters.org.au; Sieben Linden – http://siebenlinden.org/en/ecovillage-2/history;

Ecovillage at Ithaca – http://ecovillageithaca.org/live; Litfin, 'Svanholm', Ecovillage Book – http://ecovillagebook.org; Findhorn – https://www.findhorn.org/aboutus/faq/#livethere

57. For discussions of the implications of demanding diversity: 'Who's moving in?', Svanholm, Denmark, 2016 – http://svanholm.dk; Tony Sirna, 'Diversity @ Dancing Rabbit', Dancing Rabbit Ecovillage, 2016 – http://www.dancingrabbit.org; Adonia Lugo, 'Los Angeles Eco-Village'; Lois Arkin, 'Diversity issues in Los Angeles Eco-Village', *Fellowship of Intentional Communities* (blog), 7 June 2012 – http://www.ic.org/diversity-issues-in-los-angeles-eco-village

58. Matthew Daly, 'Quantifying the environmental impact of eco-villages and cohousing communities: a systematic literature review'. Paper for the Institute for Sustainable Futures, Sydney: University of Technology Sydney, p. 20.

59. Jesse Sherry, 'Community Supported Sustainability: How Ecovillages Model More Sustainable Communities', doctoral thesis submitted to the State University of New Jersey, May 2014, pp. 188, 192–93, 242.

60. Litfin, *Ecovillages*, pp. viii, 18, 187–204; Boyer, 'Grassroots innovation for urban sustainability'.

61. Mildred Gustack Delambre, 'Sustainable communities of practice and eco-villages as mediation tool for degrowth practices', in *Conference Proceedings of the 2nd Conference on Economic Degrowth*, 26–29 March 2010, Barcelona – http://www.barcelona.degrowth.org/fileadmin/content/documents/Proceedings/Gustack-Delambre.pdf

62. Welsh Assembly Government, 'Extract' [4.15.1–4.23.2] from TAN6, in Lammas, *Planning for Sustainable Rural Communities*, Technical Advice Note 6, July 2010 – http://lammas.org.uk/wp-content/uploads/2013/03/One-Planet-Development.pdf

Chapter 7

URLs accessed 20 May 2017, unless stated otherwise.

1. Michael LaFond and Larisa Tsvetkova (eds), *CoHousing Inclusive: Self-organized, Community-led Housing for All*, Berlin: JOVIS, 2017.

2. Dick Urban Vestbro, 'Concepts and terminology', in Dick Urban Vestbro (ed.), *Living Together – Cohousing Ideas and Realities Around the World: Proceedings from the International Collaborative Housing Conference in Stockholm 5–9 May 2010*, pp. 21–29, esp. pp. 21–22; Chris Coates, 'Where did it all start?', in Chris Coates, James Dennis and Jonathan How, *Diggers and Dreamers: The Guide to Communal Living 25th Anniversary Edition*, London: Diggers and Dreamers Publications, 2015, pp. 79–84.

3. Bill Metcalfe, 'Utopian struggle: preconceptions and realities of intentional communities', in Marcus Andreas and Felix Wagner (eds), *Realizing Utopia: Ecovillage Endeavors and Academic Approaches*, Munich: Rachel Carson Centre Perspectives, 2012, pp. 21–29, esp. pp. 22–23, 28.

4. Maayan Lubell, 'The new rise of Israel's Kibbutzim: more young families opt for communal life', *Haaretz*, 3 June 2015 – http://www.haaretz.com

5. Vestbro, 'Concepts and terminology', p. 29; Bill Metcalf (ed.), *From Utopian Dreaming to Communal Reality: Cooperative Lifestyles in Australia*, Sydney: University of New South Wales Press, 1995, p. 140.

6. Danny Milman, 'The history of cohousing – where it all began: cohousing in Denmark', 2014, Canadian Cohousing Network – http://cohousing.ca/history-of-cohousing

7. Margrethe Kahler, 'Collective housing and well-being', in Vestbro (ed.), *Living Together*, pp. 93–104, esp. pp. 95, 97; 'About Munksøgård', Munksøgård – http://www.munksoegaard.dk/en/about.html

8. Dick Urban Vestbro, 'History of cohousing – Internationally and in Sweden' in Vestbro (ed.) *Living Together*, pp. 42–55, esp. pp. 50–54; Dick Urban Vestbro 'Cohousing in Sweden, history and present situation', March 2014, Kollectivhus – http://www.kollektivhus.nu/pdf/SwedishCohousing14.pdf; Inga-Lisa Sangregorio, 'Collaborative housing from a woman's perspective', in Vesbro (ed.), *Living Together*, pp. 114–23; Kerstin Kärnekull, 'Thirty-three years from the start: time for new initiatives!', in Vesbro (ed.), *Living Together*, pp. 124–32, esp. pp. 127–9; Workshop 16, 'More Cohousing through cooperation between user groups, housing companies and municipalities', in Vestbro (ed.) *Living Together*, pp. 159–63, esp. pp. 160–62; Dick Urban Vestbro and Liisa Horelli, 'Design for gender equality: the history of co-housing ideas and realities', *Built Environment* 38(3), pp. 315–35, esp. p. 328; Monica William-Olsson and Kerstin Kärnekull, 'Färdknäppen: Coplanning and CoHousing for the second half of life', in pp. 68–83, esp. p. 81; Lidewij Tummers, 'The re-emergence of self-managed co-housing in Europe: A critical review of co-housing research', *Urban Studies*, 53(10): 2023–40, esp. p. 2032; Matthieu Lietaert, 'The growth of cohousing in Europe', 16 December 2007, Cohousing – http://www.cohousing.org/node/1537

9. Christiane Droste, 'German co-housing: an opportunity for municipalities to foster socially inclusive urban development?', *Urban Research & Practice*, 8(1), 2015, pp.79–92, esp. p. 80; Peter Ache and Micha Fedrowitz, 'The development of co-housing initiatives in Germany', *Built Environment*, 37(3), pp. 395–412, esp. pp. 411.

10. Droste, 'German co-housing'; Lidewij Tummers, 'The re-emergence of self-managed co-housing in Europe', esp. p. 2036.

11. Albrecht Göschel, 'Collaborative housing in Germany', in Vestbro (ed.) *Living Together*, pp. 71–78, esp. pp. 75–77; Droste, 'German co-housing'.

12. Tummers, 'The re-emergence of self-managed co-housing in Europe', esp. p. 2030.

13. Ines Peborde, 'Michael LaFond: Co-Housing in Europe #3: The Case of Berlin', *New Europe: Cities in Transition.EU* – https://citiesintransition.eu

14. Janelle Orsi, Neal Gorenflo and Yassi Eskandari-Qajar, *Policies for Shareable Cities: A Sharing Economy Policy Primer for Urban Leaders*, San Francisco: Shareable & Sustainable Economies Law Centre, 2013, esp. p. 23.

15. Ibid, p. 29.

16. Robin Goodman, Anitra Nelson, Tony Dalton, Melik Cigdem, Michelle Gabriel and Keith Jacobs, *The Experience of Marginal Rental Housing in Australia*, AHURI Final Report No. 210, Melbourne, Australian Housing and Urban Research Institute, 2013, esp. pp. 95–96.

17. ERM Australia, *Co-operative Ownership Models for Residential Parks: Final Report*, Pyrmont (NSW): Environmental Resources Management Australia, August 2006.

18. Hannah Aldridge, Theo Barry Born, Adam Tinson and Tom MacInnes, *London's Poverty Profile 2015*, London, Trust for London and New Policy Institute, 2012,

p. 46 – http://www.londonspovertyprofile.org.uk; DCLG, *Dwelling Stock Estimates: 2015, England*, Housing Statistical Release, London, Department for Communities and Local Government, 28 April 2016, p. 5.

19. CABE, *Improving the Design of New Housing: What Role for Standards?*, London: Commission for Architecture and the Built Environment, 2010, p. 7.

20. Droste, 'German co-housing', pp. 79, 85; Kristien Ring, 'Memo developers: affordable apartments don't have to be unliveable dog boxes', *The Age*, 24 November 2016 [originally *The Conversation* (site)] – http://www.theage.com.au; Iqbal Hamiduddin and Nick Gallent, 'Self-build communities: the rationale and experiences of group-build (*Baugruppen*) housing development in Germany', *Housing Studies*, 31(4), 2016, pp. 365–83, esp. pp. 367, 381.

21. Clay Lucas, 'Walls to building green housing tumble in Berlin', *The Age*, 8 April 2016 – http://www.theage.com.au

22. Stattbau GmbH, *Wohnen im Gemeinschaft: Von der Idee zum gemeinsammen Haus/Living in Community: From the Idea to the Joint Home*, Berlin: Stattbau, 2012, pp. 34–37.

23. Droste, 'German co-housing', p. 85.

24. Institute for Creative Sustainability, 'CoHousing Berlin' and 'Info', id22 – http://id22.net/en

25. Michael LaFond and Thomas Honeck (eds), *CoHousing Cultures: Handbuch für Selbstorganisiertes, Gemeinschaftliches Und Nachhaltiges Wohnen/Handbook for Self-Organized, Community Oriented and Sustainable Housing*, Berlin: JOVIS, 2012, p. 17.

26. Hamiduddin and Gallent, 'Self-build communities', p. 376; 'Ten selfmade qualities', in Kristien Ring with Franziska Eidner (eds), *Selfmade City*, Berlin: JOVIS, 2013, pp. 28–46, esp. p. 28.

27. Clay Lucas, 'Walls to building green housing tumble in Berlin', *The Age*, 8 April 2016 – http://www.theage.com.au; Ines Peborde, 'Michael LaFond: co-housing in Europe #3: the case of Berlin', *New Europe: Cities in Transition.EU* – https://citiesintransition.eu/interview; arch daily, 'Coop Housing at River Spreefeld/Carpaneto Architekten + Fatkoehl Architekten + BARarchitekten', 15 January 2015, *ArchDaily* – http://www.archdaily.com/

28. Peborde, 'Michael LaFond'.

29. Droste, 'German co-housing', pp. 83, 85.

30. Lucas, 'Walls to building green housing tumble in Berlin'; Peborde, 'Michael LaFond'.

31. Lidewij Tummers, 'The re-emergence of self-managed co-housing in Europe', esp. pp. 2024, 2030–31.

32. Droste, 'German co-housing', p. 83; Mike Eliason, 'Baugruppen: proactive jurisdictions', *The Urbanist* (blog), 14 May 2014 – https://www.theurbanist.org

33. 'Mühlenviertel: district development with building communities', in LaFond and Honeck, *CoHousing Cultures*, pp. 100–15, esp. pp. 109, 113, 115; Lidewij Tummers, 'Understanding co-housing from a planning perspective: why and how?', *Urban Research & Practice*, 8(1), 2015, pp. 64–78, esp. p. 73.

34. Lietaert, 'The growth of cohousing in Europe'.

35. Menno Vergunst and Johan Vlug 'Vrijburcht (Free Castle)', in LaFond and Honeck, *CoHousing Cultures*, pp. 167–79.

36. Jasmine Dale, Robin Marwege and Anja Humburg, 'Low impact living: More than housing', draft abstract for book chapter in Anitra Nelson and Francois

Schneider (eds), *Housing for Degrowth* (London: Routledge, forthcoming), 14 December 2016.

37. OnePlanet, 'New milestone – 23 individual One Planet Development smallholdings now up and running in Wales!', 1 July 2016, and 'Approved applications' and 'Current applications', 22 May 2017, One Planet Council – http://www.oneplanetcouncil.org.uk; see also, Stephan Cartwright, 'The 23 One Planet developments in Wales', The One Planet Life – http://theoneplanetlife.com/the-23-one-planet-developments-in-wales

38. Simon Lee, 'Grand Designs, Series 17, Episode 6: The self-sufficient hobbit-style house in Pembrokeshire Built for £27K', *Homes&Property* – http://www.homesandproperty.co.uk

39. Land Use Consultants and the Positive Development Trust, *Practice Guidance: One Planet Development Technical Advice Note 6: Planning for Sustainable Rural Communities*, October 2012, Cardiff: Planning Division, Welsh Government, see esp. Paragraph 1.5.

40. Welsh Government, '4.15 One Planet Development (–4.23)', in *Technical Advice Note 6: Planning for Sustainable Rural Communities*, July 2010, pp. 24–27, esp. pp. 24–25.

41. Land Use Consultants and the Positive Development Trust, *Practice Guidance*, pp. 2–5, 19–20, 45.

42. Ibid, p. 5.

43. Simon Fairlie, 'What is stopping low impact going mainstream?', in Sarah Bunker, Chris Coates, Martin Field and Jonathan How, *Cohousing in Britain: A Diggers and Dreamers Review*, London: Diggers and Dreamers Publications, 2011, pp. 133–42, esp. 137–39; Jenny Pickerill, *Eco-Homes: People Places and Politics*, London: Zed Books, 2016, pp. 127–28.

44. 'Threshold Centre', in Chris Coates et al., *Diggers and Dreamers*, p. 184; Radical Routes – http://www.radicalroutes.org.uk

45. Lilac, 'LILAC', UK Cohousing Network – http://cohousing.org.uk/group/lilac; Paul Chatterton, 'Towards an agenda for post-carbon cities: lessons from Lilac, the UK's first ecological, affordable cohousing community', *International Journal of Urban and Regional Research*, 37(5), 2013, pp. 1654–74, esp. pp. 1662–64; Ecology Building Society, *What We Lend On*, 2015 – https://www.ecology.co.uk (includes details of cases of communal build loans); Alice Grahame, 'Councils look to radical alternatives to solve the UK's housing crisis', *The Guardian*, 6 May 2015 – https://www.theguardian.com

46. Round the Bend Conservation Co-operative – http://www.roundthebend.org.au; Anitra Nelson (2001) 'Two models of residential conservation: communal life in an Australian box ironbark forest', *International Journal of Heritage Studies*, 7(3), pp. 249–72; Jayne D'Arcy, 'Bend of Islands: the super-secret suburb you've never heard of', *Domain*, 8 November 2016 – http://www.domain.com.au

47. 'About' and 'The ELZ', Bend of Islands Conservation Association – https://bendofislands.wordpress.com

48. For this eco-neighbourhood section, see Robin Allison, *Sustainable Town Centres and Communities*, Winston Churchill Memorial Trust Research Report, May 2009 – https://www.scribd.com/document/17760519/Robin-Allison-Sustainable-Town-Centres-and-Communities-2009

49. Graham Meltzer, *Sustainable Community: Learning from the Cohousing Model*, Victoria BC: Trafford, pp. 84–91, esp. pp. 85, 87.

50. Nilmini De Silva, 'Torri Superiore: realising a dream in an abandoned medieval village' , 20 September 2013, *Logical and Intuitive* – http://www.polisplan.com. au; Ecovilliaggio Torri Superiore – http://www.torri-superiore.org/en

51. Pescomaggiore: Eco Villaggio Autocostruito – http://www.pescomaggiore.org; Francesca Fois and Giuseppe Forino, 'The self-built ecovillage in L'Aquila, Italy: community resilience as a grassroots response to environmental shock', *Disasters*, 38(4), 2014, pp. 719–39.

52. Orsi et al., *Policies for Shareable Cities*, p. 28; Charles Durrett and Katie McCamant, 'Yarrow Ecovillage: cohousing as a building block to the ecovillage', *Communities*, 171 (Summer 2016), pp. 41–43, 77.

53. *Gemeinschaft Templehof* 'English' – https://www.schloss-tempelhof.de/service/ english; Iris Kunze and Flor Avelino, *Social Innovation and the Global Ecovillage Network: Research Report*, TRANSIT: EU SSH.2013.3.2-1 Grant agreement #613169, 2015, esp. pp. 32–52.

54. Westbeth Artists Housing, 'About', *Westbeth: Home to the Arts* – http://westbeth. org/wordpress/

55. Mike Lydon and Anthony Garcia, *Tactical Urbanism: Short-term Action for Long-term Change*, Washington DC: Island Press, 2015.

56. Yaella Depietri, Giorgos Kallis, Franscesc Baró and Claudio Cattaneo, 'The urban political ecology of ecosystem services: the case of Barcelona', *Ecological Economics*, 125, 2016, pp. 83–100, esp. pp. 95–96; Parc de Collserola – http:// www.parcnaturalcollserola.cat/en

57. Zsófia Glatz and Bence Komlósi, 'Co-housing developments for resilience in housing: knowledge transfer to increase the number of co-housing developments', *Architecture and Resilience on the Human Scale: Cross-Disciplinary Conference Sheffield 10–12 September 2015 Proceedings*, pp. 93–100, esp. pp. 93, 95.

58. Ache and Fedrowitz, 'The development of co-housing initiatives in Germany', p. 407.

59. Michael LaFond, Adam Furman, Thomas Honeck and Rolf Novy-Huy, *experimentcity europe: a New European Platform for Cohousing*, 2015, Berlin: id22 and Hattingen: Stiftung trias; Forum Gemeinschaftliches Wohnen – http:// www.fgw-ev.de

60. Kosha Joubert, 'Ecovillages and the beautiful world we could live in', and Ross and Hildur Jackson, 'Global Ecovillage Network: 1991–2015', in Kosha Joubert and Leila Dregger, *Ecovillage: 1001 Ways to Heal the Planet*, Axminster: Triarchy Press, 2015, pp. 17–21 and pp. 217–27, respectively.

61. Helen Jarvis, Kath Scanlon and Melissa Fernández Arrigoitia with Paul Chatterton, Anna Kear, Dermot O'Reilly, Lucy Sargisson and Fionn Stevenson, *Cohousing: Shared Futures*, June 2016, Newcastle upon Tyne: ESRC Collaborative Housing and Community Resilience, School of Geography, Politics and Sociology, Newcastle University Daysh Building –https://ukcohousing.files. wordpress.com/2016/06/cohousing_shared_futures_final-web.pdf

62. Helen Jarvis, 'On community-led development', experimentsincommunity, 2 February 2015 – https://experimentsincommunity.wordpress.com

63. Arunima Malik, Jun Lan and Manfred Lenzen, 'Trends in global greenhouse gas emissions from 1990 to 2010', *Environmental Science and Technology*, 50(9), pp. 4722–30.

64. Matthew Daly, 'Practicing sustainability: lessons from a sustainable cohousing community', paper presented to the State of Australian Cities Conference, Gold Coast (Queensland), 9–11 December 2015 – http://soacconference.com.au

65. Heather Lovell, 'Eco-communities', in Susan J. Smith (ed.), *International Encyclopedia of Housing and Home*, Vol. 2, Amsterdam: Elsevier, 2012, pp. 1–5, esp. p. 2.

66. Geseko von Lüpke, 'Ecovillages: islands of the future?', in Andreas and Wagner, *Realizing Utopia*, pp. 73–78, esp. pp. 76–77.

67. Joubert, 'Ecovillages and the beautiful world we could live in', p. 19.

Chapter 8

Unless otherwise stated, URLs accessed 27 May 2017.

1. Gabrielle Gwyther, 'Paradise planned: community formation and the master planned estate', *Urban Policy and Research*, 23(1), 2005, pp. 57–72, esp. pp. 57–59.

2. The sources that inform this whole section follow. Currumbin Ecovillage – https://theecovillage.com.au and SV, *Business Models for Enabling Sustainable Precincts: Ecovillage at Currumbin – A Model for Commercial Viability in an Eco-Village Development*, Melbourne: Sustainability Victoria, 2011; 'Ecovillage at Currumbin', Fellowship for Intentional Community, accessed 12 December 2016 – http://www.ic.org/directory/the-ecovillage-at-currumbin

3. Yolande Strengers, 'Bridging the Divide Between Resource Management and Everyday Life: Smart Metering, Comfort and Cleanliness', PhD thesis submitted to School of Global Studies, Social Science and Planning, RMIT University, Melbourne, September 2009, pp. 113, 220.

4. Anir Upadhyay and Richard Hyde, 'Does sustainable housing contribute to Quality of Life for residents? A study of the ecovillage at Currumbin', paper presented at 12th APRU Doctoral Students Conference, Tsinghua University, Beijing, China, January 2011, pp. 1, 6–7, 9; Ben O'Callaghan, 'A Quality of Life study of ecologically sustainable housing in south east Queensland, Australia', PowerPoint Presentation, 13 March 2015 (personal communication from author); 'Currumbin Ecovillage', Trovit, accessed 13 December 2016 – http://australia.trovit.com/property/currumbin-ecovillage; 'Currumbin Valley', Domain – https://www.domain.com.au/sale/currumbin-valley-qld-4223/; ABS, *6416.0 Residential Property Price Indexes: Eight Capital Cities, Sept. Quarter 2016*, Canberra: Australian Bureau of Statistics, 2016 – http://www.abs.gov.au

5. Upadhyay and Hyde, 'Does sustainable housing contribute to Quality of Life for residents?'; O'Callaghan, 'A Quality of Life study of ecologically sustainable housing'; Ben O'Callaghan, Heather Green, Richard Hyde, David Wadley and Anir Upadhyay, 'Exploring the influence of housing design and occupant environmental attitudes on energy and water usage', *Architectural Science Review*, 55(3), 2012, pp. 176–85, esp. 180–81; 'WestWyck EcoVillage', Bioregional, 15 December 2016 – http://www.bioregional.com

6. PIA, *Planning a Clean Energy Future: A Case Study – The Ecovillage at Currumbin*, Kingston (ACT): Planning Institute of Australia.

7. L. Blundell, 'Case study: Ecovillage – a model for normal living in the future', 30 July 2009, *The Fifth Estate* – http://www.thefifthestate.com.au/articles/4214/4214

8. Ben O'Callaghan, 'Smart Urban Villages Model', Smart Urban Villages – http://www.smarturbanvillages.com/our-model

9. O'Callaghan et al., 'Exploring the influence of housing design and occupant environmental attitudes on energy and water usage'.

10. See, for instance, Felix Wagner, 'Ecovillage Research Review', in Marcus Andreas and Felix Wagner (eds), *Realizing Utopia: Ecovillage Endeavors and Academic Approaches, Rachel Carson Center Perspectives*, 8, Munich: Rachel Carson Centre of the Ludwig Maximilian University, 2012, pp. 81–94.

11. Compare US McCamant and Durrett Architects and Cohousing Solutions – http://www.cohousingco.com/home and http://cohousing-solutions.com/about-us/our-team – with European approaches in Michael LaFond and Thomas Honeck (eds), *CoHousing Cultures: Handbuch für Selbstorganisiertes, Gemeinschaftliches Und Nachhaltiges Wohnen/Handbook for Self-Organized, Community Oriented and Sustainable Housing*, Berlin: JOVIS, 2012.

12. Kirsten Robb, 'Welcome to Victoria's most sustainable community: the Cape at Cape Patterson', *Domain*, 20 December 2015 – http://www.domain.com.au; The Cape – http:// www.liveatthecape.com.au

13. Andreas Ruby, 'Inductive urban development', zanderrotharchitekten – http://www.zanderroth.de/en/profil/konzept

14. Clay Lucas, 'Brunswick apartment plan third project in high-profile green Nightingale series', *The Age*, 2 October 2016 – http://www.theage.com.au

15. Katherine Sundermann, 'From Berlin to Melbourne: residents shaping their cities', *Assemble Papers*, 6 ('Future Local'), September 2016 – http://assemble papers.com.au/category/bluecity/

16. 'BedZED', Bioregional (Home) 15 December 2016 – http://www.bioregional.com/bedzed/

17. Neil McMahon, 'The share market', *The Age*, 10 February 2013 – http://www.theage.com.au/

18. Nightingale Housing – http://nightingalehousing.org

19. Sunderman 'From Berlin to Melbourne'; Andrea Sharam, Lyndall Elaine Bryant and Thomas Alves, 'Identifying the financial barriers to deliberative, affordable apartment development in Australia', *International Journal of Housing Markets and Analysis*, 8(4), 2015, pp. 471–83; Andrea Sharam, Lyndall Bryant and Tom Alves, *Making Apartments Affordable: Moving from Speculative to Deliberative Development*, 2015, Hawthorn (Victoria): Swinburne Institute for Social Research, Swinburne University of Technology.

20. On planning hurdles, see Nightingale Housing; on car parking, see Elizabeth Jean Taylor and Reuben van Bemmel-Misrachi, 'The elephant in the scheme: planning for and around parking in Melbourne, 1929–2016', *Land Use Policy*, 60 (2017), pp. 287–97; Cameron Jewell, 'Urban Coup X Nightingale promises a deep green community', *The Fifth Estate*, 20 September 2016 – http://www.thefifthestate.com.au; Emily Braham, 'Ecovillages come to town', *Sanctuary*, 33 – http://www.sanctuarymagazine.org.au

21. Clay Lucas, 'No parking, no air con, no real estate agents, no worries'; Clay Lucas, 'Architects and investors hope to revolutionise apartment living in Melbourne', *The Age*, 15 January 2015 – http://www.theage.com.au/; 'Suburb profile report for Brunswick VIC (3056)'; *Your Investment Property*, 15 December 2016, 6 April 2016 – http://www.yourinvestmentpropertymag.com.au/top-suburbs/vic-3056-brunswick.aspx; Suburb Profile 'Brunswick Victoria 3056', *Domain*, 15 December

2016, https://www.domain.com.au/suburb-profile/brunswick-vic-3056; Andrew Maynard and Mark Austin, 'Nightingale 3.0' at Austin Maynard Architects, accessed 3 January 2016 – http://www.maynardarchitects.com

22. Nightingale Housing – http://nightingalehousing.org; Andrew Maynard and Mark Austin, 'Nightingale 3.0', Austin Maynard Architects, accessed 3 January 2016 – http://www.maynardarchitects.com/Site/houses_1/Pages/Nightingale.html

23. Maitiú Ward, 'Better together: The Commons', *Architecture Australia*, January 2015 (#1), posted 23 March 2015 – http://architectureau.com/articles/the-commons-1/; MEF, *Sustainability at The Commons*, Brunswick: Moreland Energy Foundation, pp. 2, 6, 14, 16, 18, 26 and 28.

24. Alice Grahame, 'Councils look to radical alternatives to solve the UK's housing crisis', *The Guardian*, 6 May 2015 – https://www.theguardian.com; Walter Segal 100 – http://www.segalselfbuild.co.uk/home.html; Self-Build Government-Industry Working Group, *An Action Plan to Promote the Growth of Self Build Housing*, July 2011, National Custom and Self Build Association – http://www.nacsba.org.uk, esp. pp. 6–7 – http://www.buildstore.co.uk/ActionPlan/Govt-Action-Plan-July-2011.pdf

25. Daisy Froud, 'Is Peter Barber's Hafer Road really co-housing?', *The Architects' Journal*, 19 July 2016 – https://www.architectsjournal.co.uk

26. Clay Lucas, 'Walls to building green housing tumble in Berlin', *The Age*, 8 April 2016 – http://www.theage.com.au; roedig.schop architekten, '3xgrün – Wohnen im Holzhaus', roedig.schop architekten GbR – http://www.roedig-schop.de

27. Media release, 'CommBank reveals eight alternate pathways to home ownership', Commonwealth Bank of Australia, 7 November 2016 – https://www.commbank.com.au

28. Rachel Botsman and Roo Rogers, *What's Mine Is Yours: The Rise of Collaborative Consumption*, New York: HarperCollins, 2010; Rachel Botsman, 'Collaborative economy: a transformative lens, not a start-up trend', Collaborative Consumption, 27 November 2014 – http://www.collaborativeconsumption.com; Tom Slee, *What's Yours Is Mine*, NYC: OR Books, 2016; Hilary Osborne, 'Uber loses right to classify UK drivers as self-employed', *The Guardian*, 28 October 2016 – https://www.theguardian.com; Renate van der Zee, 'The "Airbnb effect": is it real, and what is it doing to a city like Amsterdam?', *The Guardian*, 6 October 2016 – https://www.theguardian.com; Sofia Ranchordas, 'Does sharing mean caring? Regulating innovation in the sharing economy', *Social Science Research Network*, September 2014; Juliet Schor, *Debating the Sharing Economy*, Great Transition Initiative, October 2014, pp. 6, 7, 13 – http://greattransition.org/publication/debating-the-sharing-economy; Elliot Fishman, Simon Washington and Narelle Haworth, 'Bike share: a synthesis of the literature', *Transport Reviews*, 33(2), 2013, pp. 148–65.

29. Duncan McLaren and Julian Agyeman, *Sharing Cities: A Case for Truly Smart and Sustainable Cities*, Cambridge (Massachusetts): The MIT Press, 2015.

30. Ibid, pp. 5, 7–9, 219–23.

31. Janelle Orsi, Neal Gorenflo and Yassi Eskandari-Qajar, *Policies for Shareable Cities: A Sharing Economy Policy Primer for Urban Leaders*, San Francisco: Shareable & Sustainable Economies Law Centre, 2013, esp. pp. 22–29 – http://www.shareable.net

32. Enkeleda Kadriu and Gabriele Wendorf, 'How can German housing cooperatives contribute to reducing climate change', European Network for Housing Research conference, Toulouse, 5–8 July 2011 – https://www.enhr.net/enhrconferences. php; on the UK, see Nic Bliss (compiler), *1,001 Co-Operative and Community-Led Homes: The Housing Revolution Starts Here*, Liverpool: The Federation of Co-Operative Housing, undated – http://www.cch.coop

33. D. Clapham, 'Cooperative housing/ownership', in Smith (ed.), *International Encyclopedia of Housing and Home*, pp. 243–47.

34. Clapham, 'Cooperative Housing/Ownership'; Hilary Silver, 'Cooperative Housing', in Andrew T. Carswell (ed.), *Encyclopedia of Housing*, 2nd edn, Thousand Oaks, CA: Sage Publications, pp. 101–07.

35. Kadriu and Wendorf, 'How can German housing cooperatives contribute to reducing climate change', esp. p. 1; Möckernkiez: Genossenschaft für Selbstverwaltetes, Soziales und Ökologisches Wohnen eG – http://www. moeckernkiez.de/quartier-moeckernkiez/wohnen/projekt; on the 'landlord-tenant dilemma' see Trivess Moore and Tony Dalton, 'Structuring housing provision for urban sustainability', in *Sustainability Citizenship in Cities: Theory and Practice*, London: Routledge, 2016, pp. 80–92.

36. These paragraphs on Murundaka draw from: Neil McMahon, 'The share market', *The Age*, 10 February 2013 – http://www.theage.com.au; Sophie Jordan, *Cohousing: A Sustainable and Affordable Housing Alternative?* Honours thesis submitted to RMIT University, Melbourne, October 2012, esp. pp. 16, 26–27, 32, 39 and 43; 'Co-op Models', Common Equity Housing Ltd – http://www.cehl.com. au; Matthew Daly, 'Practicing sustainability: lessons from a sustainable cohousing community', paper presented at State of Australian Cities Conference 2015, Gold Coast, 9–11 December, esp. p. 11 – http://soacconference.com.au/ wp-content/uploads/2016/02/Daly.pdf

37. 'Sunwise Co-op', Fellowship of Intentional Communities – http://www.ic.org/ directory/sunwise-co-op; Shareable – http://www.shareable.net/about

38. Robert Morris, 'Buddying Up', in Chris Coates, James Dennis and Jonathan How (eds), *Diggers and Dreamers: The Guide to Communal Living* (25th anniversary edn), London: Diggers and Dreamers Publications, 2015, pp. 71–78; Withington Co-Operative Eco-House – http://withington.coopliving.net

39. Radical Routes – http://www.radicalroutes.org.uk

40. Tony Smetham, 'Life afloat', in Sarah Bunker, Chris Coates, James Dennis and Jonathan How, *Low Impact Living Communities in Britain: A Diggers and Dreamers Review*, London: Diggers and Dreamers Publications, 2014, pp. 101–10.

41. Shay Soloman, *Little House on a Small Planet*, 2nd edn, Guildford (Connecticut): Lyons Press, 2010; Lloyd Kahn, *Tiny Homes: Simple Shelter*, Bolibas (California): Shelter Publications, 2012.

42. National Geographic, 'Pictures: Amsterdam's lean, green shipping container homes', National Geographic – http://www.nationalgeographic.com

43. Rick Mayes 'All you need is a Tipi?', in Bunker et al., *Low Impact Living Communities in Britain*, pp. 31–40.

44. Chris Coates 'Eco-mobile', in Bunker et al., *Low Impact Living Communities in Britain*, pp. 79–86, esp. 81–82, 84.

45. Wurruk'an: 'Seeding a new earth story' – http://www.wurrukan.org/web/; Samuel Alexander, 'Residencies available at the Wurruk'an Ecovillage and Permaculture

Farm (Victoria)', *Permaculture Research Institute*, 29 June 2016 – http://permaculturenews.org

46. B. A. Norrgard, 'framework of a tiny house community', a bed over my head, 15 April 2017 – http://www.abedovermyhead.com/framework-tiny-house-community; Cat Johnson, 'How to create a tiny village', Shareable, 23 February 2016 – http://www.shareable.net; Cat Johnson, '11 tiny house villages redefining home', Shareable, 17 September 2014 – http://www.shareable.net

47. Melia Robinson, 'Inside the Las Vegas trailer park that Zappos multimillionaire CEO calls home', Business Insider Deutschland – http://www.businessinsider.de

48. Kristy Totten, 'Living small: At Downtown's Airstream Park, home is where the experiment is', 5 February 2015, *Las Vegas Weekly* – http://lasvegasweekly.com

49. Airstream – https://www.airstream.com; Cat Johnson, 'How to live off-the-grid in a tiny house', Shareable, 31 March 2014 – http://www.shareable.net/blog

50. Tumbleweed Tiny House Company, 'Some of what you'll find in your copy of *The Small House Book*', *The Small House Book*, accessed 1 December 2014 – http://www.tumbleweedhouses.com/pages/books

51. Jay Schaefer quoted in Kristy Totten, 'Living small'.

52. Robin Goodman, Anitra Nelson, Tony Dalton, Melek Cigdem, Michelle Gabriel and Keith Jacobs, *The Experience of Marginal Rental Housing in Australia*, Final report, Melbourne: Australian Housing and Urban Research Institute, 2013, p. 78 – http://www.ahuri.edu.au

53. Robin Goodman, Anitra Nelson, Tony Dalton, Melek Cigdem, Michelle Gabriel and Keith Jacobs, Marginal rental housing – What is it, and how should it be managed? *AHURI Research & Policy Bulletin*, 177, August 2014, p. 3.

54. Cat Johnson, 'New report says the number of coworking spaces grew over 10x in 5 years', Shareable, 13 December 2016 – http://www.shareable.net/blog

55. Cat Johnson, 'Look out coworking. Here comes big money', Shareable, 13 May 2106 – http://www.shareable.net/blog

56. Tim Mahleberg, 'Co-living is demolishing the line between work and life', The Conversation, 7 July 2016 – https://theconversation.com/

57. Cat Johnson, '11 affordable housing alternatives for city dwellers', Shareable, 7 July 2014 – http://www.shareable.net/blog

58. Leo Hollis, 'Why startup urbanism will fail us', Shareable, 4 August 2014 – http://www.shareable.net/blog

59. Natalia Fernández (Steve Herrick trans.), 'How to put an end to the urban commons and "sharing" once and for all', Las Indias in English, 16 January 2016 – https://english.lasindias.com

60. Anitra Nelson and Frans Timmerman (eds), *Life Without Money: Building Fair and Sustainable Economies*, London: Pluto Press, 2011.

61. Quote from 'Sharing Cities Network', Shareable, accessed 15 December 2016 – http://www.shareable.net/sharing-cities

62. Juliet Schor, *Debating the Sharing Economy*, Great Transition Initiative, October 2014 –http://greattransition.org/publication/debating-the-sharing-economy; on market foci of cooperatives, see 'Co-operative facts and figures', ICA: International Co-operative Alliance – http://ica.coop/en/whats-co-op/co-operative-facts-figures; World Co-operative Monitor, *Exploring the Co-operative Economy: Report 2014*, International Co-operative Alliance and European Research Institute on Cooperative and Social Enterprises, 2014 – http://goo.gl/eNBjqF; on market realities and tensions, see Larraitz Altuna-Gabilondo, 'Solidarity at work: the case

of Mondragon', UNRISD News and Views, 18 July 2013 – http://www.unrisd.org/; David Bollier, 'The promise of "open cooperativism"', Shareable, 2 February 2105 – http://www.shareable.net/blog; Anonymous, 'Mondragon: trouble in workers' paradise', *The Economist*, 9 November 2013 – http://www.economist.com/node/21589469/; Nathan Schneider, '10 Lessons from Kenya's Remarkable Cooperatives', Shareable, 4 May 2015 – http://www.shareable.net/blog; Hollis, 'Why startup urbanism will fail us'; Tom Slee, *What's Yours Is Mine*, New York: OR Books, 2016 and Peter Richardson, 'Book Review: *What's Yours Is Mine*', *TruthDig*, 2 May 2016 – http://www.truthdig.com

63. Robert Morris, 'Buddying Up', esp. p. 73.

64. Peter Ache and Micha Fedrowitz, 'The development of co-housing initiatives in Germany', *Built Environment*, 37(3), pp. 395–412, esp. pp. 406–07.

65. Christopher T. Boyko, Claire Coulton, Serena Pollastri, Stephen Clune, Nick Dunn, Rachel Cooper and the entire Liveable Cities Team, *The Little Book of Sharing in the City*, Lancaster: Imagination Lancaster/Liveable Cities (Lancaster University), 2016, esp. p. 35.

66. P. A. Albinsson and B. Yasanthi Perera, 'Alternative marketplaces in the 21st century: building community through sharing events', *Journal of Consumer Behaviour*, 11(4), July/August 2012; Anitra Nelson, 'An impossible marriage: solidarity economy and monetary economy', United Nations Research Institute for Social Research (UNRISD) Viewpoint Series 2013, 26 March 2013 – http://www.unrisd.org

Chapter 9

Unless otherwise specified, all URLs were accessed 15 January 2017.

1. Mary Garden, 'The eco-village movement: divorced from reality', *The International Journal of Inclusive Democracy*, 2(3), June 2006 – http://www.inclusivedemocracy.org; Alexa Clay, 'Utopia Inc', 28 February 2017, Aeon: Essays – https://aeon.co/essays; Marcus Andreas and Felix Wagner (eds), *Realizing Utopia: Ecovillage Endeavors and Academic Approaches*, Rachel Carson Centre Perspectives (series), Munich: Rachel Carson Centre, 2012; Karen T. Litfin, *Ecovillages: Lessons for Sustainable Community*, Cambridge: Polity Press, 2014; Terry Leahy, 'A gift economy', in Anitra Nelson and Frans Timmerman (eds), *Life Without Money: Building Fair and Sustainable Economies*, London: Pluto Press, pp. 111–35; Jana Wendler, 'Experimental Urbanism: Grassroots Learning as Spaces of Learning and Innovation in the City', doctoral thesis submitted to The University of Manchester Faculty of Humanities, 2014.

2. Anitra Nelson and Frans Timmerman, 'Non-market socialism today', *Overland*, 207, 2012, pp. 76–81.

3. mauvaise troupe collective, *defending the zad*, (trans. Laboratory of Insurrectionary Imagination) Paris: éditions de l'éclat, esp. p. 24 (quote).

4. Kristen Ross, *Communal Luxury: The Political Imaginary of the Paris Commune*, London/NYC: Verso, pp. 1, 5.

5. Zone à Défendre, 'Statement from occupants of the ZAD struggle against the airport and its world on February 27, 2016', Zone à Défendre, 1 March 2016 – http://zad.nadir.org

6. Sabrina Bresson and Sylvette Denèfle, 'Diversity of self-managed co-housing initiatives in France', *Urban Research and Practice*, 8(1), 2015, pp. 5–16, esp. p. 5
7. Bresson and Denèfle, 'Diversity of self-managed co-housing initiatives in France', pp. 8–10.
8. Ibid, p. 11.
9. Squatting Europe Kollective (ed.), *Squatting in Europe: Radical Spaces, Urban Struggles*, Wivenhoe/New York/Port Watson: Minor Compositions, 2013; Guillermo Delgado, 'Towards dialectic utopias links and disjunctions between collaborative housing and squatting in the Netherlands', *Built Environment*, 38(3) 2012, pp. 430–42.
10. Hans Pruijt, 'Squatting in Europe', in Squatting Europe Kollective (ed.) *Squatting in Europe*, pp. 17–60, esp pp. 24–27; Claudio Cattaneo and Miguel A. Martínez López (Squatting Europe Kollective) (eds), *The Squatters' Movement in Europe: Commons and Autonomy as Alternatives to Capitalism*, London: Pluto Press, 2014.
11. Bresson and Denèfle, 'Diversity of self-managed co-housing initiatives in France', p. 15.
12. Pedro Brace, 'A simple woodland life', *Reforesting Scotland*, 45, Spring/Summer 2012, pp. 16–17, esp. p. 17; 'About Tinkers Bubble', Tinkers Bubble – http://www.tinkersbubble.org
13. Jenny Pickerill, *Eco-Homes: People, Places and Politics*, London: Zed Books, 2016, pp. 160–61.
14. Rosie Lancaster, 8min30sec-mark in Harvey Quirke, Tinkers Bubble Documentary, 2015 – https://www.youtube.com/watch?v=FmjsuPCjskc
15. Peter 'Pedro' Brace, 'Tinkers' Bubble', in Sarah Bunker, Chris Coates, James Dennis and Jonathan How, *Low Impact Living Communities in Britain: A Diggers and Dreamers Review*, London: Diggers and Dreamers Publications, 2014, pp. 53–66, esp. pp. 53, 55; Brace, 'A simple woodland life', p. 16.
16. Brace, 'Tinkers' Bubble', p. 55.
17. Simon Fairlie, 'What is stopping low impact going mainstream', in Bunker et al., *Low Impact Living Communities in Britain*, pp. 133–42, esp. pp. 135–36, 138–41; 'Planning permission' in News, 9 April 2016, Tinkers Bubble – http://www.tinkersbubble.org/News
18. Mike Zair and John Gollie in Quirke et al., Tinkers Bubble.
19. For this, and the previous, paragraph see Brace, 'A simple woodland life', esp. p. 16; 'About Tinkers Bubble', Tinkers Bubble – http://www.tinkersbubble.org; Rosie Lancaster, around the 7-min. mark in Harvey Quirke, Tinkers Bubble Documentary.
20. Pickerill, *Eco-Homes*, pp. 169–85, esp. pp. 181, 184.
21. Ibid, p. 33.
22. Robin Dunbar, 'Co-evolution of neocortex size, group size and language in humans', *Behavioural and Brain Sciences*,16(4), 1993, pp. 681–735; Sieben Linden (English sections) – http://www.siebenlinden.de; Twin Oaks – http://www.twinoaks.org
23. Marcus Andreas, 'The ecovillage of Sieben Linden', *Arcadia*, 15, 2012, Environment & Society Portal, Rachel Carson Center for Environment and Society – http://www.environmentandsociety.org/node/3917; 'Green Acres: communities reduce ecological footprints', 2016, Worldwatch Institute: Vision for a Sustainable World – http://www.worldwatch.org/green-acres-communities-

reduce-ecological-footprints; Litfin, *Ecovillages*, pp. 43, 105; Andrea Bocco's provisional ecological footprint data for 2014 emailed to author from Christoph Strünke, 8 June 2017.

24. The following sources inform this whole section on Twin Oaks. Kat Kinkade, *Is It Utopia Yet? An Insider's View of Twin Oaks Community in its Twenty-Sixth Year*, Louisa (Virginia): Twin Oaks Publishers, 1994; Kat Kinkade with the Twin Oaks Community 'Labour credit Twin Oaks Community', in Nelson and Timmerman (eds), *Life Without Money*, pp. 173–91; David Sheen (dir.), Culture of Community (interview with 20-year member Valerie Renwick) Pt I, Twin Oaks – http://www.twinoaks.org/photos-videos/video-gallery

25. Twin Oaks and Valerie Renwick, 'About income sharing', Twin Oaks – http://www.twinoaks.org/about-income-sharing

26. Paxus, 'How sustainable is Twin Oaks?', Your Passport to Complaining (is Your Willingness to do Something About It), 8 November 2014 – https://funologist.org/2014/11/08/how-sustainable-is-twin-oaks/

27. Rae Cooper, Meraiah Foley and Marian Baird, *Women at Work: Australia and the United States*, Sydney: United States Studies Centre at the University of Sydney, 2016, p. 16.

28. Pickerill, *Eco-Homes*, pp. 246–47.

29. 'Visiting: once you've arrived', Twin Oaks – http://www.twinoaks.org

30. Sheen (dir.), Culture of Community (interview with 20-year member Valerie Renwick) Pt I, Twin Oaks.

31. Emma Goldman, *Living My Life*, NYC: Alfred A Knopf, 1931, p. 59.

32. Litfin, *Ecovillages*, p. 23.

33. '37 years of communal living', ufaFabrik – http://www.ufafabrik.de/en/14998/37-years-of-communal-living.html

34. ufaFabrik, 'About the ufaFabrik', ufaFabrik – http://www.ufafabrik.de/en; for a history through images, see lothwies, 30 Jahre ufaFabrik: The First Years, 2009 – https://www.youtube.com/watch?v=teRRAudvu2w

35. ufaFabrik, 'International Culture Centre', ufaFabrik – http://www.ufafabrik.de/en/14752/international-culture-centre.html

36. ufaFabrik, 'Eco-Pioneer', ufaFabrik – http://www.ufafabrik.de/en/14796/eco-pioneer.html; Litfin, *Ecovillages*, pp. 23, 86.

37. Susanne Dzeik and Sigrid Niemer (dirs), *Cycle Power Cinema – Creative Strategies of Sustainability*, ufaFabrik/Engine Room Europe, 20 May 2013 – https://www.youtube.com/watch?v=EIkvqqchqhU

38. Ibid.

39. Zavod Pekarna, New Times, New Models: Sigrid Niemer presents ufaFabrik (Germany), 2010 – https://vimeo.com/9331755; this (and the following) paragraph draw from ufaFabrik (quote from 'International Culture Centre') – http://www.ufafabrik.de/en

40. Wendler, *Experimental Urbanism*, p. 88.

41. Alessandro Coppola and Alberto Vanolo, 'Normalising autonomous spaces: ongoing transformations in Christiania, Copenhagen', *Urban Studies*, 52(6), 2015, pp. 1152–68 esp. p. 1159.

42. Tom Freston, 'You are now leaving the European Union', *Vanity Fair*, 12 September 2013 – http://www.vanityfair.com/news/politics/2013/09/christiana-forty-years-copenhagen

43. Claudio Cattaneo, 'The money-free autonomy of Spanish squatters', in Nelson and Timmerman (eds), *Life Without Money*, pp. 192–213.

44. Helen Jarvis, 'Christiania dreaming', in Chris Coates, James Dennis and Jonathan How (eds) *Diggers and Dreamers: The Guide to Communal Living 25th Anniversary Edition*. London: BCM Edge, pp. 49–62, esp. p. 57.

45. Håkan Thörn, Cathrin Wasshede and Tomas Nilson, 'Introduction: from "social experiment" to "urban alternative" – 40 years of research on the Freetown', in Håkan Thörn, Cathrin Wasshede and Tomas Nilson (eds), *Space for Urban Alternatives? Christiania 1971-2011*, Hedemore: Gidlunds Förlag, 2011, pp. 7–37.

46. Alessandro Coppola and Alberto Vanolo, 'Normalising autonomous spaces: ongoing transformations in Christiania, Copenhagen', *Urban Studies*, 52(6), 2015, pp. 1152–68, esp. pp. 1154 and 1159.

47. Coppola and Vanolo, 'Normalising autonomous spaces', p. 1162.

48. Wendler, *Experimental Urbanism*, pp. 96–98.

49. Ibid, p. 90.

50. Coppola and Vanolo, 'Normalising autonomous spaces', p. 1161.

51. Ole Lykke quoted in Freston, 'You are now leaving the European Union'.

52. Giles Tremlett, 'The Podemos revolution: how a small group of radical academics changed European politics', *The Guardian*, 31 March 2015 – https://www.theguardian.com; Sam Jones, 'Separatist movement in Catalonia steps up battle with Madrid', *The Guardian*, 27 July 2016 – https://www.theguardian.com; Dan Hancox, 'Is this the world's most radical mayor?', *The Guardian*, 26 May 2017 – https://www.theguardian.com

53. Calafou (English) – https://calafou.org/en

54. George Dafermos, 'CIC's economic ecosystem: community exchange networks and local currencies in Catalonia', P2P Foundation, 23 August 2016 – https://blog.p2pfoundation.net

55. Two interviews associated with the Barcelona case study for SHARECITY (http://sharecity.ie/): Ferne Edwards with Anitra Nelson, 'Interview with Didac Costa' Girona, 24 August 2016; Ferne Edwards with Anitra Nelson, 'Interview with Carolina Zerpa' Barcelona, 26 August 2016.

56. This section draws mainly from personal recollections and Calafou (English) – https://calafou.org/en – especially 'About' and 'Visitors' (quote).

57. Anitra Nelson, '"Your money or your life": money and socialist transformation', *Capitalism Nature Socialism*, 27(4), 2016, pp. 40–60, esp. pp. 49–50.

58. Joana Conill, Amalia Cárdenas, Manuel Castells, Sviatlana Hlebik y Lisa Servon, *Otra Vida es Posible*, Barcelona: UOC Ediciones, 2012.

Index